CONSPIRACY

ABOUT THE AUTHOR

Ian Shircore is an author, lecturer and broadcaster, with fifteen books to his name on subjects ranging from marketing psychology and the history of telecommunications to the poetry and song lyrics of the late, great Clive James. He is a sought-after ghostwriter and runs the well-known Right for your Reader and Right for the Web writing training courses.

CONSPIRACY

The greatest cover-ups and unsolved mysteries

IAN SHIRCORE

First published in the UK by John Blake Publishing
an imprint of Bonnier Books UK
4th Floor, Victoria House,
Bloomsbury Square,
London WC1B 4DA
England

Owned by Bonnier Books
Sveavägen 56, Stockholm, Sweden

www.facebook.com/johnblakebooks
twitter.com/jblakebooks

First published in paperback as *Conspiracy!* in 2012

Paperback: 978-1-78946-616-4
eBook: 978-1-78946-664-5

All information is correct at time of publication

British Library Cataloguing-in-Publication Data:

A catalogue record for this book is available from the British Library.

Design by www.envydesign.co.uk

Printed and bound in Great Britain by Clays Ltd, Elcograf S.p.A.

1 3 5 7 9 10 8 6 4 2

John Blake Publishing is an imprint of Bonnier Books UK
www.bonnierbooks.co.uk

This is for all the whistleblowers, leakers and Freedom of Information activists who have helped cut through so many long-established myths and demystify the world around us

ACKNOWLEDGEMENTS

This book's ability to uncover new perspectives is a tribute to the awesome power of technologies like the internet and DNA profiling and the new techniques of open-source intelligence (OSINT). It is also a tribute to the genuine efforts of people, courts and some governments to shine a light into some very dark corners.

Specifically, I would like to thank all those persistent individuals whose Freedom of Information requests have unearthed so much new evidence, the anonymous footsoldiers of WikiLeaks and Bellingcat and the enlightened organisations, like America's independent National Security Archive, that have made thousands of previously secret documents available to all online.

CONTENTS

INTRODUCTION

**Yesterday's secrets make
today's news**

Ten years ago, anyone who took much of an interest in the subject of conspiracies was seen as slightly weird. I remember one book signing where a woman came up to me and asked me to sign a copy of the first edition of this book for her sister. 'Her name's Jakki,' she said. 'J-A-K-K-I. She'll love this. She believes in *everything*.'

No one should ever believe in everything. A lot of the most well-known conspiracy theories – about aliens landing in a flying saucer at Roswell, about Illuminati plots to achieve world domination, about shape-shifting lizards from outer space, about the 'murder' of Princess Diana and Elvis having faked his death, about simulated moon landings and 9/11 being a gigantic false flag operation, staged by the American government to justify George Bush's War on Terror – are fairy stories. They just don't fit the facts.

But we've just lived through an extraordinary decade. We've seen a string of big, ugly, dangerous conspiracies that were only too real.

We've seen Vladimir Putin's Russia interfere in US presidential elections to help Donald Trump into the White House. We've seen angry QAnon followers, egged on by Trump, attack the Capitol building. We've seen Moscow try to blame the Ukrainians for the deaths of 298 people on a Malaysian airliner blasted out of the sky in 2014 by a Russian missile.

And we've seen the growth of completely bogus conspiracy theories, like the outrageous suggestion, put forward by self-appointed 'truth-seekers' and eagerly backed by certain anti-gun control activists, that no children at all died in the Sandy Hook school massacre and that the grieving parents were really professional actors.

The problem is, of course, that the flood of conspiracy theories seeking to explain every major event makes it harder all the time to separate truth from fiction and facts from fantasy.

The vocabulary of conspiracies – 'false flags', 'fake news' and 'crisis actors' – has become mainstream. It's no surprise any more when the Russians bomb a maternity hospital in Mariupol and immediately claim, through their embassy in London, that the Ukrainians did it to make them look bad.

But this kind of stuff is not necessarily as modern as we think.

Way back in the 1960s, the US military came up with Operation Northwoods, a gruesome plot to unleash bomb blasts and gun attacks on the streets of Washington and Miami, blame Havana and use this as an excuse to invade Cuba. The Northwoods plans were backed and approved by the Joint Chiefs of Staff, and it was only when they reached President John F Kennedy's desk that they were firmly vetoed. Unsurprisingly, there have even been suggestions of a connection between the generals' anger about this and JFK's assassination eighteen months later.

Hitler's fig leaf of an excuse for invading Poland and starting

World War II was a classic false flag op. It was a series of raids on German border posts in which a handful of guards were killed. But the Führer had ordered the raids. The attackers were SS troops dressed in stolen Polish uniforms and the defenders hadn't always been told what was happening, so the first deaths of the war were Germans shot by Germans.

A CATALOGUE OF HORRORS

In the mid- to late twentieth century, the world champions of conspiracy and cover-up were the Americans and their secret services, led by the CIA. Thanks to declassified documents, careful research and a few deathbed confessions, what we know now about the CIA's activities, including the long history of MKULTRA experiments with mind-control drugs, hypnotism and torture, is jaw-dropping. What we don't know – which may well include involvements in several major assassinations – could be even more startling.

But Britain, too, has had its own dark secrets.

The Porton Down research labs, eight miles from Salisbury, which moved so fast in 2018 to identify the novichok nerve agent used to poison Sergei and Yulia Skripal, had secretly sprayed chemicals and germ warfare agents from planes over cities like Swindon, Southampton and Norwich. When the boffins at Porton wanted to test the effects of the new sarin nerve poison, in 1953, they did it by dripping the stuff onto the arms of young soldiers, while telling them it was all to do with finding a cure for the common cold. One 20-year-old kid died within an hour, and it took his family fifty years to get confirmation of the truth about what had happened to him.

The British government covered up the dangerous near-meltdown of the nuclear reactor at Windscale in 1957, Europe's worst nuclear accident until Chernobyl.

The police buried the evidence of the two different blood groups that pointed to two different serial killers during the three-year hunt for the Yorkshire Ripper.

The powers that be fudged the facts around the unlikely suicide of Iraq weapons inspector Dr David Kelly in 2003, after he'd cast doubt on the famous 'sexed-up dossier' about Saddam Hussein's weapons of mass destruction, and made sure a proper inquest was never held.

Worst of all, perhaps, because of the sheer injustice and the huge number of people whose lives were ruined, was what was done to hundreds of honest British sub-postmasters who were wrongly accused of theft, fraud or false accounting in a long-running saga that stretches right up to the present day and is only just reaching its climax. The harm was so great that the total compensation bill – to be paid by the Post Office, or, in the last resort, by the UK government – has been estimated at more than £1 billion.

SOME NEW ANSWERS, MANY NEW QUESTIONS

Conspiracies – real and imagined – have shaped the world we live in. MI5, MI6, the hyperactive CIA and the coolly efficient Mossad, the bloodstained KGB and its orphan child, the FSB, have all pushed and pulled the destinies of rulers and nations. So have fakers and manipulators, business moguls, politicians and gangsters.

Just glancing through the first few conspiracy cases examined in this book, you can see many of the key themes emerging. Ghastly crimes, sneaky cover-ups and botched investigations form the basis of most of the chapters, with a lot of political manipulation and Secret Service skulduggery in the background. Famous names – Marilyn Monroe, John Lennon, Elvis Presley, Princess Diana, even Glenn Miller – attract conspiracy theories like a magnet attracts iron filings. But sometimes the stories are true and the official versions are false. Marilyn Monroe was demonstrably murdered, whatever the law said, and the proof is right there in her autopsy report.

This is not meant to be a dull reference book, so bunching the assassinations together or having one section dedicated to air crashes and another to CIA plots didn't seem right. In the end, the running order has been chosen with an eye to pacing and readability, with surprise as the key ingredient. If you are not being shocked or surprised every couple of pages, this book is not doing its job.

Bug-eyed monsters, rampant paranoia and far-fetched 'Elvis lives' stories have given conspiracy theories a bad name. When you've got wild-eyed obsessives who believe everything's a conspiracy versus sneering Establishment figures who insist that nothing is, the argument is never going to get far.

But an idea is not responsible for the people who believe in it and there really are a lot of legitimate, unanswered questions still to be tackled. The newest evidence available today usually comes to us via WikiLeaks, declassified internet archives or Freedom of Information requests. Some arrives courtesy of mischievous or conscience-driven ex-spooks like Peter Wright, who wrote *Spycatcher*, and Edward Snowden, now stripped of his US passport and exiled in Russia. Some comes from anonymous 'leaktivists', like the mole who released the Panama Papers in

2016, raising questions about the financial dealings of all sorts of people, from Putin's friends and Xi Jinping's brother-in-law to Mark Thatcher and several members of the Spanish royal family.

I have no secret or privileged sources. Almost all the documents and images referred to in the text – including, for example, the Monroe autopsy, the secret Operation Northwoods plans, the scientific papers for and against the COVID lab leaks theory and the judges' rulings on the UK sub-postmasters scandal – can easily be found online with a few carefully chosen keywords.

Every day sees more fanciful conspiracy theories and fake news thrown into the mix. But every day brings us new information and new opportunities to assemble the evidence needed to sort the wheat from the chaff. We owe it to ourselves – and perhaps to our children – to expose the real conspiracies and debunk the nonsense. In the end, the truth matters, especially when those with vested interests are out to hide it from us.

1

BRITAIN'S SUB-POSTMASTERS

COMPUTER SAYS 'FRAUD!'

Between 2000 and 2014, more than 700 British sub-postmasters and post office counter staff were convicted of theft, fraud, false accounting and similar charges. More than twenty were sent to jail. One man was wrongly accused of stealing £208,000 and received a prison sentence of more than three years. Tracy Felstead, a counter assistant at Camberwell Green Post Office, who was nineteen at the time, was convicted and spent three months in a cell in Holloway. Sub-postmaster Seema Misra, who was pregnant, was found guilty of stealing £75,000 and given a fifteen-month sentence. One post office veteran, fifty-nine-year-old Martin Griffiths, who had been a sub-postmaster for fourteen years, left a note for his family and stepped out in front of a bus, after being falsely accused of stealing £61,000.

Most of those convicted were sub-postmasters, the self-employed men and women contracted to run the country's 10,000 local post offices, selling stamps and National Lottery tickets, handling passport and TV and driving licence applications and providing various financial services.

The problems had begun in 1999, when the Post Office introduced Horizon, a £1 billion computer accounting and stock-taking system for branch post offices designed by ICL/Fujitsu. Almost immediately, the people in the front line started to notice unexplained discrepancies and glitches, including duplicate entries and missing sales records. There were even cases where phantom transactions appeared to have taken place overnight, in locked post offices, when no one was around. When the sub-postmasters queried these snags with the Post Office and asked for help, they were told the new IT system was '100 per cent robust' and had been thoroughly tested. If the cash balances and other figures produced by Horizon seemed worryingly random, the people at the tills must be doing something wrong.

Over the next few years, dozens, then hundreds, of sub-postmasters were informed that there were major deficits in their accounts, often running into tens of thousands of pounds, sometimes into six figures.

No one could argue with Horizon. No detailed explanations were ever offered about just how and where the shortfalls had appeared. The sub-postmasters were simply given the option of repaying the money that was alleged to be missing or facing prosecution. In court, no evidence of fraud or false accounting was required, other than the Horizon data. It was unassailable, and almost every charge resulted in a conviction.

All these cases were brought to court by the Post Office's own private prosecutions department, meaning that the organisation took three roles – as victim, investigator and prosecutor – bypassing the checks and balances that would have been provided by the involvement of the police and the Crown Prosecution Service.

In the eight-year period from 1991 to 1998, Post Office prosecutors charged and won convictions against an average of six sub-postmasters each year.

From 2000 to 2013, that rate suddenly went up to an average of fifty-one convictions a year. That, in itself, should have rung warning bells.

There were only three possible explanations for all this. Either villainous sub-postmasters had been getting away with murder for years and the new IT system had finally exposed them. Or the arrival of Horizon had coincided with a sudden upsurge in criminality among a previously law-abiding group of small business owners generally seen as pillars of the community. Or there was something very wrong with the system Fujitsu and the Post Office had installed.

In all, 736 sub-postmasters and counter staff were convicted. Nearly 2,500 more were told there was money missing from their accounts, but that they would not be prosecuted as long as they made good the deficits.

Dozens of sub-postmasters have borne witness to the fact that the Post Office's pitiless investigators fed each of them the same lies to coerce them into paying up or making false confessions or plea bargain deals. 'You're the only one it's happened to,' the interrogators' baffled victims were told. 'No one else has had any problems – you're the only one. This has never happened before. You are alone.'

The investigators may claim they were only obeying orders. But every one of them must have known by day two on the job that what they were saying was untrue.

Many of those who were found guilty lost their businesses,

their health and their homes and had their lives and careers ruined by bankruptcy and the stigma of having a criminal record. Even the 'lucky' ones, the sub-postmasters who were not charged but found themselves having to remortgage their houses or arrange loans to pay back money they hadn't taken, suffered appallingly. As Samuel Caveen, the nephew of the late Martin Griffiths, said in 2021: 'Not everyone in the Post Office scandal was prosecuted. Some just had their livelihoods, reputations, life savings and wellbeing stolen from them.'

Throughout it all, the Post Office steadfastly maintained that it was in the right. In the face of an increasing weight of evidence to the contrary, it continued blaming the sub-postmasters. There was nothing wrong with the Horizon system, it repeated. There were no bugs or defects that could have caused the alleged shortfalls. There was no way anyone within the Post Office or at Fujitsu could ever access a sub-postmaster's accounts and make alterations to the data.

As the High Court in London has found, in a succession of recent cases, each of these claims is factually untrue.

Yet when the sub-postmasters were finally able to confront their tormentors in court, both the Post Office and Fujitsu tried to obscure the facts and stick to the party line. Written evidence was submitted that was shown to be incorrect and that was contradicted by what was later revealed under cross-examination. There were allegations, too, that the Post Office and its lawyers were indulging in 'lawfare' – deliberately complicating the legal proceedings and bumping up the costs in an attritional process aimed at exhausting the resources of the sub-postmasters' representative body, the Justice for Sub-postmasters Alliance (JFSA), and leaving it with no money to carry on fighting.

At the time of the second major High Court case, known as

the Horizon Issues trial, in December 2019, the judge, Mr Justice Fraser, identified twenty-nine separate bugs, errors and defects in the IT system. He sharply criticised the Post Office, saying its case amounted to 'bare assertions and denials that ignore what has actually occurred'. This was, he said, 'the twenty-first century equivalent of maintaining that the earth is flat'.

And he was even more damning about Fujitsu's witnesses. 'I have very grave concerns regarding the veracity of evidence given by Fujitsu employees to other courts in previous proceedings about the known existence of bugs, errors and defects in the Horizon system,' he said. 'After very careful consideration, I have therefore decided, in the interests of justice, to send the papers in the case to the Director of Public Prosecutions, Mr Max Hill QC, so he may consider whether the matter to which I have referred should be the subject of any prosecution.'

DID THE SCANDAL AMOUNT TO A CONSPIRACY?

A conspiracy, according to the Oxford English Dictionary, is 'an agreement between two or more persons to do something criminal, illegal, or reprehensible'.

The Post Office would probably claim that its assertions about the Horizon system's infallible accuracy were based on apparently factual information given to it by its trusted supplier, Fujitsu.

The government, which is the Post Office's sole shareholder and is supposed to oversee its actions via the Department of Business, Energy and Industrial Strategy, would claim that its repeated denials, over many years, that there were serious flaws in Horizon and that sub-postmasters were being persecuted were based on apparently factual information provided by the Post Office.

There is no evidence of actual collusion between these three powerful bodies to do down the sub-postmasters, so you could say there was no conspiracy. For those on the receiving end, though, it seemed as if every attempt to prove their innocence was met by a closing of ranks and a concerted refusal to listen. There will be long legal arguments about whether the Post Office's actions were criminal or illegal, but no one could argue that they were not reprehensible – either negligent, reckless or deliberately oppressive.

COMPENSATION PAYMENTS COULD COST UP TO £1 BILLION

In 2021, seventy-two sub-postmasters had their convictions quashed. At the first landmark hearing, in April, thirty-nine people's names were cleared and the judge ruled that the original verdicts were 'an affront to the public conscience'.

One particularly important piece of background evidence, which was not disclosed in connection with several earlier trials and was finally revealed in 2020, was the advice written by Simon Clarke, a barrister working with Post Office solicitors Cartwright King in 2013. For many people, this looks like the crucial evidence that the Post Office acted in deliberate bad faith when it continued to fight the sub-postmasters in court.

The Clarke advice pointed out to the Post Office that a senior Fujitsu engineer, Gareth Jenkins, had failed to disclose known flaws and bugs in the Horizon system in relation to the successful prosecutions of a number of sub-postmasters. After the Post Office had begun a series of weekly conference calls to discuss Horizon issues, Simon Clarke was told that its Director of Security had given orders for the minutes of these calls to be shredded. Post Office executives do not deny this, though they insist that no minutes were actually destroyed.

The Horizon affair is now seen by many as the most widespread and shameful miscarriage of justice in Britain's recent legal history. In 2020, a relatively toothless 'independent inquiry' was set up to investigate the whole sorry mess. In May 2021, this was upgraded to become a full-scale statutory inquiry, which means it has the power to force witnesses to give evidence under oath. The Justice for Sub-postmasters Alliance is refusing to take part, saying a slow-moving inquiry will hold up the process of getting justice and further delay the compensation payments the sub-postmasters are entitled to. For its part, the UK government has now agreed to make interim compensation payments of £100,000 available to each person who was wrongly convicted.

One key figure in the fight to expose this shameful tale is a freelance journalist called Nick Wallis. He has been investigating the cover-up for more than a decade, interviewing dozens of victims and Post Office employees, politicians, accountants and lawyers and trawling through endless transcripts, court documents and audit reports. Many of his discoveries have been featured in a string of BBC radio and TV programmes that have gradually brought the issue into the spotlight and he has written a chilling book on the subject, *The Great Post Office Scandal*.

Nick Wallis knows more than anyone about various aspects of this sordid affair that have yet to be made public, and he has a fine ear for a telling quote. In his award-winning BBC Radio 4 series *The Great Post Office Trial*, made in 2020, he talked to one of the Post Office's former legal advisers.

This man pointed out that the whole ugly story was by no means over. Even when all the wrongful convictions have been quashed and all the victims have been financially compensated, there will still be the little matter of establishing who was responsible for inflicting this grotesque injustice on so many innocent people. So far, not one individual at the Post Office or Fujitsu or in government has been prosecuted or publicly rebuked, or even admitted responsibility.

'Everyone involved in the prosecution process has a duty to comply with the rules,' the legal expert told the BBC. 'And a deliberate failure to comply with the rules usually amounts to a perversion of the course of justice. I can probably name half a dozen people, with hindsight, who should be very worried.'

2

COVID-19

DID THE VIRUS LEAK FROM
THE WUHAN LAB?

In January 2020, reports started reaching the West of a mysterious flu-like disease spreading in the Chinese city of Wuhan. The images coming out of Wuhan seemed apocalyptic. Videos showed people collapsing in the street. Infected locals were forcibly locked into their apartment buildings and the doors welded shut. Drones patrolled the city, barking out police orders to anyone found disobeying the lockdown laws. An emergency thousand-bed hospital was built in ten days.

Soon the virus had spread far beyond China. Just two months later, in March 2020, the World Health Organization (WHO) declared the outbreak a global pandemic. By April 2022, nearly 500 million people worldwide had been infected by COVID-19, and more than six million had died.

With the aid of the internet, conspiracy theories about COVID started spreading at warp speed. In the first stages of the pandemic, before vaccines were developed, one popular conspiracy theory had it that the disease wasn't even real. It was a big lie, invented by a global elite intent on terrifying, cowing and controlling the world's population.

Other conspiracists conceded that the disease was real enough, but claimed that it was a Chinese bio-weapon. Or possibly it was just a mild bug, no more virulent than the flu. Or maybe it was being spread by 5G cellphone towers.

In December 2020, after the first vaccines came on the market, a rash of vaccine conspiracy theories began to circulate.

A lot of the zanier vaccine rumours revolved around the figure of Bill Gates. Thanks to his work through the Bill and Melinda Gates Foundation, Gates had long been known as a proponent of mass vaccination programmes. Early on in the COVID crisis, conspiracy hunters pounced on a public comment Gates had made about the possible introduction of a COVID 'digital certificate'. 'Eventually,' he said, 'we will have some digital certificates to show who has recovered or been tested recently or, when we have a vaccine, who has received it.' According to many online sages, this was all the proof they needed that Gates and other members of the global elite planned to use vaccination needles to insert their microchips into the upper arms of everybody in the world.

Other conspiracy theorists asserted that the COVID vaccine itself would injure or kill you, unless you were lucky enough to be given 'the placebo'. But why would the global elite bother to give some people placebos, if it was using vaccines for nefarious purposes? This wrinkle in the theory was not explained. In any case, the early COVID conspiracy theories were swiftly disproved by developments in the real world.

COVID was a real disease all right. Six million people do not die of an imaginary ailment. As for vaccines, by late spring 2022, twelve billion doses had been administered globally, and almost

60 per cent of the world's population had been vaccinated. No mass onslaught of deaths or injuries had occurred as a result of this vast vaccination effort. On the contrary: the vaccines had done their job, significantly reducing the virus's power to cause serious illness and death.

Moreover, many people who refused vaccines on ideological grounds ended up contracting COVID, and some of them, inevitably, died. Some of these people were courageous enough to publicly recant their conspiracist views on their deathbeds, urging others not to make the same fatal mistake they'd made.

But there is one conspiracy theory about COVID that has never been wholly refuted.

This is the proposition that the coronavirus outbreak was triggered by a leak from a research lab in Wuhan, China, and that there has been a concerted international effort to cover this up. Perhaps a naturally occurring virus that was being studied in the laboratory had managed to escape and infect researchers and others. Or, more ominously, an existing virus had been genetically engineered – for experimental purposes or as a potential bio-weapon – and had then made its escape or been intentionally released.

To begin with, the 'lab leak' theory was derided as a bizarre notion on a par with the tales about 5G phone masts. At one point, major social media platforms like Facebook went so far as to censor all discussion of it.

But in May 2021, President Joe Biden revealed that the US intelligence community was divided about the viability of the lab-leak theory and called for the question to be more thoroughly investigated. Many months later, no one can say for sure whether the lab-leak hypothesis is true or false. What we can say is that it's a potentially valid explanation for what happened, and that the evidence on both sides of the argument needs to be weighed with some care.

AT FIRST, EVERYTHING POINTED TO AN ORIGIN IN NATURE

When the initial coronavirus outbreak began in Wuhan, experts immediately pinpointed the city's Huanan Seafood Wholesale Market as the likely source of the disease. As well as seafood, the crowded market sold live animals such as mink, masked palm civets, porcupines and raccoon dogs and could have provided a suitable environment for a virus to make the leap from animals to humans. SARS-CoV-2 – the virus that causes COVID-19 – originated in bats, and proponents of the wet-market theory believe that it leapt to humans via an intermediate animal host, which has not yet been identified. (The pangolin, or scaly anteater, was originally considered a prime suspect, because it is the only other species that has been found to harbour a close SARS-CoV-2 relative, though this was later ruled out.)

To begin with, there seemed to be near-total consensus among experts that SARS-CoV-2 emerged naturally – 'zoonotically', in the jargon – by making that leap from animals to humans. Many scientists believe that a SARS-CoV-2 progenitor virus jumped from animals to humans and then 'ping-ponged' back and forth, steadily adapting to its new host.

Very early on, in February 2020, *The Lancet* published a statement, signed by twenty-seven eminent scientists, that roundly condemned the lab-leak hypothesis. 'We stand together to strongly condemn conspiracy theories suggesting that COVID-19 does not have a natural origin,' the statement said. 'We support the call from the Director-General of WHO to promote scientific evidence and unity over misinformation and conjecture.'

The following month, a panel of virologists who had studied the virus's genome sequence published an article in the journal *Nature Medicine*. 'Our analyses,' the scientists declared, 'clearly show that SARS-CoV-2 is not a laboratory construct or a purposefully manipulated virus.'

In May 2020, Dr Anthony Fauci, the director of America's National Institute of Allergy and Infectious Diseases, said that the evidence pointed 'very, very strongly' away from the lab-leak theory. All the signs, Fauci said, suggested the virus 'evolved in nature and then jumped species'.

Early in 2021, a World Health Organization report, written jointly with the Chinese authorities, insisted that the lab-leak theory was 'extremely unlikely'. It was far more probable, the report said, that the disease had jumped from bats to humans, perhaps by way of an intermediate animal host.

Taken together, these authoritative pronouncements seemed to settle the argument and put the lab-leak hypothesis to bed. For a long time, the noisiest proponents of the lab-leak theory were President Donald Trump and his Secretary of State, Mike Pompeo. But neither man was a scientist, to put it mildly. So their vulgar and possibly racist opinions about the origins of 'the China virus' could safely be dismissed.

BUT SOME EXPERTS SAY SARS-COV-2 IS 'TOO PERFECT'

Scientific research labs operate according to strict bio-security guidelines. The highest level of security is Biosafety Level 4, which is stipulated for labs handling highly infectious pathogens. There are a dozen BSL-4 laboratories in the US, but only two in the whole of China. One of them is the Wuhan Institute of Virology, which houses the world's most comprehensive collection of bat coronaviruses and is situated eight miles from the Huanan market, on the other side of the Yangtze River.

So what were the chances of SARS-CoV-2 arising zoonotically in a wet market in the same city that just happened to contain China's premier coronavirus lab? Proponents of the zoonotic explanation are obliged to dismiss this as a pretty big coincidence. Which doesn't mean the zoonotic theory isn't true, of course. After all, coincidences do happen.

On the other hand, lab leaks happen too. In 2014, *USA Today* revealed that more than 1,000 lab accidents involving bacteria, viruses and toxins had been reported to US regulators between 2008 and 2012. Half of these incidents were serious enough for lab staff to need medical evaluation or treatment. In five cases, lab workers had fallen ill, though fortunately none had died. 'High-containment laboratories have a whispered history of near-misses,' wrote the novelist and journalist Nicholson Baker, in a controversial, taboo-busting 2021 article about the COVID lab-leak hypothesis. 'Scientists are people, and people have clumsy moments.'

So do we have any particular reasons to suspect that a leak may have occurred at the Wuhan Institute of Virology? Well, yes. In 2018, the US sent several representatives from its embassy in Beijing to inspect conditions at the WIV's new BSL-4 facility. The embassy subsequently cabled two official warnings to Washington about lax safety and management standards at the lab.

And an unverified 2021 US intelligence report revealed that in November 2019, several weeks before the first case of the new coronavirus outbreak was officially identified, three researchers from the WIV were admitted to hospital with COVID-like symptoms.

This is circumstantial evidence, of course. It doesn't add up to proof. But if there is to be proof of the COVID origin story, it may well lie in the genome sequence of the virus itself. Some well-qualified proponents of the lab-leak theory say the SARS-CoV-2 genome has features that couldn't possibly have evolved naturally, and must therefore have been spliced into the virus in a lab.

To follow this argument, we need to understand that the Wuhan Institute of Virology was almost certainly involved in a controversial activity called 'gain of function' research. This involves obtaining viruses in the wild, then modifying them in a lab to make them more virulent or more transmissible to humans. The rationale for such work is that by supercharging viruses in a controlled environment, scientists can learn how to combat them if they should ever evolve in the wild. Critics say that the dangers of such research outweigh the benefits, because the consequences of a lab leak could be devastating to humanity.

The reasoned case for the COVID lab-leak hypothesis received a big public boost in January 2021, when Nicholson Baker published his long, densely argued cover story for *New York* magazine.

Baker quoted numerous scientists who were concerned that the lab-leak hypothesis had been prematurely dismissed. Experts from France to Taiwan, Baker revealed, had become increasingly troubled by a 'peculiar furin-like cleavage site', a spot where a human enzyme, furin (also known as PACE – Paired basic Amino acid Cleaving Enzyme) cuts the protein.

As has repeatedly been reported, SARS-CoV-2 is like a ball covered with spikes. Each of these protein spikes features an unusual cluster or 'insertion' of four amino acids that constitute the furin cleavage site and make the virus uniquely capable of leaping from cell to cell and person to person, and of burrowing deep into the human lung. The spike protein of SARS-CoV-2 has to be cleaved by furin before it becomes fully functional.

Baker's *New York* article attracted plenty of popular media attention. But the whole scientific world was rocked in May 2021 when one of America's most honoured and distinguished biologists, Nobel Prize-winning Caltech Professor David Baltimore, commented that the nature of the furin cleavage site was the 'smoking gun' that implied that the virus had escaped from a laboratory.

This was dynamite. 'These features make a powerful challenge to the idea of a natural origin for SARS2,' said Baltimore. Suddenly, the lab leak theory had real heavyweight backing.

Within weeks, though, Baltimore backtracked on his dramatic phrasing, recognising that the key words 'smoking gun' had overstated his opinion. What he'd meant, he said, was that the furin cleavage site raised legitimate doubts about the origin of SARS-CoV-2. 'I believe that the question of whether the sequence was put in naturally or by molecular manipulation is very hard to determine, but I wouldn't rule out either origin,' he told the *Los Angeles Times*.

But if David Baltimore had softened his stance, others kept the debate bubbling. 'The furin cleavage site in the COVID virus sticks out like a sore thumb,' the science writer Nicholas Wade wrote in January 2022, pointing out that the peculiar 'set-up' in the COVID cleavage site has never been found in any other coronavirus in any other species. The 'precision' involved in the virus's set-up, Wade noted, 'is unusual in nature'.

Scientists do not disagree about that point. It is unusual.

The question is, how did this unusual insertion find its way into the virus's genome? Some sceptics have claimed it is highly improbable – perhaps even impossible – that this oddly perfect combination of amino acids could have evolved spontaneously, in the wild. On the other hand, they say, it is entirely thinkable that this 'insert' could have been spliced into the virus in a lab.

Other experts have pooh-poohed this argument. They point out that the SARS-related coronaviruses are in the beta genus, one of four in the *Coronaviridae* family. Several members of that genus have furin cleavage sites, which appear to have evolved repeatedly. One SARS-CoV-2-related virus, according to a 2020 paper in *Current Biology*, has three of the four amino acids that make up the furin cleavage site. And that, say the authors, is 'strongly suggestive of a natural zoonotic origin' for the COVID virus.

The lab-leak debate took another explosive turn in mid-2021, when the *Washington Post* published emails dating back to early 2020 between Dr Anthony Fauci and Dr Kristian Andersen, a Scripps Research professor and a member of an international expert panel that had studied the recently published genome sequence of SARS-CoV-2. 'Some of the features (potentially) look engineered,' Andersen wrote in a note to Fauci, adding that he and his fellow panellists 'all find the genome inconsistent with expectations from evolutionary theory'.

Just weeks after this email exchange, though, both Andersen and Fauci were publicly dismissing the lab-leak hypothesis as close to meritless.

Why? What had happened to change their minds? The plot thickened in early 2022, when a Congressional Committee published details of a conference call that had taken place on 1 February 2020, involving members of the expert panel, Fauci and Dr Francis Collins, then Director of America's National Institutes of Health.

Emails exchanged in the wake of the conference call suggested that several members of the expert panel continued to lean towards the lab-leak theory. They just couldn't get past the suspiciously 'perfect' length – exactly twelve units of RNA – of the 'insert' on the furin cleavage site. 'I just can't figure out how this gets accomplished in nature,' wrote Professor Robert Garry of Tulane University. 'It's stunning. Of course, in the lab it would be easy to generate the perfect twelve base insert that you wanted.'

Another of the experts, Dr Mike Farzan of Scripps Research, felt the same way. Unable to quote directly from Farzan's redacted email, the committee paraphrased its contents thus: 'He is bothered by the furin cleavage site and has a hard time explain[ing] that as an event outside the lab (though there are possible ways in nature, but highly unlikely).'

Elsewhere in his email, Farzan declared himself to be '70:30 or 60:40' in favour of a lab-leak explanation.

Given that these experts felt this way in February 2020, why did several of them, including Professor Garry, put their names, just one month later, to the *Nature Medicine* article which weighed into the lab-leak debate with the categorical statement that 'Our analyses clearly show that SARS-CoV-2 is not a laboratory construct or a purposefully manipulated virus'?

What had happened in the interim to lead the experts to reach this fresh and seemingly conclusive verdict?

It is possible, of course, that further inspection of the genome had changed their minds. But emails released by the Congressional committee suggest the possibility of a more political motive. On 2 February 2021, Dr Francis Collins wrote in an email to Fauci and others, 'A swift convening of experts in a confidence-inspiring framework (WHO seems really the only option) is needed, or the voices of conspiracy will quickly dominate, doing great potential harm to science and international harmony.'

If some American scientists decided to downplay the lab-leak hypothesis for political reasons, this unfortunately put them on the same side as the Chinese government, which has gone to extreme lengths to discourage open discussion of the virus's origins.

Back in April 2020, when Australia's foreign minister called for an international inquiry into the origins of COVID-19, China retaliated immediately by imposing heavy tariffs on Australian exports. The Australian wine industry alone took a billion-dollar hit as a result.

During the pandemic's second year, however, the taboo surrounding the lab-leak theory slowly began to lift. In May 2021, a group of eighteen prominent scientists published a letter in *Science* magazine declaring that, in light of all the available evidence, the zoonotic theory and the lab-leak theory 'both remain viable'.

In the same month, President Joe Biden revealed that America's intelligence agencies were currently split between those theories. They 'do not believe there is sufficient information to assess one to be more likely than the other', Biden said, adding that he had asked the intelligence community to 'redouble their efforts' to resolve the question once and for all.

Biden's statement helped to confer a new respectability on the lab-leak hypothesis. The *New York Times*, which had previously been in the habit of calling it a 'debunked' theory, now started calling it an 'unproven' one.

Even Anthony Fauci revised his public position. 'I keep an open mind,' Fauci said in June 2021. 'It could have been a lab leak.'

As of 2022, that is still the reasonable position to take. The assumption that COVID-19, the greatest global pandemic for a century, had a natural origin is arguably supported by SARS-CoV-2's genomic make-up and the early epidemiological pattern, with the first cases tightly clustered around one market in a city of eleven million people. But neither the zoonotic theory nor the lab-leak hypothesis has been proved beyond reasonable doubt. It may take years or decades before the question is resolved, if indeed it ever is.

In the meantime, we should probably follow Anthony Fauci's example. When the evidence, one way or the other, is inconclusive, keeping an open mind is the only sane option.

3

PIZZAGATE, QANON AND THE PRESIDENT

THE PATH THAT LED TO THE CAPITOL

On 7 October 2016, just a month before the US presidential election between Donald Trump and Hillary Clinton, WikiLeaks broke a story that may have changed the eventual result. The website had somehow got hold of some 50,000 emails hacked from the personal account of John Podesta, the chair of the Clinton campaign. WikiLeaks initially released 2,000 of the choicest emails as a kind of teaser, drip-feeding further instalments to the public over the next few weeks and thus ensuring the story would continue to dominate the news cycle.

Podesta's emails contained some embarrassing revelations about infighting in the Democratic Party. But did they also include coded messages pointing to far deeper secrets? Conspiracy theorists were convinced they did. On websites like the anarchic imageboard 4chan, and the more respectable Reddit, amateur cryptologists combed the leaked documents for clues.

In one email exchange, Podesta had proposed having a 'Hillary pizza party' as a fundraiser. 'Hillary doesn't seem like the type to host a pizza party', someone on 4chan observed. 'Unless by Pizza they mean Cheese Pizza.' On 4chan, 'cheese pizza' was routinely used as code for child pornography, presumably because the two phrases begin with the same initial letters.

Maybe the author of this original post was just trying to be funny, when he or she casually speculated that Hillary Clinton was into child pornography. On a site like 4chan, it can be hard to tell. In any case, once the theme of paedophilia had been raised, other 4channers couldn't get enough of it. Applying their own creative approach to codebreaking, they came to the conclusion that the leaked emails were studded with encrypted references to child abuse.

For example, many of Podesta's personal emails contained recipe ideas and culinary references, ostensibly because he was a keen Italian cook. It wasn't long before an anonymous 4chan wag proposed that 'cheese' might be Podesta's code-word for little girls, and 'pasta' his term for little boys, while 'walnut' – one of the chairman's preferred ingredients – must mean 'person of colour'.

As for pizza, it happened that several emails in the WikiLeaks dump had been sent to Podesta by a man named James Alefantis, the owner of a Washington pizzeria called Comet Ping Pong. The implications were clear, at least to 4channers. Obviously, they decided, John Podesta and Hillary Clinton must be running a child porn and slavery ring out of the basement of Alefantis's restaurant.

This theory rapidly acquired its own hashtag – #pizzagate. On 4 November, just four days before Donald Trump won the presidential election, the pizzagate hashtag started trending on Twitter. Staff at Comet Ping Pong began to receive death threats. James Alefantis got hundreds in the space of a few days.

Then Alex Jones, the heavyweight champion of American conspiracy theory, jumped on the bandwagon. On his Infowars website, Jones alleged that Hillary Clinton was 'one of the most vicious serial killers the planet's ever seen'. He spoke of 'all the children Hillary Clinton has personally murdered and chopped up and raped' – presumably not in that order. 'Pizzagate is real,' Jones told his audience. 'You have to go investigate it for yourself.'

A week later, a twenty-nine-year-old warehouse worker named Edgar Maddison Welch decided to do exactly that. Armed with a semi-automatic AR-15 and a handgun, Welch drove 360 miles from his home in North Carolina to Washington, where he planned to 'self-investigate' the situation at Comet Ping Pong. 'Raiding a pedo ring, possibly sacraficing [sic] the lives of a few for the lives of many,' he texted a friend.

Having slipped into the pizzeria, Welch looked around for the enslaved children in the basement. But there were no children. There wasn't even a basement. Welch discharged his AR-15 three times, hitting nobody, before surrendering to police. 'The intel on this wasn't 100 per cent,' Welch later conceded.

You might think Welch's well-publicised fiasco would have been enough to scotch the idea that Hillary Clinton was a child sex-slaver. But you'd be wrong. On the internet, the theory continued to fester and mutate, even after Donald Trump had been installed as president.

In October 2017, a series of cryptic messages started appearing on 4chan, posted by someone using the handle 'Q Clearance Patriot'. Before long, this poster became known simply as Q.

Q claimed to work at the US Department of Energy, where employees with 'Q-level clearance' enjoy access to top-secret information. According to Q, Trump hadn't forgotten about his famous promise to lock Hillary up for corruption 'on a scale we've never seen before'. Far from it. Behind the scenes, Trump was apparently waging a secret war against a vast and shadowy 'liberal cabal' devoted to trafficking children on an industrial basis. The Cabal had roughly 100,000 members, hailing from America's political and entertainment elite. Key members included Hillary and Bill Clinton, Barack Obama, Oprah Winfrey and Tom Hanks.

Q's posts rapidly proliferated, totalling about 5,000 over the next few years. For a high-level government employee, Q certainly seemed to spend a lot of his waking hours online. Since he – or she – frequently spoke in riddles, Q's loyal band of followers, who called themselves QAnon, had ample opportunity to engage their own creativity in the never-ending quest to nail down Q's exact meaning.

As QAnon mythology ramified, members of the cult began to develop their own distinctive lingo. Q's posts were known as 'Q drops'. 'The Storm' was Q-speak for the glorious and supposedly imminent day when Trump would order mass arrests of the Cabal's leading members, deporting them to Guantanamo Bay for trial and probable execution. QAnon believers identified one another by means of various slogans and loyalty oaths, including 'Where we go one, we go all' and 'Trust the plan'.

As for its ideological content, QAnon theory embraced claims that made the wilder assertions of pizzagate look downright pedestrian. Pizzagate believers had merely contended that Hillary Clinton and her allies were paedophiles and sex traffickers. According to QAnon lore, the Cabal was actually sucking the blood of children. Or rather, it was into harvesting a substance called adrenochrome from their pituitary glands. This miraculous elixir helped Hollywood's stars maintain their youthful glow, which explained why so many celebs had started to look drawn and haggard during the COVID-19 era, when the pandemic created inevitable supply-chain issues in the child-harvesting industry.

Another key tenet of QAnon mythology was the belief that John F Kennedy Jr, far from having perished in a plane crash in 1999, was alive and kicking. Some of the faithful believed that Kennedy and Q were one and the same person. Others predicted that the resurrected Kennedy, son of JFK and a staunch Democrat throughout his life, would publicly out himself in time to become Trump's running mate in 2020.

Like the pizzagate theory before it, QAnon theory spread rapidly from 4chan to less specialised platforms like YouTube and Twitter. Before long it had gone troublingly mainstream. In December 2020, a poll found that 17 per cent of Americans claimed to believe in the existence of 'a group of Satan-worshipping elites who run a child sex ring [and] are trying to control our politics and media'.

Alarmingly, QAnon ideology began to seep into Republican politics. QAnon signs and T-shirts became a frequent sight at President Trump's rallies. Asked for a comment about his QAnon fans, Trump called them 'people who love our country'. In Georgia, a hard-core QAnon believer, Marjorie Taylor Greene, fought and won the Republican primary for a safe Congressional district. Trump's presidency, said Greene, presented 'a once-in-a-lifetime opportunity to take this global cabal of Satan-worshipping paedophiles out'. Trump approved, calling Marjorie Taylor Greene 'a future Republican star'.

Meanwhile, General Michael Flynn, who served briefly as Trump's National Security Advisor before falling victim to the administration's Russia scandal, seemed to go all-in on QAnon. At a Fourth of July barbecue in 2020, Flynn filmed himself reciting the QAnon loyalty oath – 'Where we go one, we go all' – with a group of friends. The general then uploaded the video to Twitter, complete with a QAnon hashtag.

When Trump was voted out of office without ever initiating 'The Storm', QAnon believers were angry and frustrated. Along with an assortment of other ticked-off Trump fans, they headed to Washington for a giant 'Stop the Steal' rally on 6 January 2021, when a joint session of Congress was due to certify Joe Biden's victory. 'Big protest in DC on January 6th,' Trump tweeted. 'Be there, will be wild!'

Wild it certainly was. At noon on the big day, Trump addressed his followers at a gathering near the White House. 'We won this election and we won it by a landslide,' he said, before urging the crowd to march to the Capitol and 'stop the steal'.

'I'll be there with you,' he added, inaccurately.

In the event, the crowd didn't merely march *to* the Capitol. They marched all the way into it. The resulting scenes appalled the world and left five people dead. The QAnon presence was heavy. One of the key insurrectionists was Jake Angeli, the so-called QAnon Shaman, who turned up wearing a fur hat with a pair of buffalo horns and brandishing a spear. 'Q Sent Me,' said a placard tied to the spear's shaft.

Also among the rioters was a thirty-five-year-old Californian woman named Ashli Babbitt. 'No Biden the kid raper,' Babbitt had tweeted a week before flying to Washington to make her protest in person. 'Nothing will stop us,' she elaborated, a day before the protest-cum-insurrection. 'They can try and try and try but the storm is here and it is descending upon DC in less than 24 hours.'

Babbitt was shot dead the next day by a Capitol police officer, as she and a group of fellow rioters, ignoring repeated orders to stop, tried to clamber into the Speaker's Lobby of the Capitol through a broken window. According to true believers, Babbitt died a martyr. But if QAnon theory wasn't true, then Babbitt wasted her life on an idea that was bogus at the very best and, at worst, a deliberate hoax.

QANON SHAMAN ADMITS: 'I WAS WRONG. PERIOD.'

The pizzagate and QAnon conspiracy theories were riddled with predictions and assertions that turned out to be factually untrue.

As Edgar Maddison Welch discovered when he raided Comet Ping Pong, there were no child sex slaves in the pizzeria's basement. Indeed, the ground-floor restaurant had no basement. To his credit, Welch was quick to concede that his online information sources had been off the mark. His mission was 'incredibly ill-advised', he admitted, shortly before embarking on a chastening four-year prison sentence.

As for Q, the list of his – or her – failed prophecies is long. Q's very first Q drop, in late 2017, had knowingly claimed that Hillary Clinton's arrest was imminent. 'Expect massive riots organized in defiance and others fleeing the US to occur,' Q wrote. But Q's intel was as dodgy as his syntax. The long-promised 'Storm' never materialised. Nor has John F Kennedy Jr made a shock return to public life.

On closer inspection, most of Q's output consists of second-hand material cobbled together from older conspiracy theories, dressed up with rhetoric stolen from bad Hollywood movies. The rallying cry 'Where we go one, we go all' comes from a 1996 Ridley Scott flop called White Squall. Q's obsession with paedophilia was nothing more than a rerun of a discredited pizzagate trope. And the stuff about sucking children's blood, along with the movement's general overtones of anti-Semitism, recycles themes notorious from the fraudulent *Protocols of the Elders of Zion,* a document originating from Tsarist Russia which was exposed as a grim hoax more than one hundred years ago.

As for adrenochrome, it's true that there is a chemical compound by that name. But the idea that it's some kind of wonder drug is a myth derived from Hunter S Thompson's dope-addled road trip novel *Fear and Loathing in Las Vegas.* 'There's only one source for this stuff,' says the wacky narrator of that book, '…the adrenaline glands from a *living* human body. It's no good if you get it out of a corpse.'

When Terry Gilliam made *Fear and Loathing* into a film, Thompson told him that all the stuff about adrenochrome's magical properties was simply made up.

And here's another reason to doubt the truth of QAnon theory. Even Alex Jones thinks it's bullshit. 'Q tells us stuff and all of it's lies,' an exasperated Jones was heard to say in early 2021. General Michael Flynn eventually jumped off the Q bandwagon too, declaring the whole thing 'a disinformation campaign to make people look like a bunch of kooks'.

Even Jake Angeli, the QAnon Shaman himself, came to see the error of his ways. 'I was wrong. Period,' Angeli said, while awaiting trial. Getting indicted, Angeli explained, had 'permitted me to start reanalyzing my life'. Donald Trump was 'not honourable', the ex-Shaman ruefully concluded, before starting a forty-one-month prison sentence. 'He let a lot of peaceful people down.'

Moreover, the evidence suggests that Q isn't even a single person. Linguistic analysts have concluded that Q's earlier and later posts were written by two distinct individuals. And a recent

HBO documentary offered compelling evidence that Q, or one of the Qs, was a young man named Ron Watkins, one-time administrator of the website 8kun, where Q began exclusively posting in 2018. Watkins, now in his early thirties, has no apparent credentials apart from a high school diploma, and certainly doesn't enjoy Q-level clearance at the US Department of Energy.

But if Ron Watkins authored the 8kun Q drops, then who was the real Q, the original Q?

Given the mountain of evidence that the first Q was no more reliable than the second one, the question can perhaps be phrased in a different way. Who cares? Once we know that the whole thing was nothing more than a twisted, fevered fantasy, the question of authorship is hardly important.

DID QANON HYSTERIA HAND BIDEN THE PRESIDENCY?

In 2021, the Associated Press launched an investigation into Donald Trump's claim that the 2020 election had been a Big Steal. AP set teams of investigative reporters to work in six battleground states where Trump's team alleged that the vote had been flipped by fraud.

In the immediate aftermath of the election, the US Attorney General William Barr, a Trump loyalist, and officials in each of the fifty states had found no evidence of widespread fraud or irregularities in the election. But AP wanted to dig deeper.

And guess what? The Associated Press reporters found that a certain amount of voter fraud had actually taken place.

In Wisconsin, a convicted felon had cast a ballot despite being legally ineligible to vote. All he wanted to do, he said, was register his support for the president. A woman in Arizona had voted on behalf of her mother, who had died a month before Election Day. A Las Vegas businessman whose company had hosted a Trump rally joined the clamour against election fraud but later pleaded guilty to casting a vote in his dead wife's name. In several cases, people were found to have voted twice – once by mail, and once in person.

In all, across the six states in question, AP identified 475 instances of potential fraud, out of a total of 25.5 million votes cast. So President Trump wasn't wholly wrong. Voter fraud was really a thing.

But did 475 suspect votes – some for Biden, some for Trump – scattered across six different states, amount to a Big Steal? Not by a long shot. More than 81 million Americans voted for Joe Biden, as against 74.2 million for Donald Trump, in the first election since 1992 where an incumbent president had missed out on a second term.

If Biden's overall margin of victory was impressive, though, the situation in the three closest states (Wisconsin, Georgia and Arizona) had been on a knife edge, with a total margin, across the three, of just 43,000 votes. These three states have 37 electoral college votes between them, while Biden's winning margin was just 74. And in the event of a tie, Trump would still have been president.

It is quite possible that the gothic paranoia of the QAnon and pizzagate believers – with their lurid, obsessive insistence that the Democrats were motivated by murderous and paedophilic tendencies, rather than just the politician's usual self-serving lust for power – may have revolted and turned off more than 43,000 voters in these key counties. In which case, it could well be true that these noisy conspiracists inadvertently ushered their sworn enemy, Joe Biden, into the White House.

4

JIM MORRISON

THE END OF A LONG-RUNNING MYSTERY

Jim Morrison, the legendary lead singer of psychedelic rock band The Doors, was a troubled man. Swamped by bouts of depression and addicted to a range of dangerous substances, he was certainly not in peak physical condition. But despite his rock 'n' roll lifestyle, it came as a shock to music fans around the world when Morrison died in Paris on Saturday, 3 July 1971. According to the French police, the 27-year-old star had died of natural causes.

The story of Jim Morrison's death involved two key witnesses. Both told completely different tales and one must have been lying. The problem was that, for many years, there were very good reasons to regard both as potentially unreliable sources.

One of these witnesses was Pamela Courson, Morrison's long-term partner. She spent the evening and night in their rented flat in the rue Beautreillis, where Morrison officially died. Her version of events said that Jim went to have a bath while she fell asleep and that she discovered his dead body slumped in the tub the following morning.

The other version came from Sam Bernett. He was a friend of

Morrison's, later a journalist, TV front man and vice president of Disneyland Paris, but at that time manager of the Rock And Roll Circus club in Paris. This was a bar that had seen performances by Pink Floyd, the Beach Boys and Cat Stevens and had been a Parisian haunt of the Beatles, the Stones, Clapton and Hendrix. It was a heavy place – 'gangsters, nightlife, bad cops, mafia… and a lot of fighting', according to one ex-employee.

The difficulty with Pamela Courson's story is that it is implausible. Courson herself was an unstable and heavily addicted heroin user, who killed herself with a massive overdose three years later. Her story of a simple, though tragic, death by natural causes has always seemed hard to accept, especially in view of what followed.

On the morning of 3 July, an incurious French doctor, Max Vassille, carried out a brief examination of the body at the flat and decided there was no reason to suspect foul play and that a full autopsy was not necessary. He signed the death off straight away as being from natural causes, the result of a heart attack. The media scrum, which was always looking to find new stories about the cherub-faced exhibitionist, was not even told he was dead for three days.

Courson's tale was always an oddly limp and downbeat account, the chief feature of which seemed to be that no one was at fault for anything or in any danger of facing any kind of criminal prosecution.

The key problem with the other version of events, Sam Bernett's story, was the fact that it took thirty-six years to emerge.

Apart from that, though it was bizarre, far-fetched and melodramatic and involved hard drugs, threats and suppression of the truth, it seemed to fit the times, the milieu and the people involved rather better.

After his thirty-six-year silence, Bernett finally produced a book in 2007 called *The End – Jim Morrison,* in which he told how the star died in his club from a heroin overdose. He described it all vividly – how it happened, where it happened, exactly who was there and how the people involved set about making sure Morrison's death wouldn't be known about until he was found back in his own bathroom the next day.

There was never any way of reconciling these two stories, of course. Either Courson or Bernett was lying. Or could it have been both?

Whispers that Jim Morrison wasn't really dead arose instantly and kept cropping up for many years. It was the usual sub-Elvis stuff – that he had faked his own death to go off and live a life of peace and meditation in some unknown land, that he was fleeing from gangsters who had vowed to cut him up and auction the pieces, or that he needed five, ten or maybe thirty years of privacy to create his great masterwork.

As with Elvis, the problem was always the body. If you are going to fake your own death on a given day, you need a fresh, warm substitute corpse who looks like you and has a similar medical history, available more or less instantly. That's unless you choose a faked death, like disappearing in the sea or up a mountain, where providing a body isn't necessarily part of the equation.

Like him or loathe him – and there are many music fans who believe Morrison always was a strictly second-rate talent, compared with the dead gods of rock – Jim Morrison certainly had the knack of attracting attention, even in death.

His grave lies near those of Oscar Wilde, Edith Piaf, Balzac, Sarah Bernhardt and Chopin in the Père Lachaise Cemetery in Paris, and it's the most visited of them all.

There's not much doubt that Jim Morrison died and that the

body that ended up in the bath in Paris was his. If there was a conspiracy, it was to do with covering up how and where he died and how he came to be in the bathtub the next morning.

A CONSPIRACY TO PLAY DOWN THE ROCK STAR'S DEATH

Everything about the investigation – or lack of it – into Jim Morrison's death raises question marks and eyebrows.

One of the most-recognised faces on the planet drops dead at twenty-seven and the official follow-up lasts a matter of hours. The medical examiner doesn't see anything worth further investigation in the unchallenged idea of a millionaire twenty-seven-year-old running a warm bath, climbing into it and never getting out again. Only in Paris, perhaps…

Rock stars can die young of natural causes. Much fitter specimens – footballers like Cameroon and Manchester City's Marc-Vivien Foé and the Ivory Coast and former Newcastle United midfielder Cheick Tioté, for example – sometimes drop dead in their twenties or early thirties. But Jim Morrison had been piling on the weight during his time in Paris and his personal fitness regime was not calculated to carry him through to a ripe old age.

The thinking girl's pin-up always took care to muddy the waters about his substance abuse, often pontificating loudly about the evils of drugs. Few people believed for one moment that he was clean. It was a pose, and Morrison had a narcissistic liking for poses that would help him appear deep and confusingly enigmatic.

Jim Morrison was certainly good at cultivating his image and exploiting his bad boy persona. He was convicted of obscenity for supposedly exposing himself on stage at a concert in Miami in 1969, though there has been controversy ever since about whether this actually happened.

More than forty years later, in December 2010, Florida's authorities granted him a posthumous pardon, at the urging of the retiring state governor, a Doors fan. At the time of the pardon, Doors drummer John Densmore told a reporter he had been an eyewitness to nothing. 'Jim was charged with the wrong thing,' he said. 'He was drunk and disorderly, but he didn't whip it out.'

In the end, the most likely explanation for Jim Morrison's death seemed to everybody to be the most banal – that he died of a drug overdose, probably accidental, while his heroin-stupefied girlfriend slept in the room next door.

Even this, of course, would have involved an element of conspiracy, as Dr Vassille, Pamela Courson and Morrison's friends sought to obscure the truth and promote the idea that it was a blameless heart attack that killed him.

'WE SAW NOTHING. WE HEARD NOTHING. WE SHUT UP, OK?'

But the much more colourful truth about Morrison's death may have been revealed at last in the vivid account offered by nightclub manager Sam Bernett, backed up by a well-known French photographer and a British 1960s pop icon, Marianne Faithfull.

Vague rumours had rumbled on for years that Jim Morrison had died of an overdose at the Rock And Roll Circus club and that his dead body had been bundled back across Paris and home to the flat – some said rolled up in a carpet.

But Sam Bernett's 2007 book certainly fleshed out the story, giving details of times, names and places that hadn't been seen before.

According to Bernett, Jim Morrison walked into the Rock And Roll Circus at around 1 a.m. on 3 July 1971.

'I greeted Jim as I always did. He didn't look in great form and immediately went to his usual spot at the bar and ordered a bottle of vodka. I was used to talking about everything with him – from Janis Joplin to the beatniks – but that night it was just small talk. He'd come in to pick up heroin for Pam. He was always collecting drugs for her and the club was full of dealers.'

He claims he saw Morrison doing a drugs deal in the club that night with two regular dealers he knew, both young Frenchmen in their twenties.

'Jim disappeared into the toilets at around 2 a.m. Then, about half an hour later, a cloakroom attendant came up and told me someone was locked in one of the cubicles and wasn't coming out. I got a bouncer to smash the door down.'

What Bernett saw next, in a cubicle of the women's toilets, was vivid and unforgettable. In his book, he wrote, 'I recognised the US Army combat jacket and the riding boots from the Camargue region, which he never took off. It was Jim Morrison, with his head between his knees, his arms dangling. We were mesmerised. Seeing Jim in such a bad way was awful.

'We were certain he'd been snorting heroin because there was foam coming out of his lips, as well as blood. He was scared of needles, so he never injected drugs. He just snorted them.'

A doctor Sam Bernett knew was at the club and he rapidly examined Morrison's body. 'He pushed Jim's head back, lifted his eyelids, opened his mouth and put his ear to his chest to listen for his heartbeat,' Bernett said. 'He looked for marks and bruises on the body and arms. It was a quick and professional examination and his diagnosis was very confident. "This man is dead," he said. "He appears to be the victim of a cardiac arrest."

The two French drug dealers from the bar who had given Jim Morrison the heroin arrived in the toilet and argued that he had 'just fainted' and that they would take care of him.

Sam Bernett says there was a brief disagreement about what should happen next before the two dealers simply lifted Morrison's body out of the cubicle, wrapped a blanket round him and carried him through the cloakroom and out of the street door of a neighbouring club.

That was the last Bernett saw of his friend Jim. Word was that he was taken back to the flat, stripped and put in a very hot bath, in the hope of either reviving him or at least warming the body and making it hard for anyone to pinpoint the time of death.

Among those who later admitted helping spirit Jim Morrison's body away was Patrick Chauvel, now an internationally respected war photographer. 'We carried him in a blanket and got him the hell out of there,' Chauvel said. 'The five or six people who knew – who were there that night – agreed to just forget about it.'

When they got back to the bar, Bernett claims the right-hand man of the club's owner, Paul Pacini, made it clear to him that nothing was to go any further. Or else.

'Since Morrison's friends want to take him with them, we have nothing more to do with this story,' he told him. 'The club has no responsibility for what happens here. It was a sad accident, certainly, but that's fate. So we saw nothing. We heard nothing. We shut up, OK? It's what we better do to avoid a scandal.'

Sam Bernett's book even gave the name – Count Jean de Breteuil – of the man whose heroin killed Jim Morrison.

De Breteuil was to die soon of his own heroin overdose. That night, however, he just wanted to get clear of any trouble following Morrison's death. He left the club and grabbed his girlfriend, Marianne Faithfull, the English rock princess and ex-partner of Mick Jagger, and the couple flew to Casablanca.

Marianne Faithfull's testimony, in her autobiography, *Faithfull*, provided powerful support for Bernett's version of the Jim Morrison conspiracy. She pulled no punches.

'Jean was a horrible guy, someone who had crawled out from under a stone. Somehow I ended up with him… it was all about drugs and sex.'

When de Breteuil got a call from Pamela Morrison [Courson] and said he had to go very quickly, Faithfull wanted to go with him. She wanted to meet Jim Morrison but de Breteuil refused to take her and said he'd only be away a couple of hours.

'He came back in the early hours of the morning in an agitated state and woke me up. Then, for no apparent reason, he beat me up. "Get packed."

'"Why? Where are we going?"

'"Morocco."

'He was scared for his life. Jim Morrison had OD'd and Jean had provided the smack that killed him. Now he was a small-time heroin dealer in big trouble.'

Although some of the details of all this have still not been confirmed, the French police were initially impressed enough to consider reopening the case. This hasn't happened, however, and it would have been extremely unusual under French law, as cases cannot normally be reopened after more than twenty years.

There's still one question left unanswered. If what Sam Bernett has said was true, why did he wait so long to unveil what must have been the burning secret of his life?

'I was 26 in 1971,' he told journalists in 2007. 'Today I'm past 60 and I want to get rid of my heavy burden.'

When cynics pointed out that a brisk-selling book about an iconic and long-dead rock star can form a useful pension contribution for a Frenchman in his early sixties, Bernett just shrugged. 'I'm not tarnishing anything. I am simply telling the truth. At least everything is now out there to be discussed. I've said what I have to say.'

5

MKULTRA

THE CIA BOFFINS WHO MADE THE
WORLD DOUBT AMERICA

Sixty years ago, a secret CIA report moaned about how restricting the range of technologies available for its black ops and other secret work was.

'As of 1960, no effective knockout pill, truth serum, aphrodisiac or recruitment pill was known to exist,' the document complained.

But this shopping list – straight out of the pages of a James Bond fantasy – was something the CIA had already started working on. Creating the pharmaceutical secret weapons a real-life 007 might wish for was the job of a crack team of spooks and boffins involved in the MKULTRA research and testing programme.

What about memory erasers? Intelligence enhancers? Instant sobriety tablets? Or undetectable assassination pills that mimicked heart attacks or strokes?

In the conspiratorial world of the 1950s and 1960s, everything was denied, everything was untraceable and even the funding for the CIA's advanced research programme was carefully disguised and hidden away from public scrutiny. What was actually going on and how this last 6 per cent of the agency's research budget was spent was even kept secret from the CIA's own top brass.

For many years, the US government ridiculed the idea that MKULTRA existed. When the few documents about it that had survived the shredder were eventually declassified or released under the Freedom of Information Act, even those who had been most suspicious were staggered to glimpse the kind of cruel, unethical and illegal experiments that had been funded by their taxes.

Apart from trying to develop truth drugs and aphrodisiacs, the researchers had enthusiastically tried out experiments in hypnotic programming and electro-shock brainwashing. When they talked about a 'recruitment pill', they were hoping for a mind-control drug that would override victims' free will and make them do exactly as they were told.

They wanted to turn spies into double agents, make prisoners reveal secrets and, ideally, find ways to create remorseless, brain-washed zombie assassins who would kill without pity or memory.

Drugs, of one sort or another, seemed the most promising tools for this kind of work. They tested other approaches, too, like radiation treatments and implanting electrodes into people's brains to see if their behaviour could be modified. Other guinea pigs were disoriented by being deprived of sleep or locked in sensory deprivation chambers. They even brought in stage magicians and hypnotists, to see what could be learned from their techniques.

But the most exciting psycho-warfare tool was the CIA's drug of choice, LSD.

In the early 1950s, little was known about LSD, except that it seemed incredibly powerful, concentrated and unpredictable.

Wide-ranging CIA experiments in the quest for 'special interrogation' tools had not had a lot of success. They'd tried ether and alcohol, morphine and heroin, amphetamines, cocaine and their own concoction, TD (as in 'truth drug'), a tasteless, odourless extract of cannabis.

But 1951 saw the start of a CIA love affair with acid that was to last for many years. The potential of LSD seemed limitless. In the right dose, under the right circumstances, this might be the truth drug the spooks had been looking for.

It could be an unstoppable weapon. What if a cupful of acid, a few million doses, could be slipped into a city's water supply? The answer was that it couldn't – or, rather, that the chlorine in public water supplies would neutralise the drug. But what about treating, say, the water supply of an airfield or a battleship?

Under the umbrella of MKULTRA, CIA staff tested LSD on each other and on hundreds of volunteers. But they also tested it on thousands of totally unwitting, non-consenting victims, including servicemen, prisoners, hospital patients and punters visiting prostitutes in special CIA-run brothels that were set up in San Francisco.

This last project, known poetically as Operation Midnight Climax, gave the CIA new insight into how sex and entrapment could be used in Secret Service work, as well as people's reactions to LSD, as two-way mirrors let the hardworking agents study everything that happened. Midnight Climax was one of the longest projects, running from 1955 to 1963, when the CIA's Inspector General called a halt after being shocked to discover details about it during a routine activity review.

Doctors working on CIA contracts did things no doctor should ever do.

In one of the worst cases, black inmates at a prison hospital in

Lexington, Kentucky – one of fifteen large institutions used for MKULTRA experiments – were given LSD day after day, non-stop, for two and a half months, with doubled and quadrupled doses to overcome their growing tolerance to the drug.

This was one of many trials that were subcontracted out, with funds channelled via the National Institute of Mental Health to a civilian doctor, Dr Harris Isbell.

Ironically, Dr Isbell was a member of the US Food & Drug Administration's expert Advisory Committee on the Abuse of Depressant and Stimulant Drugs. Few people realised quite how deep his knowledge of his specialist subject went.

Like many MKULTRA trials supposedly justified by concern for US national security, this treatment of prisoners and addicts was clearly unethical and tantamount to torture. It was carefully and deliberately concealed from Congress and the public at the time and the conspiracy to keep it hidden for ever came within an ace of succeeding.

For years, despite the number of people involved, there were no whistleblowers. The conspirators – spooks, the military, bio-chemists, doctors and academics, prisons and hospitals, drug companies and forty-four colleges and universities – seemed to have managed to keep the lid nailed down on a potentially huge scandal.

STATE-SPONSORED CONSPIRACIES ACT IN OUR NAME

Maybe it all depends on definitions. At one level, all our national security and Secret Service operations are about a conspiracy – and it's one that involves us.

We give the CIA, MI6 and the rest of them the licence to

do what we wouldn't do and don't even want to think about, in order to protect us and our children. And we just hope that, when it eventually comes to light, it won't be too awful.

That's the shock of a world war, or even a smaller conflict like Vietnam. Suddenly, we can't opt out and delegate the killing and cruelty to other people. Conscription comes and suddenly people like us have to get involved.

In recent years, the CIA has still been behaving almost as badly as it was in the Cold War period – in Iraq, in Afghanistan and Pakistan, and, above all, with its disgraceful programme of 'extraordinary rendition' flights, secret prisons on overseas territories and outsourced torture of terror suspects and others.

These activities are not just shameful for the CIA's subcontractors, including the Secret Services of Britain and other allies. They are shameful for us, too, as they are being done in our name. We want the results, if they keep us safe, but we don't want to know about how they are achieved. But is it a conspiracy? Does that count? Probably not quite.

In the same way, some would argue that MKULTRA was just a secret intelligence service doing what it has to do and roping in the resources it needs to carry out those tasks.

MISSED DOCUMENTS REVEAL MKULTRA'S SECRETS

The original motive for the CIA's research programmes was the belief that some US prisoners returning after the Korean War had been brainwashed by the Communists.

It was feared they might have been programmed to commit sabotage or assassinations. America needed to know if this was possible. And, if it was, America wanted to be able to do it, too.

MKULTRA was run by Dr Sidney Gottlieb, head of the CIA's Technical Services Division and a real-life Dr Strangelove who had studied the files of the monstrous Nazi medical experiments at the Dachau concentration camp. But it was largely the brainchild of Richard Helms, whose steady climb up the hierarchy eventually led to the top role, as Director of Central Intelligence (and, later, a suspended two-year sentence for lying to Congress).

Helms was enchanted with the imagined military and subversive potential of LSD. He referred to it as 'dynamite' and encouraged the use of 'P-1', as it was officially coded, in interrogation and overseas operations for more than ten years from 1955 onwards.

A pet idea was that foreign leaders should be slipped acid before big speeches or meetings to make them appear uncoordinated and incoherent in public. You can see the appeal. A world statesman whose speech started sounding like lines from 'I Am the Walrus' would surely forfeit much of his international credibility.

It was Helms who ordered the deliberate destruction of all the files and records relating to MKULTRA on 31 January 1973, claiming it was because of 'the burgeoning paper problem'. Clearly untroubled by any sort of conscience, he gave a more candid explanation a couple of years later: 'Since the programme was over and finished and done with, we thought we would just get rid of the files as well, so that anybody who assisted us in the past would not be subject to follow-up questions, embarrassment, if you will.'

It was only persistent sleuthing by the *New York Times* that brought some details of MKULTRA to the surface in 1974, leading to investigations by President Gerald Ford's Rockefeller

Commission and the Senate's Church Committee. These led the president to sign the first Executive Order on intelligence activities, banning assassinations and experiments on people without their consent.

Even then, the cat was not entirely out of the bag, though the discovery process was helped in June 1977, when it turned out that Helms's attempt to erase the past had been bungled. Seven large boxes with 20,000 MKULTRA documents that had been missed by the cover-up squad were unearthed, filling in many of the details CIA witnesses had found it so hard to remember under oath.

These documents have now been declassified and many are available online, including a remarkable collection of interesting and chilling reports that can be browsed in their original form. A simple Google search for 'MKULTRA documents' brings up a mass of jaw-dropping detail.

Altogether, MKULTRA covered 149 'subprojects', as they were called. It was directly responsible for several deaths and for physical or psychological damage to thousands of volunteers and non-consenting victims. The lies and secrecy around it also made a huge contribution to leading millions of Americans to lose faith in themselves and their government.

No one knows now whether CIA MKULTRA brainwashing and programming techniques had a hand in the great unresolved mysteries of the twentieth century, including the Kennedy assassinations, the killing of Martin Luther King, the murder of John Lennon, the Ronald Reagan shooting and the mass suicide of over 900 people in Jonestown. Doubt and cynicism reign, casting forward a pall of confusion that covers both tragedies like 9/11 and flagrantly criminal activities like extraordinary rendition. The CIA is firmly established as standing for Conspiracy In Action and half the world believes America is out to do it down. It's a big, bad legacy from a small project that started with just $25 million, a few grammes of LSD, a bunch of mad scientists and a dark conspiracy to make sure Washington didn't know what was being done in its name.

6

DR DAVID KELLY

**FAR TOO MANY UNANSWERED
QUESTIONS**

**As the helicopter slowly clattered its way through the darkness,
the crewmen knew what they were looking out for in the fields
and woods below them.**

Criss-crossing the Oxfordshire night in a tight search pattern,
they were looking for a man – or a body.

The UK's leading chemical and biological warfare expert,
Mr Anthrax himself, the top specialist from the secretive Porton
Down laboratories, had gone missing. But if he had had an
accident – or worse – in the countryside down there, they would
find him. The helicopter had modern thermal imaging search
and rescue equipment. In skilled hands, that doesn't miss much.

Dr David Kelly was a former UN weapons inspector in Iraq,
a veteran of thirty-seven rounds of that high-stakes cat-and-
mouse game. He had been accused of leaking information to
the BBC that cast doubt on the British government's reasons
for invading Iraq. He knew about the famous 'sexed-up dossier'
that claimed Saddam Hussein had weapons of mass destruction

(WMDs) that could be used at forty-five minutes' notice and he had indicated to BBC reporter Andrew Gilligan that this key claim was simply not true.

As a result, two days earlier, on 15 July 2003, he had been called before Parliament's Select Committee on Foreign Affairs for a very uncomfortable televised public grilling, followed by a private session with the British intelligence services at a safe house outside London.

Dr Kelly was in the spotlight and under intense scrutiny – as his wife, Janice, said, a 'distressed' man.

But that doesn't mean that he killed himself. When he went out for his usual afternoon walk on nearby Harrowdown Hill, round about three on the afternoon of Thursday, 17 July 2003, nothing seemed out of the ordinary. He had been working in his study all morning – even booking tickets to fly to Iraq a week later, on 25 July – and had arranged to meet his daughter, Rachel, that evening, so the day was unfolding in a fairly routine way. Curiously, despite the intense media interest, the pressmen who had been doorstepping the house had gone.

It was only when he hadn't come home much later – after midnight – that Janice Kelly called the police. Recognising that he was a man under pressure, they began a search that included putting up the police helicopter.

According to the search pattern the pilot was flying, it must have been nearly three o'clock in the morning when the helicopter, with its heat-seeking search equipment, flew over the edge of the woods on Harrowdown Hill. The crew saw nothing to report.

Yet, a few hours later, around 9 a.m., volunteer searchers Paul Chapman and Louise Holmes and their dog, Brock, found Dr Kelly's body, dead but still warm, slumped against a tree at the edge of the wood.

There were cuts on Dr Kelly's left wrist, apparently made with his blunt and bloody pruning knife that lay, with his wristwatch, on his left side. There was a certain amount of blood, as the deepest of the cuts had severed the small ulnar artery on the little finger side of the wrist, and some vomit around his mouth. There were also three blister packs that had held a total of thirty coproxamol tablets, though there was only one tablet left.

The suspicion, naturally, was that Dr Kelly had given way to the pressure he found himself under and committed suicide.

But there were a number of disturbing factors about this death. They have emerged slowly, over the years, so no one has had all the information at one time until now.

For example, it was not until a Liberal Democrat MP, Norman Baker (later a junior transport minister in Britain's coalition government), made a Freedom of Information Act request in 2007 that it came out that the bloodied knife found next to Dr Kelly had no fingerprints on it – neither his, nor those of anyone else.

It has since emerged that there were also no prints on the tablet packs. Nor were there any on the blood-smeared bottle of Evian water found by the body. Nor were there any gloves to be found nearby.

Again, it took another FOI request, by author Garrick Alder in 2008, to flush out the details and times of the unsuccessful helicopter search. The flight record from Bedfordshire and Thames Valley Police forces, which shared the twin-engined Eurocopter, states: 'Area search included bridlepaths from Longworth north to the River Thames, east to Newbridge and back to Kingston Bagpuize.'

At 2.50 a.m., the Longworth-Thames leg of the search took the helicopter right over Harrowdown Hill, where Dr Kelly was found the next morning. Nothing was spotted down below. Yet the Home Office pathologist, Dr Nicholas Hunt, later told the Hutton Inquiry that Dr Kelly's death occurred between 4.15 p.m. and the early hours of the morning. The latest time he could have died was 1.15 a.m.

If Dr Kelly was down there on the edge of the wood, recently dead, the helicopter crew would have hoped to find him. If he wasn't yet there, but was already dead somewhere else, the suicide scenario is obviously wrong.

Over the years, the mystery surrounding his death has never been resolved. There is still a niggling, bubbling suspicion that this 'suicide' was actually something far worse.

One reason for scepticism is the fact that there never was a completed inquest into Dr David Kelly's death – nor a properly constituted public inquiry, under the Public Inquiries Act 1921, which would have done the same job.

The local coroner's inquest was opened on 21 July 2003, but adjourned and never reopened. The Hutton Inquiry was technically 'an ad hoc non-statutory judicial inquiry' set up 'urgently to conduct an investigation into the circumstances surrounding the death of Dr David Kelly'. At the time, it was widely believed the inquiry would perform the functions of an inquest.

Hutton reported on 28 January 2004, largely exonerating the government and blaming the BBC for its handling of the Kelly/WMD affair. It adopted the conclusion of the pathologist, Dr Hunt, that the cause of death was as recorded on the death certificate '1(a) Haemorrhage, 1(b) Incised wounds to the left wrist, and 2 Coproxamol ingestion and coronary artery atherosclerosis'.

This was surprising in itself. The death certificate had been completed and the cause of death registered as 'haemorrhage' on

18 August 2003, five weeks before the Hutton Inquiry ended, at a time when Hutton was still taking new evidence to find out what had happened.

Dr Kelly's death certificate says an inquest took place on 14 August – which is simply untrue – and it has not been signed by a doctor or a coroner, which makes the document technically invalid. The Oxfordshire coroner later decided, at a quick fifteen-minute hearing, not to resume his adjourned inquest.

But Hutton was not a 'real' public inquiry with powers to examine the case fully, take evidence under oath and cross-examine witnesses so that it could take the place of a coroner's inquest. Evidence-taking seemed haphazard. There were seventy-four witnesses at the Hutton Inquiry but the police officer in charge of the investigation, Chief Inspector Alan Young, wasn't one of them.

Lord Hutton had never sat as a coroner (and had only led one very minor inquiry before) and the way he dealt with the case didn't fulfil the basic legal requirements for investigating unnatural deaths. Coroners have to answer five questions about any unusual or unexpected death. These are, broadly:

1) Who died?
2) Where?
3) When?
4) How? (What was the immediate cause of death?)
5) Why? (A verdict is needed, stating by what means the deceased came by his death.)

The Hutton Inquiry didn't even cover these basics. It didn't specify where Dr Kelly died and there is certainly room for doubt about how he met his end.

Even the time of death raises some odd questions. Dr Nicholas

Hunt, who later carried out the post-mortem, first saw the body at the scene at 12.10 p.m. A key part of his job was to find out when Dr Kelly had died, but he didn't get round to taking the necessary rectal temperature measurement until 7.15 p.m., seven hours after first examining the body.

The earlier a temperature reading is taken, the more sure you can be about the time of death. Because of the long delay, the pathologist was only able to say that Dr Kelly had been dead for eighteen to twenty-seven hours before the temperature was measured. This meant death had occurred between 4.15 p.m. on the Thursday afternoon and 1.15 a.m. on the Friday morning.

THE MAN WITH 'A BRAIN THAT COULD BOIL WATER'

In January 2010, it emerged that Lord Hutton had taken the unprecedented step of requesting, after his inquiry ended, that all the medical records, post-mortem documents and police photographs relating to Dr Kelly's death should be kept locked up for seventy years. Despite this, the post-mortem report was released by the Ministry of Justice in October 2010. To everyone's surprise, it seemed to make the official account of Dr Kelly's suicide more, rather than less, plausible. Many people wondered why it had ever been held back, though Lord Hutton appeared to have thought this would help to protect Dr Kelly's family.

The pressure that had been building up on David Kelly certainly could have driven almost anyone to suicide.

When he died, there was an unopened letter on the desk in his study from a senior personnel man at the Ministry of Defence, Richard Hatfield, making it clear that he was going to have to shut up and stop leaking secrets or airing his opinions in public. If he didn't, he'd be disciplined or even sacked.

The letter – the text of which is available on the Hutton Inquiry website – had already sat there, unread, for a week, but Dr Kelly had a pretty good idea what was inside. There had already been an interview with Richard Hatfield and various warning phone calls from other MoD people. The dodgy dossier business was bad enough, but the MoD was even more worried about what was to come next. Dr Kelly had written 40,000 words of a detailed book about his career and the powers that be did not want to see that published unvetted.

His attitude to his work was careful and measured, though Defence Ministry sources made some clumsy attempts to play down his importance or present him as a Walter Mitty character or a loose cannon. In the 1990s, his UN weapons inspectorate boss had nominated him for a Nobel Peace Prize. A colleague described him admiringly as having 'a brain that could boil water'.

In June 2003, six weeks before his death, Dr Kelly had made his last trip to Iraq, to examine two trailers that were said to be mobile germ weapon plants. They weren't, he concluded, though more recent information, mainly from WikiLeaks, has shown there were plenty of chemical weapons still to be found. The scale may have been smaller than expected, but it turns out that Saddam still had access to weapons of mass destruction right up to the time Iraq was invaded.

To many people's surprise, America's secret Iraq War logs, made public by WikiLeaks in September 2010, revealed that more WMDs, including chemical agents, mustard gas shells and 'neuroparalytic weapons', were still being discovered in Iraq in 2004, 2007 and right up to 2008. Small-scale chemical weapons laboratories were also found and there was some evidence that AQI (al-Qaeda in Iraq) had used chemical weapons in attacks on coalition soldiers.

LITTLE BLOOD – AND A BODY THAT MOVED

Dr David Kelly had become an embarrassment to the Labour government of Tony Blair. He had been a thorn in the side of the Iraqis for many years and had already been warned by the Russians that he was on an Iraqi Secret Service hit list. He was also, apparently, someone the Chinese Secret Intelligence Service particularly disliked and had placed on a target list.

We know that he freelanced as an adviser for several other intelligence services – including Mossad, the CIA and the FBI, the French and Germans, the Australians and the Japanese – but we have no way of knowing how well or badly these relationships were going. All we can know for sure is that, because of who he was and what he did, there could easily have been some very serious people who were out to get him.

And there are simply too many unusual and unlikely aspects of David Kelly's death for the outstanding puzzles just to be left unresolved. Unless the British authorities and secret service agencies already know the answers, there could still be long-standing national security issues at stake, even now. The loose ends still need to be tied up.

For example, though the searchers on Harrowdown Hill said they'd found Dr Kelly's body slumped against the base of a tree, it then seems to have moved several feet in the course of the next half-hour or so.

One of the two experienced paramedics who were on the

scene before 10 a.m. was David Bartlett. He recalled the body as being well away from the tree trunk.

'He was lying flat out some distance from the tree. He definitely wasn't leaning against it. I remember saying to the copper, "Are you sure he hasn't fallen out of the tree?"

'When I was there, the body was far enough away from the tree for someone to get behind it. I know that, because I stood there when we were using the electrodes to check his heart.

'Later, I learned that the dog team said they had found him propped up against the tree. He wasn't when we got there. If the earlier witnesses are saying that, then the body had obviously been moved.'

Bartlett and his crew partner, Vanessa Hunt, checked the body over and confirmed that life was extinct at 10.07 a.m. They were both amazed by how little blood they saw around Dr Kelly's body.

Like Bartlett, Hunt had attended many slashed-wrist suicide attempts over the years. In all cases, there was arterial blood everywhere. But only one of the attempts she'd encountered had succeeded.

'That was like a slaughterhouse,' she said. 'Just think what it would be like with five or six pints of milk splashed everywhere. If you slit your wrists, that is the equivalent amount of blood you would have to lose.'

In the woods on Harrowdown Hill, the picture was strikingly different.

'There was no gaping wound,' she said. 'There wasn't a puddle of blood around.'

The elements of the Kelly case – political, military, judicial, medical and highly confidential – were always bound to make it controversial. Anything short of maximum transparency was always going to feed conspiracy theories.

But the handling of this explosive mixture was secretive, careless and provocative. Many years later, there are still completely unexplained questions about the search, the evidence-gathering, the inquiry procedures and the aftermath.

Why, for example, did policemen and three others (assumed to be officers from MI5's Technical Assessment Unit) come to the house so early on the Friday morning, well before Dr Kelly was known to be dead? Why were Janice Kelly and her daughters asked to go outside and wait in the garden, while the visitors carried out a search so thorough that it included stripping wallpaper off the sitting-room walls?

Why were colleagues of Dr Kelly apparently 'warned off' and told not to go to his funeral?

And why didn't the man in charge of the police investigation, Chief Inspector Alan Young, give evidence at the public inquiry?

Perhaps the oddest fact of this strange case is a detail that has obsessed conspiracy theorists for years. The search for the missing scientist was codenamed Operation Mason by Thames Valley Police. The date-stamped incident file headed 'Operation Mason' appears to have been opened at Thames Valley Police HQ at 2.30 p.m. on Thursday, 17 July.

But that was almost ten hours before Dr Kelly was reported missing and some time before he left home to go for his routine afternoon walk.

Just eighteen and a half hours later, before a single policeman had set eyes on the body or had a chance to confirm Dr Kelly's identity, the last entry was made in the file: '9.00 a.m. 18.07.03. Body recovered.'

Thames Valley Police representatives have since claimed the Kelly file was only ever intended to cover the period of the incident itself and was timed and dated retrospectively.

Sceptics, including Norman Baker MP, have pointed out that the 'sexed-up dossier' affair and Dr Kelly's grilling by parliamentary committees and MoD officials were hardly going to be irrelevant to a possible verdict of suicide. As Baker said, any investigation that took 2.30 p.m. on Thursday 17 July as its starting point would be 'woefully inadequate'.

With the passing of time, even the most suspicious and controversial issues start to fade from view. But occasionally some new element thrusts the fate of Dr Kelly back into the spotlight. In 2018, an award-winning investigative journalist called Miles Goslett stirred things up again with a new book entitled *An Inconvenient Death: How the Establishment Covered up the David Kelly Affair*.

Goslett has a nose for trouble – he was the first to expose Jimmy Savile's predatory sexual abuse of women and children – and he highlighted many of the inconsistencies in the official account. His book also pointed out the oddly chilling fact that Dr Kelly's patient records disappeared from his dentist's surgery on the day he died, only to reappear in her filing cabinet again three days later.

Alongside the secrets of the Operation Mason file, the missing fingerprints and the whole catalogue of unanswered questions surrounding Dr Kelly's presumed suicide, this is the kind of detail that will always continue to feed mistrust and speculation. But if this case teaches us one thing, it is that searching for the truth is very difficult indeed when politicians, police and those involved in the justice system have all decided it should be buried safely out of sight.

7

OPERATION NORTHWOODS

EVIL IN THE AIR, TERROR ON THE STREETS

The vicious, murderous plan was finally exposed, in all its chilling detail, less than six months before the 9/11 attacks on the Twin Towers of New York's World Trade Center.

Airliners were to be hijacked and other aircraft blown up. Bombs were to be planted in public places. Gunmen would mount assassination attempts on key individuals. Ordinary citizens were to feel the dread and anxiety of a terror campaign targeting several major cities, including the capital.

The victims who would be exposed to the threat of terror and suffer the results of bombings and violence were the people of America, specifically those in Miami and Washington DC.

But the conspirators behind the plans for this despicable terror campaign were their own leaders, America's top generals.

Operation Northwoods was an extraordinary false flag operation aimed at justifying an American invasion of Fidel Castro's Communist Cuba. And it was dreamed up, planned out and signed off as a serious proposal in 1962 by the US Joint Chiefs of Staff, under the chairmanship of General Lyman L Lemnitzer.

This breathtakingly insane plan also included bright ideas like faking the downing of a chartered airliner over Cuba, using an empty, pilotless, radio-controlled aircraft.

Real passengers – 'a group of college students' was suggested – would board a plane for Jamaica or Venezuela, painted and numbered to look identical to an airliner owned by a CIA front company. The disguised plane and the real one, already being flown by remote control, would rendezvous over the ocean. The disguised plane, carrying the students, would quietly sneak back to a remote airfield, unload its passengers and be repainted to resume its normal identity, while the radio-controlled aircraft flew on into Cuban airspace.

Once there, it would send out Mayday distress calls saying it was being attacked by Cuban fighters, before being detonated in a spectacular explosion, with the apparent loss of dozens of innocent lives.

There was also a scheme to sink an unmanned, radio-controlled US ship off the coast of Cuba and pretend that many sailors on board had been killed.

'Conduct funerals for mock victims,' the provisional plan suggested. A further embellishment carried the note: 'Casualty lists in US newspapers would cause a helpful wave of national indignation.'

Many more bloodcurdling ideas were listed.

'We could sink a boatload of Cubans en route to Florida (real or simulated),' the generals proposed.

Credibility would be important, though, and some people might have to pay a price for that.

'We could foster attempts on lives of Cuban refugees in the United States, even to the extent of wounding,' the top brass continued.

Not one of the military leaders seems to have had qualms about the proposals, which were forwarded as 'a preliminary submission suitable for planning purposes', with the recognition that individual projects would be considered on a case-by-case basis.

The declared aim was to put the US in the position of 'suffering justifiable grievances' in order to get world and United Nations opinion firmly behind military action.

'These suggestions provide a basis for development of a single, integrated, time-phased plan to focus all efforts on the objective of justification for US military intervention in Cuba,' the planning memorandum concluded.

Within a couple of days of the meeting at which the generals gave their approval, the detailed proposal document was put before President John F Kennedy by his Secretary of Defense, Robert McNamara.

JFK's reaction to the Operation Northwoods plan was less than sympathetic. Like McNamara, he was appalled by the generals' gung-ho enthusiasm for provoking a war. He soon got rid of Lemnitzer as chairman of the Joint Chiefs of Staff, though the general's career hardly skidded to a halt. He was moved to Europe and became NATO's Supreme Allied Commander for the next six years. As late as 1975, long after his retirement, Lemnitzer was brought back by President Gerald Ford as a member of his Foreign Intelligence Advisory Board.

DID ANGRY GENERALS DECIDE JFK WAS ANTI-AMERICAN?

The key point about the plan for Operation Northwoods is that, despite the astonishing willingness of all the country's top soldiers to set out on a campaign of state-sponsored terrorism on the American mainland, nothing actually happened.

This time, the checks and balances in the system worked. The executive dismissed the whole idea, and President Kennedy told Lemnitzer face to face that the US was not about to use military force against Cuba.

All this was only a few months after the disastrous CIA-backed assault on Cuba that ended in defeat for the anti-Castro Cubans at the Bay of Pigs, with hundreds of battlefield deaths and executions and the capture of 1,200 prisoners.

The dramatic and embarrassing failure had made a deep impression on the president. After the Bay of Pigs, JFK told a reporter, 'The first advice I'm going to give my successor is to watch the generals and to avoid feeling that because they are military men their opinions on military matters are worth a damn.'

Kennedy was disgusted with the Bay of Pigs fiasco. He sacked CIA Director Allen Dulles and famously said he wanted to 'splinter the CIA into a thousand pieces and scatter it to the winds'. He moved fast to take responsibility for paramilitary operations away from the spooks and give it to the Joint Chiefs of Staff, in the hope that they would plan and behave better. Operation Northwoods was the clearest possible proof that that strategy hadn't worked.

Whether Kennedy's objections to the idea of a staged terror campaign on US soil were partly moral or wholly practical, his scrapping of the Northwoods proposals made him bitter enemies among the generals, to go alongside his sworn foes in the CIA. Those who think there may have been a mega-conspiracy behind the JFK assassination eighteen months later point to the Bay of Pigs and Operation Northwoods as crucial moments when powerful forces in the US began to believe their president was becoming – in their terms – dangerously anti-American.

THE CONSPIRACY THAT PROVES ANYTHING'S POSSIBLE

Operation Northwoods was kept firmly out of sight for many years, and it was not until 1997 that the first declassified papers were released that hinted at the existence of this carefully concealed conspiracy.

In late April 2001, a single damning document was published. This was the complete Memorandum for the Secretary of Defense, dated 13 March 1962 and originally marked 'Top Secret – Special Handling – Noforn [no foreign nationals]', with the full details of the thinking behind Operation Northwoods.

General Lemnitzer was usually careful to make sure the documentation about anything he didn't want to own up to was destroyed or 'lost'. But even Lemnitzer couldn't snatch back everything. The Secretary of Defense, Robert McNamara, had kept his copy of the memo, the only absolute proof that these detailed plans had been approved by the Joint Chiefs of Staff and reached the highest levels of government. (The original fifteen-page document is now available online – just search for 'Operation Northwoods pdf'.)

As well as unleashing terror on the streets of Florida and Washington, the Northwoods proposals included the idea of using Cuban dissidents or American forces in Cuban uniforms to sabotage or mortar the US naval base at Guantanamo Bay.

Disguised US aircraft could make night raids on the Dominican Republic, dropping Soviet-made incendiary bombs to implicate Cuba. Adapting American F-86 Sabre jets to create 'reasonable copies' of Russian-built MIG fighters would take 'about three months' and would offer scope for all kinds of airborne confusion and mayhem.

All the time, the idea was to build up a picture of the Cuban regime as 'rash and irresponsible and an alarming threat to the peace of the Western Hemisphere', in order to provide a pretext for a large-scale US military intervention before the end of 1962.

In the event, these hare-brained notions were never put into practice, as President Jack Kennedy and Secretary of Defense Robert McNamara threw them out.

But the fact that these highly specific and cynically ruthless plans were unanimously endorsed by America's top generals, albeit sixty years ago, is a chilling reminder.

Bizarre, manipulative and bloodthirsty plots don't just exist in the minds of paranoid and embittered conspiracy theorists. They can also exist in the minds of generals, politicians and others who may have the power and resources to turn them into reality.

Very often, there is less to an apparently suspicious chain of events or circumstances than meets the eye. Coincidence and cock-up are momentous, shaping forces in human affairs. But sometimes there truly is more going on than they ever want you to know.

8

MALAYSIA AIRLINES FLIGHT MH17

PUTIN'S LESSON – 'KEEP LYING TILL YOU DROWN OUT THE TRUTH'

In the summer of 2014, the Donbas region in southeastern Ukraine was a dangerous place to be. The previous November, a popular revolution in Kyiv had ousted the Ukrainian president, the Putin-friendly autocrat Viktor Yanukovych. Russia responded by annexing the Crimea and invading parts of eastern Ukraine. In Donbas, armed conflict raged between Ukrainian forces and Russian-backed rebels, supplied with military hardware ferried in across the nearby Russian border.

In this perilous context, some commercial services had been rerouted to avoid passing over Ukraine. But thirty-seven airlines – including BA, Lufthansa, KLM, Singapore Airlines and several US carriers – continued to fly over the war zone, following advice that said flights above 32,000 feet were safe from the skirmishes below.

On 17 July 2014, Malaysia Airlines Flight 17 from Amsterdam to Kuala Lumpur entered Ukrainian airspace, following a flight path 33,000 feet above the conflict.

More than 160 airliners had already flown, one after another, through Donbas airspace that day. But MH17 just happened to be in the wrong place at the wrong time.

At 4.20 p.m. Kyiv time, just 50km short of the Russian border, it disappeared abruptly from the radar screens. The plane, a Boeing 777, had disintegrated in mid-air over Ukrainian territory, scattering debris over an area of fifty square kilometres. All 298 people on board – 15 crew and 283 passengers – were killed. More than half the plane's passengers were Dutch, but many citizens of Malaysia, Australia and the UK were also among the dead.

Considering the location, there were immediate suspicions that the crash had not been an accident. These suspicions intensified when Ukraine's intelligence service, within hours of the disaster, released a damning series of intercepted voice recordings, which apparently captured phone conversations between Russian-backed separatists on the ground in the immediate aftermath of the crash. If the recordings were authentic, they made it crystal clear that the separatists, having mistaken the Boeing for a Ukrainian transport or military plane, had shot it down with a ground-to-air missile. Russian sources insisted the voice recordings weren't genuine. On Russia's state-controlled TV channels, various different stories about the disaster were put out.

Initially, Russian TV reported that the aircraft was a Ukrainian transport plane. Then Russia conceded that the plane was indeed a passenger aircraft, but asserted that it had been shot down by a Ukrainian ground-to-air missile, or perhaps by a Ukrainian fighter jet.

At one point a Russian official even made the outrageous claim that the bodies found in the wreckage were 'not fresh', and that the CIA had loaded the plane with corpses and flown it over the war zone as a false flag provocation – an idea that seemed to echo the Americans' notorious Operation Northwoods plan from the 1960s.

FOUR BUKS CAME FROM RUSSIA – ONLY THREE RETURNED

If Russia's conspiracy theories about MH17 seemed vague and contradictory, the evidence of Russian complicity was solid from the start. The day after the crash, US intelligence sources confirmed that the plane had been hit by a ground-to-air missile. By that stage, Ukrainian intelligence had already released recordings of several purported communications between Russian-backed separatists on the ground. Translated transcripts of these intercepts were published around the world, and they seemed to provide slam-dunk proof that pro-Russian rebels – who referred to themselves as 'Cossacks' – stationed at Chernukhino (Chornukhyne) had been responsible for the tragedy:

Male voice: Yes, Major.
Major: Well, the Chernukhino lads shot down the plane.
Male voice: Who shot it down?
Major: From the Chernukhino roadblock. The Cossacks at
Chernukhino.
Male voice: Yes, Major.
Major: Well, the plane fell apart in the air, near the
Petropavlovskaya coal mine. The first casualty 200
[military jargon for 'dead body'] has been found.
A civilian.

Male voice: Well, what do you have there?

Major: Basically, it was 100 per cent a civilian aircraft.

Male voice: Are many people there?

Major: [Curses] The debris fell right into the backyard.

Male voice: What kind of aircraft?

Major: I have not figured this out yet because I haven't been close to the main body of the debris. I am only looking where the first bodies began to fall. There are the remnants of internal brackets, chairs and bodies there.

Male voice: I see. Any weapons there?

Major: Nothing at all. Civilian things, medical bits and bobs, towels, toilet paper.

In a separate recording, another of the Russian-backed separatists was heard to say, 'Regarding the plane shot down in the area of Snezhnoye-Torez. It's a civilian one. Fell down near Hrabove. There are lots of bodies of women and children. The Cossacks are out there looking at all this. They say on TV it's a Ukrainian AN-26 transport, but it's got Malaysia Airlines written on the plane. What was it doing in Ukrainian territory?' To which his commander replied: 'That means they were bringing in spies. They shouldn't be [curses] flying. There's a war going on.'

The authenticity of these radio intercepts has never been seriously challenged. And the story they told was reinforced in 2016, when an international investigation team, led by Dutch prosecutors, announced the findings of a two-year inquiry into the MH17 disaster. Having assessed an 'immense body of evidence', including eyewitness testimony, satellite and radar data and video and audio recordings, the investigators concluded that MH17 was downed by a Russian-made Buk SA-11 missile, fired from an area controlled by pro-Russian fighters.

Satellite imagery proved that the long-range surface-to-air missile system had been transported into Ukraine from Russia on the day of the crash, with four missiles clearly visible. It was then taken back across the border afterwards, with just three missiles on board.

Dutch prosecutors charged four men – three Russians and one Ukrainian – with murder. When Moscow refused to extradite the accused men to the Netherlands, they were tried *in absentia*.

Another reason to doubt the Russian narrative is that there *was* no coherent Russian narrative. Russia's story kept changing. To begin with, Russian state TV reported that the aircraft that had been destroyed was a Ukrainian transport plane. Then came the story that the Ukrainian military had shot the plane down, either from the ground or in the air. One state-owned Russian channel portrayed the incident as a botched Ukrainian attempt to assassinate Vladimir Putin, who happened to have been on a flight from Brazil to Moscow when MH17 was struck. And let's not forget the obscene fantasy about the CIA filling the plane with dead bodies.

Clearly, these stories couldn't all be true. To add to the confusion, in the twenty-four hours following the disaster, Twitter was flooded with 65,000 tweets blaming the incident on the Ukrainian government. It later emerged that this Twitter campaign had been orchestrated by professional trolls working for Russia's Internet Research Agency – the same troll farm that Russia would employ, two years later, to cause havoc in the run-up to America's presidential election.

So what was going on?

This chaotic mixture of confusion and self-contradiction was not accidental. In fact, confusion was precisely the effect the Russians were aiming to achieve.

MH17 LIES SHOW HOW MOSCOW'S PROPAGANDA WORKS

In the wake of the MH17 disaster, the world was getting a glimpse of how Russian propaganda works in the age of Vladimir Putin. Old-school propagandists plied their trade by hammering away at a single false narrative. But, as Yale philosopher Jason Stanley, author of *How Fascism Works*, points out, post-modern Russian propagandists take a different approach. Their aim is to sow confusion by broadcasting 'a cacophony of opinions and outlandish possibilities'. The idea is that if the cacophony of half-truths and outright lies is cranked up loud enough, the facts will be rendered inaudible. 'Objective truth is drowned out,' as Professor Stanley puts it.

In the West, Russia's fevered attempts to obscure the truth about MH17 didn't fool anyone for long. These days there is broad international acceptance that the plane was brought down by pro-Russian separatist forces, probably with help from a Russian missile crew, using a Russian weapon. But in Russia itself, the regime's disinformation campaign yielded alarming results. According to a poll conducted by Moscow's independent and respected Levada Center two weeks after the crash, 82 per cent of Russians blamed Ukraine for shooting down the plane.

A year after the MH17 disaster, Vladimir Putin sat down for a series of interviews with the American film-maker Oliver Stone. When Stone raised the subject of MH17, Putin had his reply ready. 'As far as I know, right away after this terrible catastrophe, one of the Ukrainian air controllers – I think he was a specialist originating from Spain – announced that he had seen a military aircraft in the corridor assigned for civil aircraft. And there could have been no other military aircraft than the ones controlled by the Ukrainian authorities.'

There it was, straight from the horse's mouth. Twelve months on from the crash, Russia was ready to commit itself, at last, to a single theory or narrative about MH17. The plane had been shot down from the air by a Ukrainian military aircraft. What's more, there seemed to be some evidence to support this claim, in the form of the testimony of the 'specialist originating from Spain'.

So who was the specialist in question? In the hours after MH17 came down, a Twitter user with the handle @spainbuca had published a series of tweets, in Spanish, that did indeed appear to support the story told by Putin. Claiming to be an air traffic controller employed at Kyiv's Boryspil International Airport, @spainbuca told the Twittersphere that moments before MH17 vanished from his radar, he had observed two Ukrainian fighter jets flying beside it.

By the time Putin tried to sell it to Oliver Stone, though, the story of the Spanish air traffic controller had long been viewed as suspect.

Almost immediately after the MH17 disaster, @spainbuca's Twitter account had been suspended, apparently because he had violated the platform's spam policies. And Ukrainian authorities had quickly confirmed that there were no Spaniards employed in Ukrainian air traffic control at the time of the crash.

The plot thickened when it emerged that several months before publishing his MH17 tweets, a Spaniard using the @spainbuca Twitter handle had made a mysterious appearance on RT Spanish, the Spanish-language TV channel operated by RT, Russia's Moscow-based propaganda mouthpiece. To protect his identity, the producers had blurred out the Spaniard's face and had given him a fake name, 'Carlos'. They had, however, shown his true Twitter handle – a slip that subsequently enabled a sharp-eyed journalist to link him to the MH17 story.

So what was 'Carlos' doing on a Russian propaganda channel, two months before the downing of MH17? Well, he was there to talk in negative terms about the Ukrainian revolution. He claimed that protestors in Kyiv had threatened his life, forcing him to flee Ukraine.

In other words, the enigmatic Carlos, aka @spainbuca, seemed to be in the habit of spreading anti-Ukraine propaganda. To say the least, this cast a shadow of reasonable doubt over his subsequent tweets about Ukraine's involvement in the MH17 crash.

In 2018, Radio Free Europe tracked down the elusive Carlos. He turned out to be a Spanish ex-convict whose real name was Jose Carlos Barrios Sanchez. Confronted about his MH17 tweets, Sanchez confessed that he'd never really worked in Ukrainian air traffic control. Indeed, he hadn't even been in Ukraine when MH17 was shot down. Russian propagandists, he alleged, had employed him as a professional troll. They 'told [me] what I had to write' on Twitter, Carlos said, and they'd paid him US $48,000 for his troubles.

Mind you, Carlos never furnished any hard evidence for this assertion, despite claiming that he had bank records to back it up. 'In the end,' Radio Free Europe reported, 'all we got was Carlos's word.'

That was a worry, given that Carlos had already established himself as a serial liar. On the other hand, so had Vladimir Putin.

On the subject of MH17, Russia's official word is even more worthless than Carlos's.

Timothy Snyder, another Yale professor and a Russian- and Ukrainian-speaking expert on disinformation techniques, has pointed out that the ultimate aim of all Putin's propaganda is to make people abandon the idea that truth is even attainable. Bombarded with contradictory stories, they just give up and lapse into cynicism. 'No one really ever tells the truth,' he says. 'Perhaps there is no truth. So let us simply repeat the things we like to hear, and obey those who say them.' As Snyder concludes, with bitter understatement, 'That way lies authoritarianism.'

9

ROBERT F KENNEDY

WAS THIS REALLY A LONE ASSASSIN?

Senator Robert F Kennedy, younger brother of America's greatest martyr since Abraham Lincoln, was shot on 5 June 1968. It was five years after the assassination of President Jack Kennedy and a year to the day after the start of the Israeli/Arab Six Day War. It was also just two months after the murder of Dr Martin Luther King.

Younger, taller, more handsome and with fewer compromises on his political record than JFK, Bobby Kennedy was popular and in tune with the times. He had once been an active supporter of McCarthyism's anti-Communist witch-hunts, but by 1968 he was strongly for black civil rights and against the war in Vietnam. He had already shown, as Attorney General in JFK's 'Camelot' administration, that he was determined to take on organised crime and the mafia.

At the age of just forty-two, he looked to many people like America's next president.

RFK was gunned down in the crowded kitchen pantry of the Ambassador Hotel in Los Angeles as he and his team went from the party celebrating his victory in the California Democratic primary to a press conference in another part of the hotel. The route through the building had been changed at the very last moment on the orders of Kennedy's security chief, Bill Barry.

His attacker, Sirhan Sirhan, was a Christian Palestinian refugee who saw Bobby Kennedy as pro-Jewish and objected to his promise to sell fifty Phantom fighters to Israel.

'RFK must die,' Sirhan had written in his diary. 'Robert F Kennedy must be assassinated before 5 June '68.' The date planned for the shooting was no accident, as this was the anniversary of the Six Day War.

Sirhan was tried, convicted of murder and sent to prison for life. A politically motivated fanatic, people assumed, or a lone nut. But there was enough that didn't ring true to launch dozens of alternative explanations and conspiracy theories over the years. Could it have been the mafia, the CIA, white racists or red spies? Sirhan claims to recall nothing about the shooting and pleaded insanity in court, which led to the idea that he might have been a 'Manchurian Candidate' assassin, hypnotised by others to attack and kill without fear or remorse.

IT SEEMED LIKE A STRAIGHTFORWARD SHOOTING

Bobby Kennedy was shot at by Sirhan Sirhan in front of a crowd of witnesses, including a young Australian journalist from the *Daily Mirror,* John Pilger.

Pilger was just feet away, so close that the woman who was standing right next to him suffered a bullet wound to the head. There were seventy-seven people crammed into the pantry area at the time. Bullets taken from Kennedy's body were later identified by their rifling marks as almost certainly being from Sirhan's gun, an Iver Johnson .22 Cadet 55-A.

It seemed like an open-and-shut case. Sirhan was caught red-handed, pinned down by bodyguards and arrested on the spot. In his pocket was a newspaper clipping about Kennedy's support for Israel. He was a strange, distracted, obsessive man, violently anti-Jewish and quite capable, it seemed, of carrying out this crime. There seemed to be no reason to go looking for other suspects or to think that Sirhan was anything other than a lone assassin. Why should anyone suppose there was a conspiracy?

BUT COULD THERE HAVE BEEN A SECOND GUNMAN?

Bobby Kennedy had a lot of enemies, with vast economic, political and military firepower. He had bitter personal foes within the powerful Teamsters Union, including union leader Jimmy Hoffa, and in the CIA.

Many Southerners hated him for his stand on civil rights. He was feared and detested by the mafia, which had suffered when he was Attorney General and looked like having an even rougher ride if the charismatic and ruthless RFK won the Democratic nomination and became president. If there really had been a conspiracy behind the assassination of Jack Kennedy five years earlier, those plotters could be sure Bobby would try to strip away the cover-up and avenge his brother. So there was no shortage of potential conspirators. But the existence of people who would be pleased, rather than shocked, at RFK's death does not make a conspiracy. Even the strongest motives prove nothing.

The reasons to believe this was not a lone assassin are far more solid. And the most powerful evidence is the most concrete. Sirhan's gun – the cheap Iver Johnson revolver – could hold eight bullets. The number of bullets fired and found at the scene, embedded in bodies, ceiling panels or the pantry's doorframe, was nine, at least. Some counts make that thirteen or even fourteen bullets, and the *Los Angeles Free Press*, which reported this, backed up its claim with a photograph of the pantry doorframe, showing several holes. There were simply too many bullets for the official story to be true.

The LA coroner, Thomas Noguchi, certainly had his doubts. He performed the post-mortem and saw the crucial evidence of the doorframe before it was inexplicably destroyed by the LAPD. He later wrote in his autobiography, 'Until more is precisely known, the existence of the second gunman remains a possibility. Thus, I have never said that Sirhan Sirhan killed Robert Kennedy.'

Noguchi's autopsy report specified the actual cause of death as a fatal shot with a .22 calibre gun held close to the back of the head, behind the right ear. It was so close there were powder burns, but nobody has ever claimed Sirhan got that near. According to the autopsy report, two more bullets hit Kennedy from behind, one entering through his back, the other tearing through his armpit.

Forty years on from Sirhan's attack and Robert Kennedy's death, John Pilger repeated his eyewitness account in a radio interview.

'He was wrestled to the ground and then there were other shots. There's no question that there was another gunman, because one of the people who was hit – just grazed – was standing next to me and that happened after Sirhan Sirhan had been wrestled to the ground. So that's the interesting thing. There was another assassin or another several assassins.'

The newest forensic evidence concerns the one and only sound recording of the shooting, captured entirely accidentally by a Polish journalist, Stanisław Pruszyński, who had forgotten to switch off his tape recorder after Bobby Kennedy's victory speech.

This recording was subjected to modern audio lab analysis for the first time in 2007, and the results were presented to the American Academy of Forensic Sciences in Washington the following year. At least ten, and maybe as many as thirteen, shots can be heard, in a five-second period of mayhem. That's certainly more than the eight bullets in Sirhan's revolver. And the time between some of the shots is far too short for them to have come from a single weapon. Although Sirhan continued shooting until his gun was empty, he had only fired twice before he was tackled by several bystanders and security men and thrown to the floor.

Five of the shots heard on the audio tape appear to feature the slightly different sound signature of a Harrington & Richardson 922, the only other pistol that is known to produce a similar pattern of rifling marks to the Iver Johnson 55-A. And one man who owned an H&R 922 was Thane Cesar, a hired-in security guard who was immediately behind and to the right of Bobby Kennedy at the moment when Sirhan Sirhan stepped forward to confront the senator and the shooting started. There is no doubt that Cesar had a weapon in his hand, but he always denied that it was his H&R 922, saying he was carrying his other gun – a Rohm .38 pistol – that night. LA police interviewed him briefly after the shooting, but didn't regard him as a suspect and didn't demand to see his gun.

Cesar, who died in the Philippines in 2019, at the age of seventy-seven, was an extreme right-winger who hated the Kennedy brothers for their advocacy of civil rights. That doesn't mean, of course, that he was the killer, or part of a wider conspiracy. He was never charged, but those who believe there was more to RFK's assassination than meets the eye have always suspected that the cover-up began with the blanket denial that there was more than one gunman and the refusal to properly investigate Thane Cesar's role.

10

ROSWELL

WOULDN'T THAT BE THE BIGGEST COVER-UP
OF THEM ALL?

Yes, there is intelligent life out there. According to NASA, our own Milky Way galaxy contains more than 100 billion planets. In a universe with at least 80 billion such galaxies, there will be so many stars, so many solar systems and such an unimaginable number of planets that it is bound to be so. Logic and science point that way. It takes an almost religious act of faith to believe that we are the only sentient beings in the whole of creation.

We are not alone.

No, intelligent life forms from unknown worlds do not come dropping in on us in either humanoid or lizard-like shapes, flying in stylish silver frisbees that conveniently break down from time to time to give us the chance to take a peek at them. Our ideas of what alien travellers from worlds beyond should look like are almost entirely shaped by the limited imaginations of a small handful of salaried illustrators and make-up artists working on comics and films in Britain and America just after World War Two.

And no, again, there has been no vast government-inspired conspiracy to cover up reports of contacts with aliens or to collaborate with them to form an all-powerful world government.

So far, so good. But there have been just one or two famous incidents and stories that have entered our modern mythology and stuck there for a long time. And the most famous of these is all about what happened near Roswell, New Mexico, in 1947.

It started with some 'metallic, foil-like debris' that was found by a sheep farmer on a remote ranch in New Mexico, outside the little township of Corona, on 14 June 1947.

The rancher, Mac Brazel, was puzzled, but not particularly excited about what he'd discovered. In fact, he didn't do or say anything about it until three weeks later, on the Fourth of July, when he and his wife and kids celebrated Independence Day by going back and gathering up most of the wreckage.

The next day, Saturday, he heard the radio mention sightings of 'flying saucers' or 'flying disks' for the first time and wondered if his bits of debris might be connected. So, when he was in Corona selling his wool on the Monday, he went along to see the sheriff, George Wilcox, and 'whispered, kinda confidential like' that he might have found a flying disk.

Recognising his duty to save the world, the sheriff passed the word on to the big Strategic Air Command nuclear bomber base at Roswell, seventy-five miles to the south. Roswell responded and sent an intelligence officer, Major Jesse Marcel, who took a look at the wreckage, thought it might be significant and carried most of it with him back to the base.

After examining the strange pieces of material, the Army Air Force issued the most extraordinary statement to the local press. As a result, the *Roswell Daily Record* for 8 July 1947 led with the splash headline: 'RAAF CAPTURES FLYING SAUCER ON RANCH IN ROSWELL REGION', followed by a less exciting second-deck headline that said: 'NO DETAILS OF FLYING DISK ARE REVEALED'.

The story below carried very little detail but began: 'The intelligence office of the 509th Bombardment group at Roswell Army Air Field announced at noon today that the field has come into possession of a flying saucer.'

Most of the rest of the story was about a local hardware merchant and his wife who claimed to have watched the flying disk from their front porch.

After this, the debris was flown to Fort Worth, examined and declared to be the tattered remnants of a high-altitude weather balloon, which appeared to explain the tinfoil-like, stick-like, paper-like and rubber-like qualities of the alien materials.

Brigadier General Roger M Ramey, commander of the Eighth Air Forces, issued a reassuringly bland statement the very next day, saying the wreckage came from a type of balloon used to measure the direction and velocity of winds at high altitudes. And that, as far as the official version goes, was that.

Mac Brazel instantly became something of a celebrity, which he hated. Within a couple of days, he was telling local reporters the publicity was driving him mad and that, if he ever found anything else short of a bomb, he sure wasn't going to say anything about it.

As far as the rest of the world was concerned, the happenings on Brazel's ranch faded into obscurity until they were dragged back into the spotlight by the publication in 1980 of *The Roswell Incident*, by Charles Berlitz and William Moore. This book insisted that an alien craft had crashed near Roswell and that alien bodies had been taken from the wreckage.

Over the next few years, this line was apparently supported by new witnesses and evidence, including a 1991 affidavit from Glenn Davis, a mortuary technician from Roswell.

Davis told of fielding questions from the base about very small coffins and of talking to a nurse who had supposedly been present at the foul-smelling autopsy of a creature with four-fingered hands with suckers on the fingertips, a huge head, flapped ears and so on. There were also papers from a secret US government committee called Majestic-12 that appeared to confirm the recovery of alien bodies.

It was clear that a lot of people wanted to believe. But the Davis testimony was suspiciously unverifiable, the Majestic-12 papers proved to be forgeries and people seriously interested in UFOs tended to dismiss the new Roswell stories as hype and showbiz twaddle.

MAKING AN 'ALIEN' WITH BRAINS, JAM AND ENTRAILS

While strange lights in the sky have occasionally been seen throughout human history, the 1940s and 1950s were apparently the busiest times for interplanetary travellers. During the war, there were many reports in Europe, from pilots of both sides, of 'foo fighters' – blobs of light or balls of fire that zoomed past and manoeuvred around their planes, with an agility and speed no human technology could match.

But the idea of the flying saucer was something that suddenly took off in the late 1940s.

The terms 'flying disk' and 'flying saucer' were first used in national newspapers in the US on 27 June 1947, in articles about a sustained observation of some inexplicable flying objects by a pilot called Kenneth Arnold, who had seen them over mountains in Washington State on 24 June.

This means, of course, that they were already the talk of the town and buzzwords of the week when the Roswell story broke a few days later.

The apparent official acknowledgement of a flying-disk crash on Brazel's ranch, followed by the instant squashing of the story by military top brass, has always fed suspicions of a cover-up. Yet the Roswell incident itself is actually far less convincing than many others. The term 'UFO' wasn't around until 1952, when it was invented by the USAF, but UFO stories kept on coming thick and fast.

The most likely explanation for the Roswell events is simply that the 'weather balloon' story was a partial cover-up.

From early 1947, the US Army Air Forces had begun a top-secret programme known as Project Mogul. This used clusters of rubberised high-altitude balloons to carry ultra-sensitive microphones into the upper atmosphere to listen out for the detonations of Soviet nuclear tests.

The fourth probe in this series was launched from Alamogordo, New Mexico, ninety miles west of Roswell, on 4 June 1947. In a 1994 report (*The Roswell Report: Fact versus Fiction in the New Mexico Desert*), when it no longer had any incentive to cover up Project Mogul, the USAF stated that the wreckage of this secret eavesdropping device was what Mac Brazel found on his ranch.

There were still loose ends to be tied up and the USAF duly obliged in 1997 with a further, final report entitled *The Roswell Report: Case Closed*. This took a careful look at the accounts of the supposed witnesses, particularly those who claimed to have seen the alien bodies. It suggested their memories of Roswell had got mixed up with those of a number of later incidents, including a horrific aircraft fire and a 1959 accident involving a manned balloon, and was generally welcomed as a credible and useful summary.

The least convincing aspect of the whole Roswell story is the most familiar one – the pictures and video of undersized, emaciated and apparently half-decayed corpses with near-human features and spindly limbs. These come from a blatantly faked 'alien autopsy' film released in 1995 and featuring two lovingly crafted aliens made by Manchester sculptor and model-maker John Humphreys.

Humphreys became involved when two British opportunists, Ray Santilli and Gary Shoefield, decided there would be a worldwide market for a film that apparently showed the Roswell autopsy. For Humphreys, producing something that looked right was a challenge. It took skill and patience, casts containing sheep brains set in raspberry jam, chicken entrails and knuckle joints bought from a butcher in London's Smithfield Market.

'You make an aluminium armature, which you then cover in clay, and then add all the detail. That's it, in simple terms, but it involves some complex 3D thinking,' Humphreys told the BBC in 2006. 'It had to look like an alien. But I suppose it was the detail of the anatomy that made it look real.'

701 SIGHTINGS STILL OFFICIALLY UNEXPLAINED

For all the reasonable doubts about the Roswell incident, there is no mistaking the American authorities' continuing concern about unidentified flying objects in the post-war period.

On 9 July 1947, the day after the Roswell story broke, the Army Air Force and the FBI began a review of the most credible sightings of unexplained objects in the sky. Three weeks later, they arrived at the unwelcome conclusion that the flurry of reports coming in could not all be explained away. Some were obviously the result of hysteria or alcohol. Some could be put down to natural phenomena. But that still left several puzzling questions and inexplicable events.

A month or so later, there was another assessment of the situation, by the commanding officer of the Air Materiel Command, Lieutenant General Nathan F Twining. This came to the same conclusion. There was something to be worried about. Twining called for an official multi-agency investigation, leading to the setting up of Project Sign in early 1948.

Project Sign developed into Project Grudge and the work later became focused and funded under the long-running Project Blue Book. This continued all the way through to the end of 1969, when it was scrapped on the grounds that no UFO evaluated by the Air Force had (1) threatened US national security, (2) represented technologies or principles 'beyond the range of present day scientific knowledge' or (3) been shown to be an extra-terrestrial vehicle.

Nonetheless, out of 12,618 UFO sightings reported to Project Blue Book, the project closed with 701 of the flying objects remaining forever 'unidentified'. For those who wish to adopt the 'case closed' line, 701 is a very large number of unexplained incidents.

11

RUSSIAGATE

ONE BIG CONSPIRACY –
OR TWO?

During the run-up to the 2016 presidential election, American democracy was hit by a vast and coordinated campaign of online interference. On platforms like Facebook and Twitter, a shadowy army of bots and trolls flooded cyberspace with propaganda and disinformation, all of it aimed at undermining the candidacy of Hillary Clinton. Among other improbable smears, the trolls circulated allegations that Hillary was terminally ill and/or a child-killer and/or a close blood relative of Satan.

Meanwhile, in an apparently unrelated development, huge numbers of hacked Democratic emails were released by WikiLeaks – usually at key moments of the campaign. First came a large dump of emails stolen from the servers of the Democratic National Committee. Then came a batch filched from the personal account of John Podesta, Clinton's campaign chair.

The timing of the Podesta leak was especially suspicious. It came just twenty-nine minutes after the Republican candidate's campaign was rocked by the publication of the notorious Pussygate videotape, in which Donald Trump had made a series of foul remarks about women. When the Podesta emails dropped from the sky, via WikiLeaks, media outrage about the Pussygate scandal was instantly deflected and diluted. Somebody, it seemed, did not want Trump to lose the election.

So who was behind this suspiciously coordinated hacking and disinformation campaign? According to all of America's leading intelligence agencies – including the FBI, the CIA and the National Security Agency – there was no doubt about the identity of the culprit. It was Russia. The disinformation side of the operation had been run by a sinister St Petersburg entity called the Internet Research Agency, a so-called 'troll farm' with ties to Russia's military intelligence service, the GRU. Two groups of GRU hackers had used spear-phishing techniques to capture log-in and password details and steal the Democratic National Committee and Podesta emails.

Nobody now doubts that Russia systematically interfered with the 2016 election. The key question, for conspiracy theorists and serious political observers alike, is whether Donald Trump was merely the unwitting beneficiary of this meddling or whether he was an active co-conspirator.

For the whole of his term in office, Trump was besieged by allegations that he, personally, or key members of his campaign team, had colluded with the Russians. This tenacious suspicion soon acquired a name: 'Russiagate'. In its most extreme form, the Russiagate theory held that Trump was a long-term Russian agent or asset, installed in the White House by Moscow to serve as Vladimir Putin's personal puppet.

The roots of the Russiagate story go back to a London wine bar in 2016. One night in May of that year, two men met at the Kensington Wine Rooms. One of the men was Alexander Downer, Australia's High Commissioner to the UK. The other was George Papadopoulos, a young American energy consultant who had worked briefly on the doomed Republican primary campaign of Ben Carson, before persuading the Trump campaign to hire him as a foreign policy advisor.

According to Downer's subsequent account, Papadopoulos made an extraordinary revelation during the course of the evening. He claimed that Russia had thousands of emails hacked from Democratic Party accounts. The Russians were going to release these during the campaign, he said, significantly boosting the chances of a Trump victory.

Downer didn't think much of Papadopoulos's unlikely story until July, when WikiLeaks put out 20,000 damaging emails hacked from the servers of the Democratic National Committee. Timed to coincide with the party's National Convention, the email dump wreaked havoc with the Clinton campaign. Among other things, the emails showed that the DNC had played favourites during the Democratic primaries, deliberately undermining the campaign of Hillary Clinton's left-leaning rival Bernie Sanders. In the wake of the leak, the chair of the DNC, Debbie Wasserman Schultz, was obliged to resign.

Over in London, the dumping of the Democratic emails made Alexander Downer suddenly recall, 'with a shudder', as he told the *Washington Post*'s Greg Miller, what George Papadopoulos had told him in the wine bar. Downer contacted the US Embassy and told them what he knew. As a consequence, the FBI launched a counterintelligence probe into Russia's election meddling and its possible links with the Trump campaign. With a nod to the lyrics of an old Rolling Stones hit, 'Jumpin' Jack Flash', the FBI's operation was codenamed 'Crossfire Hurricane'.

As the FBI investigation proceeded, a parallel dirt-digging operation was happening in the private sector. During the

Republican primaries, a rich anti-Trump Republican had hired a Washington research firm called Fusion GPS to build a file of damaging information about the Donald.

When Trump prevailed in the primaries, the rich Republican stopped funding the Fusion dirt-digging project. But a Washington law firm, Perkins Coie, representing the Clinton campaign, stepped in and retained Fusion to continue its enquiries. In mid-2016, Fusion hired a former British intelligence officer named Christopher Steele to investigate Trump's possible ties to Russia. Steele had served under cover in Moscow in the early nineties and been widely respected within the UK's Secret Intelligence Service. He had also led the investigation into the poisoning of the Russian defector Alexander Litvinenko with radioactive polonium in London and run MI6's Russia desk from 2006 to 2009. Pumping his intelligence sources for dirt on Trump, the ex-spy wrote a series of memos that eventually became known as the Steele Dossier.

The dossier, whose contents were later leaked by *BuzzFeed News*, contained some extremely salacious allegations. The most notorious of these concerned the so-called 'pee tape'. According to one of Steele's sources, Donald Trump, during a 2013 visit to Moscow, had consorted with prostitutes in the presidential suite of the Ritz-Carlton and had induced them to perform a 'golden showers' routine on a bed that had once been slept in by Barack and Michelle Obama. Steele's source claimed that Russian intelligence had bugged Trump's hotel room and had kept a videotape of the encounter for *kompromat* or blackmail purposes.

Less graphically, but more damagingly, an informant of Steele's also claimed to have heard, from a source close to Trump's campaign team, that there existed 'a well-developed conspiracy of co-operation between them and the Russian leadership'.

Steele's investigation intersected with the FBI's in early October 2016, when members of the Crossfire Hurricane team formally interviewed the ex-MI6 man as part of their enquiries.

Shortly after the Trump election victory in November, US intelligence chiefs met the president-elect at Trump Tower to brief him about certain urgent matters of national security. Among other things, they informed him of their conclusion that Russia had systematically interfered with the election.

After the meeting broke up, FBI Director James Comey stuck around to brief Trump in private about the Steele Dossier, whose contents the intelligence chiefs feared – correctly – were about to leak.

'I started to tell him about the allegation that he had been involved with prostitutes in a hotel in Moscow in 2013 during the visit for the Miss Universe pageant and that the Russians had filmed the episode,' Comey told ABC News' *20/20*. 'I did not go into the business about people peeing on each other. I just thought it was a weird enough experience for me to be talking to the incoming president of the United States about prostitutes in a hotel in Moscow.'

According to Comey, Trump reacted strangely. 'He interrupted very defensively,' Comey said, 'and started talking about it. You know, "Do I look like a guy who needs hookers?"'

From Trump's earliest days in power, the Russia story hung over his administration like a bad smell.

The first casualty of the affair was Michael Flynn, Trump's National Security Advisor. During the presidential transition period, Flynn had spoken several times with the Russian ambassador, Sergey Kislyak, with a view to undercutting diplomatic sanctions imposed on Russia by the Obama administration. Flynn had then lied about these conversations to several members of the Trump team, including the Vice President-Elect, Mike Pence.

Flynn resigned after only twenty-two days as National Security Advisor – a new record for brevity of tenure in the role.

A few weeks after Flynn's resignation, news broke that Jeff Sessions, Trump's Attorney General, had also had two meetings with Kislyak during the 2016 campaign. This was an inconvenient revelation, given that the US Attorney General, during his Senate Confirmation hearing, had sworn that he was 'not aware' of any communication between the Trump team and the Russian government in the run-up to the election.

Sessions didn't resign, but he did recuse himself from the Justice Department's continuing investigation into Russian election interference. Trump was incensed by Sessions' recusal, which inevitably served to fan speculation about the extent of the administration's ties to Russia.

In May 2017, Trump stunned the world by abruptly firing FBI Director James Comey. Comey retaliated by disclosing the contents of a memo he'd written after a meeting with Trump in February, the day after Michael Flynn's resignation. According to Comey's meticulous notes, Trump had urged him to shut down the federal investigation of Flynn. 'I hope you can see your way clear to letting this go,' Trump had said.

By leaking his account of that conversation, Comey clearly hoped to leave the Justice Department with no choice but to appoint a Special Counsel to get to the bottom of the whole Russia mess. He got his wish. The very next day, Robert Mueller, himself a former FBI Director, was appointed to conduct a Special Counsel investigation into Russian election interference. This was not what Donald Trump had been hoping for. According to the Mueller Report, he didn't take the news well. When the

Attorney General told him about Mueller's appointment, he slumped back in his chair. 'This is the end of my presidency,' he told Sessions. 'I'm fucked.'

The Mueller Inquiry ran for two years and took a number of key scalps. The first was George Papadopoulos, the man from the London wine bar, followed by several close Trump associates, including the flamboyant fixer Roger Stone. Stone was sentenced to forty months in jail for having served as the back channel between the WikiLeaks organization and the Trump camp, though the president commuted the sentence before Stone could serve a single day and later granted him a full pardon.

On the international front, Mueller issued symbolic indictments against thirteen foreign nationals associated with Russia's Internet Research Agency and twelve officials from the GRU.

When the Mueller Report was finally published in April 2019, it confirmed that Russia had mounted an unprecedented attack on American democracy. 'The Russian government interfered in the 2016 presidential election in sweeping and systematic fashion,' it said.

But had the Trump campaign collaborated with that effort? Was Donald Trump a Russian agent?

Oddly, people on both sides of the Russiagate argument seized on the Mueller Report as a vindication of their beliefs.

So who was right?

MUELLER COULD NOT PROVE COLLUSION

Robert Mueller and his team spent two years looking everywhere for evidence of a conspiracy. In the end, they found no absolute proof of collusion between Trump and the Kremlin and certainly no evidence to substantiate the Steele Dossier's more lurid claims.

Mueller did not recommend charging Donald Trump, or any of his associates, with acting as agents of the Russian government. As the Mueller Report flatly stated, 'The investigation did not establish that members of the Trump Campaign conspired or coordinated with the Russian government in its election interference activities.'

For supporters of Trump, and for many neutral observers, too, that was the report's most telling sentence. There was no conspiracy to be found, they concluded. Russiagate was all smoke and no fire.

WAS THE BOOT ON THE OTHER FOOT?

Believers will reply that there was an awful lot of smoke.

Some of it hung around the person of Paul Manafort, one-time chair of the Trump campaign. Manafort initially struck a plea deal with Mueller and his team. But he lied to investigators so prolifically that Mueller eventually announced the deal was off. In August 2018, Manafort was found guilty of tax and bank fraud and sentenced to seven and a half years imprisonment. In December 2020, after losing the election, Trump granted him a presidential pardon.

One of Robert Mueller's more sensational lines of inquiry had concerned Manafort's relationship with a Russian-Ukrainian political consultant named Konstantin Kilimnik, whom the FBI believed 'to have ties to Russian intelligence'. Manafort had been in frequent contact with Kilimnik during Trump's campaign and had shared confidential campaign information with him, including internal polling data. This may not have been a smoking gun, exactly. But it was certainly deeply troubling.

Eighteen months after publication of the Mueller Report, the bipartisan (but Republican-controlled) Senate Select Committee on Intelligence published its own 1,000-page report on Russian election interference. The SSCI report contained further damning revelations about the Manafort-Kilimnik connection. 'Kilimnik is a Russian intelligence officer,' it said. 'Some evidence,' the report also noted, 'suggests Kilimnik may be connected to the GRU hack-and-leak operation related to the 2016 election.'

Tantalisingly, the report added that there was a 'possibility' that Manafort was connected to that operation, too. Unfortunately, much of the text in this section of the report has been heavily redacted, so the precise nature of Manafort's possible link to Russia's hack-and-leak activities remains unknown.

Did the SSCI report put the Russiagate conspiracy theory back on its feet? Not exactly. But it certainly gave believers in the theory some new threads to cling to. In many respects, the Senate report went further than Mueller in suggesting a high level of coordination between the Trump campaign and Russian intermediaries.

The SSCI's report also dispelled some of the mystery surrounding WikiLeaks' publication of the Podesta emails. Remember the suspicious timing of the initial email dump? Remember how it occurred just twenty-nine minutes after the release of the Pussygate tape?

Well, the SSCI found that this timing was no coincidence. It was down to the quick thinking of Trump's associate, Roger Stone. According to the committee's report, Stone called his back-channel contact moments after the Pussygate tape surfaced and sent a message urging WikiLeaks to 'drop the Podesta emails immediately'. Within half an hour, WikiLeaks had obliged.

Dodgy as that sounds, it still doesn't prove that Trump's campaign directly colluded with Russia.

But even if there was no conspiracy on the part of Trump and his team, that doesn't mean there was no Russiagate conspiracy at all.

Maybe the whole thing was a vast *left*-wing conspiracy, as opposed to a vast right-wing one.

Maybe the Russiagate idea was a deliberate hoax, a false narrative cooked up and propagated by Trump's political foes, with the uncritical assistance of America's mainstream media.

That suggestion may sound impossibly far-fetched. But in light of later developments, it's actually starting to seem distinctly plausible.

In December 2020, in the twilight hours of the Trump administration, the outgoing Attorney General, William Barr, revealed that he had secretly appointed a Special Counsel, John Durham, to investigate the way America's intelligence and law enforcement agencies had handled the Russia investigation. By granting Durham the status of Special Counsel, Barr virtually guaranteed that the Biden administration would be unable to fire him, thus ensuring that his inquiry would have a robust future.

In September 2021, Durham handed down his first indictment, charging a Washington lawyer named Michael Sussmann with having lied to FBI investigators. Sussmann was a partner at a Washington law firm, Perkins Coie. Does that name ring a bell? Back in 2016, the same firm, working for the Clinton campaign, had retained the services of the research outfit Fusion GPS, thereby indirectly sponsoring the creation of the Steele Dossier.

Several months after Perkins Coie started funding the Fusion GPS research, Michael Sussmann met a senior FBI official to pass on allegations about a 'mysterious computer back channel' linking servers at the Trump organization with Alfa Bank, Russia's largest private bank. In his indictment, Durham alleged that Sussmann had shopped this story to the FBI under false pretences, assuring investigators that he wasn't working for 'any client', when in fact he was working for Hillary Clinton's presidential campaign. Sussmann pleaded not guilty to the charge.

In November 2021, Durham made another interesting move. He arrested an American-based Russia analyst named Igor Danchenko and charged him with having lied to the FBI. Who was Danchenko? According to Durham's indictment, he was the 'primary' intelligence source for the allegations contained in the Steele Dossier. Danchenko stood accused of lying to the FBI (and also presumably to Steele) about the identities of his supposed informants. Durham alleged that Danchenko, far from having 'deep cover' sources in Russia, had actually sourced several of the dirt file's most sensational stories from a Democratic operative and Clinton ally in the US. Like Sussmann, Danchenko entered a plea of not guilty.

Taken together, Durham's early indictments seemed to tell an ominous story, as, indeed, they were clearly intended to. They suggested that the famous Steele Dossier might have been a Democratic stitch-up from first to last. 'The Danchenko indictment,' as CNN put it, 'raises new concerns about the circular nature of portions of Steele's work, and how it fitted into a larger effort by Democrats to dirty up Trump.' Democratic operatives, CNN noted, had 'paid for the research, funnelled information to Steele's sources and then urged the FBI to investigate Trump's connections to Russia'.

'Democrats' hidden hand revealed,' said the subhead of the CNN story. Coming from CNN – hardly the most Trump-friendly of media outlets – this was a major concession. Indeed, CNN's report went on to admit that Durham's investigation was inspiring a 'reckoning' among news organisations that had hyped the Russiagate story, including CNN itself.

Trump has always dismissed the Steele Dossier allegations as 'fake news'. 'It was a group of opponents that got together, sick people, and they put that crap together,' he said back in 2017, when the dossier first appeared online. At the time, that sounded like a typical Trump Hail Mary. Now it's beginning to sound rather less unlikely. It's almost certain that many of the Steele allegations were fabricated, somewhere along the line. But, as Christopher Steele himself said later, he had gathered together material from a range of sources, most of them unverifiable.

How much of it did he believe was true?

'Seventy to ninety per cent,' he told a *Guardian* reporter.

The main allegations – that Putin and Russia wanted Trump to beat Clinton and that Trump campaign staff had many secret conversations with Russian contacts – may not have been as eye-catching as the tales of unseemly behaviour in the Moscow Ritz-Carlton. But they have been corroborated many times over.

In this tangled web of lies, half-truths and power politics, nothing is quite what it seems. For those with the stamina to continue unpicking the threads, there will always be more to uncover. Was there one conspiracy, or two, or more? The only certainty is that we will never know the whole story, and that Russiagate will remain what it has always been – a riddle wrapped in a mystery inside an enigma.

12

POLISH AIR CRASH

DEATH AND SUSPICION IN SMOLENSK

The tragic air crash that killed Poland's president, Lech Kaczyński, his wife and ninety-four other Polish VIPs in April 2010 was one of the worst peacetime disasters ever to hit a European Union country.

It wasn't just the number of people involved. The heads of Poland's Army, Navy and Air Force, the security services, the national bank, the Olympic committee and the Polish Church were all killed when their official plane, a Russian-built Tupolev 154, crashed in dense fog while trying to land at the Smolensk air base in Western Russia.

The country's leaders were flying to Russia for a ceremony to commemorate an earlier national tragedy – the cold-blooded, pre-planned slaughter of 22,000 Poles in 1941. The victims of the original massacre were soldiers, doctors, teachers, lawyers and engineers, all executed seventy years before at Katyn and other places in the Soviet Union by Joseph Stalin's secret police. Smolensk North, sixteen miles east of Katyn, had been chosen as the nearest suitable airfield.

Apart from so many of the leaders of Polish society, the

crashed plane carried a dozen relatives of the Katyn massacre victims, MPs, a much-loved Polish actor and a true national heroine, Anna Walentynowicz, the ninety-year-old ex-crane driver who had originally founded the Solidarity trade union.

Also on the plane was the controversial Deputy Defence Minister, Stanisław Komorowski. He was the man who, according to WikiLeaks, had poured scorn on the US plan to site a Patriot air defence battery with no live missiles in Poland, shouting at the Americans that his country wanted 'missiles, not potted plants'.

The president's identical twin brother and political comrade in arms, former Prime Minister Jarosław Kaczyński, would also have been on board the Tu-154 but had stayed in Poland to look after their mother, who was seriously ill.

The crash happened after the Polish pilots had been advised to divert to Minsk or Moscow on safety grounds. Instead, they ploughed on and tried to make a visual landing in thick fog on an airfield with no form of instrument landing system.

Smolensk Airport has a tricky approach, across an undulating landscape. So much so that, at the point of first impact, 1,200 yards short of the threshold, the plane was actually fifty feet below the level of the runway.

In the end, as the plane came in far too low, it hit the top of the trees, plunged into the forest and burst into flames. There were no survivors.

On the face of it, the accident looked like a clear case of pilot error. But the political dimensions involved meant that few people could accept what had happened at face value, without at least wondering whether there was some conspiracy or cover-up behind it.

The fact that the flight was a pilgrimage to Katyn seemed to encourage grim suspicions. The obscenity of the Katyn massacre had been perpetrated by Soviet Russia, at a time when it was allied to Nazi Germany. Fifteen months later, under attack by Hitler, the Soviet Union had changed sides and made a determined effort to put in place a cover-up and pretend Katyn's mass graves were the result of a Nazi atrocity. Britain and the US knew it was the Soviets but conspired to keep the secret to avoid embarrassing their new ally, Stalin. It wasn't until 1990, under Mikhail Gorbachev, that the Russians finally admitted responsibility.

'TERRAIN AHEAD – PULL UP, PULL UP!'

A catastrophe on the scale of the Smolensk air disaster is hard to take in, under any circumstances.

But one that more or less decapitates a country, taking away its president, many of its top politicians, its military and security service leaders, the president of the national bank and even its leading clergymen, all in the blink of an eye, is bound to be truly traumatic.

And the last thing anyone wants to have to deal with is any suspicion that the crash was anything but a horrific accident, caused by bad weather, bad luck and perhaps the inevitable element of human error.

Initial impressions seemed to confirm this was the case. The fog was definitely getting worse as the doomed flight neared Smolensk and the last flight in, a big military AWACS jet, had taken a quick look and diverted to Moscow's Vnukovo Airport, 250 miles away.

Twenty minutes later, as the Tupolev started its approach,

Smolensk ground control warned that visibility was terrible and conditions were not good enough for a landing. Even when the warning was repeated, though, the plane kept on coming.

Several different factors seem to have played a part in the crash. Because the Russian-built Tu-154 spent most of its days flying in and out of Western airports, it had been modified to use Western-style instrument landing systems (ILS). But there was no ILS at Smolensk – just non-directional beacons at each end of the runway. These tell pilots about their position relative to the line of the runway, but don't, crucially, give any information about height.

Like all airliners these days, the plane did have a modern terrain awareness and warning system (TAWS). These devices have virtually wiped out the dreaded controlled flight into terrain (CFIT) accidents that used to account for most aviation deaths, giving pilots the unmissable warning of a whooping siren and a voice saying 'Pull up, pull up' whenever the plane gets too low. And, although the mixed use military/civil airport at Smolensk is not on the global TAWS database, the cockpit voice recorder from the crashed Tupolev shows that the TAWS did its job.

Bilingual Russian/Polish transcripts from the black box recording show that the TAWS gave its first 'Terrain ahead' message as the plane came down through the 1,000-feet mark.

This was repeated several times before, at 300 feet, the more urgent 'Pull up, pull up' alert rang out. The warning came again and again, and was ignored seven more times over the next eighteen seconds as the plane flew on and on and eventually hit the trees. Why the crew didn't respond to the life-saving warning is still a mystery.

CYNICAL OPPORTUNISM, BUT PROBABLY NO CONSPIRACY

Many Poles, inevitably, found it hard to believe the Smolensk crash was a random, arbitrary accident. It seemed too cruel, too savage and too painfully ironic that it should have happened on the way to the cursed forest of Katyn.

In Warsaw and around the world, people reacted to the shock of the Smolensk tragedy with fear and suspicion. There is too much history between Poland and Russia for everyone to accept uncritically that the crash was a spontaneous accident, and many Poles wondered out loud if the Russian authorities could be trusted to carry out a thorough and objective crash investigation.

There were soon calls for the international community to get involved in finding out what happened in Smolensk and a petition calling for an international commission of inquiry quickly attracted 300,000 signatures.

But the rumour mill was already churning within hours of the accident and no accusation seemed too outrageous.

Film clips from the crash site posted on YouTube sparked a frenzy of sinister speculation, as they appeared to show Russian troops moving through the still-burning wreckage, swearing, laughing and firing at least four gunshots. Translations offered by those who posted the videos claimed the muffled, distant voices of the soldiers were saying, among other things, 'Look in his eyes', 'Kill them all', 'He's getting away' and 'Come here, bastard' (followed by shots).

It is obviously easy to fake or manipulate the sound on videos, but these clips clearly were filmed in the immediate aftermath of the Tu-154 crash. Some people believed the troops were firing to ward off dogs or wolves near the wreck of the fuselage or that the bangs were exploding ammunition from the Polish security guards' weapons, but others alleged that survivors of the crash were being shot.

There were accusations, later found to be true, that the raw Russian army conscripts who were supposed to be guarding the crash site had stolen credit cards and personal items from the smoking debris. There was a large cashpoint withdrawal on one of the bank cards within two hours of its owner's death, though it was another four days before the last of the human remains were recovered from the wreckage.

The dead president's twin brother identified his body in Russia, before the post-mortem examination, but some Poles later claimed that the body returned to Krakow for burial a few days later was not that of Lech Kaczyński.

Crude suggestions that Russia's political elite might have reverted to Cold War ways and arranged the death of an awkward and noisily anti-Communist and anti-Russian Polish leader were never far from the surface.

President Kaczyński had been a strong supporter of 'lustration', the process of dragging out into the light every instance of collaboration with the Communist authorities. This had caused embarrassment to many former friends of Russia – and even to Poland's first non-Communist president, Lech Wałęsa. There was certainly no love lost between Kaczyński and Russia's leader, Vladimir Putin.

The Polish prime minister, Donald Tusk, Kaczyński's political rival, had been invited to Putin's official memorial ceremony for the Katyn massacre victims on 7 April 2010, flying to Smolensk with the same plane and crew. The president's party on the crashed plane was heading for a second ceremony, three days later, which was carefully framed as an unofficial event.

Immediately after the disaster, Putin's reaction was noted by many as being unexpectedly sensitive and sympathetic. The Russian authorities gave many assurances that a painstaking crash investigation would be carried out and that the details and background data would be shared with Poland.

But, as the months wore on, Polish investigators found it harder and harder to get the information they needed. When the draft of the Russian air accident investigation report was handed to the Polish government for comment in October 2010, six months after the crash, officials were appalled and refused to accept its findings. The initial response was 150 pages of queries and criticisms and a statement by the prime minister, Donald Tusk, that some of its conclusions were 'without foundation', though the new president, Bronisław Komorowski, said he was satisfied with the explanation that it had simply been too foggy to attempt a landing.

Within hours of the crash, Russian TV stations had reported that the plane was already in trouble and dumping fuel before starting its approach to Smolensk, leaving the crew with no choice but to try to land. The cockpit voice recordings show this version to be untrue. But Russian TV commentators also referred back to reports that Lech Kaczyński had a track record of bullying pilots who refused to attempt risky landings on safety grounds. On a flight to Tbilisi, in Georgia, a couple of years earlier, he had become so furious that he fired the pilot for diverting in bad weather.

Some commentators, in Poland as well as Russia, suggested the president might have suspected a political motive behind the air traffic controllers' instructions to divert to Moscow, four hours' drive away. If he thought this was a move to spoil his big day and make it impossible for him to get to Katyn, the president might have ordered the pilots to ignore the advice and land at Smolensk as planned.

While Kaczyński probably did not put direct pressure on the crew, the cockpit voice recorder showed there were two extra people on the flight deck before the attempted landing. They are believed to have been Lieutenant General Andrzej Błasik, head of the Polish Air Force, and Mariusz Kazana, diplomatic protocol chief at the foreign ministry. They were unlikely to have been joyriding in the cockpit without a purpose and it seems quite likely that they urged the pilots on in the fatal attempt to put the plane down.

There is just one more ugly aspect of the Smolensk tragedy.

Because of the number of top military and security service officials on the plane, it quickly became obvious that the laptops, USB drives and documents on board would probably have great security implications. While soldiers secured the crash site after the accident, officers from Russia's electronic intelligence service, the Federal Agency of Government Communications and Information, combed the wreckage and searched through bags, pockets and personal belongings to find what they were looking for.

The head of Poland's military counterintelligence service, the SKW, claimed there were no 'secret codes, devices or cryptographic materials' on board, but NATO military ciphers were changed afterwards in response to this situation. The crash may have given the Russians the keys to a great deal of encrypted military information, as it is routine practice these days to intercept and hoard vast amounts of encrypted traffic, even when you have no way of reading it. When a 'break' like this occurs, it can provide access to all the information in this archived back catalogue of secret messages.

Western intelligence experts believe the Smolensk tragedy may have presented Russia with its biggest intelligence windfall for many years, including details of ultra-secret military codes used for satellite communications. But this was almost certainly a question of ruthless opportunism after the event, rather than evidence of a sinister Russian plot.

Like the many wild internet rumours of deliberately misaligned landing beacons, 'gravity waves' and fog machines – and the claim that there were no bodies in the wreckage – the suggestion of a Secret Services conspiracy to bring down the president's aircraft is simply an attempt to make sense of a pattern of events that should not have occurred. The idea that Poland's national elite was wiped out in a few seconds because of some badly judged decisions and a few wisps of fog is just too hard for many people to accept without challenge and questioning. But it does seem to be the truth.

13

7/7 BOMBINGS

IF THE DETAILS ARE WRONG,
CAN THE STORY BE RIGHT?

The 7 July bombings in London in 2005 killed fifty-six people and injured more than 700, amid scenes of nightmare carnage and horror.

The four bombs were apparently detonated by four al-Qaeda -inspired terrorists – Mohammad Sidique Khan, Shehzad Tanweer, Hasib Hussain and Jermaine Lindsay – all of them British nationals. All four men were found among the dead, making it the first time suicide bombing techniques had been used in Britain.

Three bombs exploded with devastating force in crowded late-rush-hour tube trains, at Aldgate, Edgware Road and King's Cross, at around 8.50 a.m., while the fourth blew up fifty-seven minutes later on a double-decker bus in a London square.

Responsibility for the attacks was immediately claimed by the 'Secret Organisation Group of Al-Qaida of Jihad Organisation in Europe', though this was quickly dismissed as a crude attempt to jump on the bandwagon.

But the tangled, elusive story of 7 July 2005 led many people to question what happened and who did it, and what the thinking and motives were that led to so many deaths and injuries.

The main theories were:

1) The four British Muslims planned and carried out their own suicide bomb assault on the people of London.

2) The four bombers carried out the suicide bomb attacks under direct orders from al-Qaeda planners.

3) The bombers were following al-Qaeda instructions but had not been told they would not be returning from their bomb-planting mission.

4) The four men were set up as patsies in a plot by one or more Western intelligence services aimed at boosting support for the War on Terror – or at least allowed to go ahead with their own plot, either deliberately or through incompetence.

5) The four came to London thinking they were taking part in some sort of training exercise, arrived late, then heard about the bombs. Realising they'd been framed and were meant to die in the blasts, they fled towards Docklands and Canary Wharf, in the hope of achieving safety by taking their story to the media. They were then shot dead by anti-terrorist police at Canary Wharf, while a huge cover-up operation swung into action.

The official account of what happened in Britain's worst terrorist atrocity since the Lockerbie bombing in 1988 saw the attacks as homegrown terrorism, inspired by al-Qaeda, but not planned abroad. Specific instructions from overseas masterminds were no longer suspected.

The idea that the London bombers were set up as 'involuntary suicides' also went out of fashion. Once it was noted that the 7/7 bombs did not seem to have timers, this became less likely. Cynics did point out that simply telling your terrorist there was a delay mechanism, when there wasn't one, might effectively turn a walk-away bomber into a suicide martyr. But this line of thought was greatly undermined by the two suicide videos left behind by Khan and Tanweer.

The general assumption had always been that the four men – three from West Yorkshire and one from Aylesbury, in Buckinghamshire – were suicide bombers, intent on achieving jihadi martyrdom. But there were some strange hints that they might have been expecting to come back after their mission to London.

On their journey south to London's King's Cross, they bought return train tickets and a parking ticket at Luton station. They left more bombs and detonators in the boot of one of the parked cars. They each carried a number of items – credit cards, receipts and even a passport – that made identification possible and helped lead straight back to the bomb factory in Leeds, which was still operational.

Strangest of all were the actions of Hasib Hussain, who was trying to call the other three on his mobile phone some time after their bombs had gone off. If he knew they were all on a one-way suicide mission, this would seem like odd behaviour.

Hussain seems to have decided that his bomb wouldn't work and gone to buy a new battery. He called the others, presumably to see if they'd had the same problem, though, of course, they had already been dead since ten to nine. Hussain was evacuated with the general public from King's Cross station at 8.54 a.m., obviously in response to the emergency underground. But he tried to telephone the other three, a couple of times each, over the next twenty minutes or so.

Unable to get back into the tube, he apparently went to get a bite to eat in McDonalds, then got on a number 91 bus towards

Euston, got off again and boarded the ill-fated number 30 that was finally blown up in Tavistock Square.

HOW MUCH DID THE POLICE AND MI5 KNOW?

The two 'alternative narratives' of what happened on 7/7 that attracted most attention were both centred on conspiracies involving Britain's Secret Services.

The more complicated and outlandish scenario had the men arriving in London with their rucksacks, thinking they were either delivering drugs or taking part in a training drill, with no thought of killing on their minds. But in this version they had been tricked, by MI5 or another agency, into behaving exactly as bombers would behave and becoming the fall guys in a false flag terror operation designed to justify clampdowns or attacks on Muslims at home and abroad.

When three bombs went off in the tube, the suspects recognised they were in mortal danger and hurried to give their story to the press to put themselves in the spotlight, so that they could not be killed off so easily. They got as far as Docklands, the spooks caught up with them and they were shot dead.

This bizarre Hollywood scenario had some convinced supporters and was the subject of several YouTube 'exposés'. Apart from the lack of witnesses or evidence, other than second-hand hearsay and contradictory emails, this story had a lot of other objections to overcome.

Leaving aside questions about whether such an outrage could ever happen in Britain, this hypothesis had trouble accounting for Hasib Hussain on the number 30 bus, DNA evidence from the blast sites, Khan and Tanweer's suicide videos and even, ironically, the lack of CCTV footage of the men progressing towards Canary Wharf.

For those who were happy to assume that police, doctors and ambulance crews, train passengers, forensic scientists, transport staff, office workers in buildings at Canary Wharf and everybody else were all in on one gigantic conspiracy, no scenario was impossible.

Most people, however – even those with doubts about the official story – believed this was an imaginative leap too far.

In the same way, relatively few people were prepared, without some concrete proof, to believe that the four bombers had blown themselves up as part of an MI5, CIA or Mossad plot.

What was harder to disbelieve was the idea that the security services might have had some warning – or even specific foreknowledge – of the attacks and somehow failed to stop the bombers and protect the public.

Mohammad Sidique Khan and Shehzad Tanweer had come to the notice of police and security agencies several times before. But they were seen as fringe hangers-on, rather than potential terrorists.

Khan and Tanweer had both been watched, filmed and photographed by MI5 and police attached to Operation Crevice, the operation to stop planned fertiliser-bomb attacks on the Bluewater Shopping Centre and London's Ministry of Sound nightclub. They had been observed and tailed home when they met fertiliser-bomb-plot ringleader Omar Khyam in February and March 2004. MI5 agents had twice followed Khan's Honda back from Crawley, in West Sussex, to West Yorkshire, a distance of 230 miles. On one occasion, this was after a Crevice gang meeting with bomb maker Momin Khawaja, who had just flown in from Canada.

The MI5 transcript of one long, fragmented conversation between Omar Khyam and Mohammad Sidique Khan, sitting with Tanweer in Khyam's bugged car, threw interesting light on the 7/7 bomber's concerns in February 2004. There was a lot of talk about how to get £20,000 or so by ripping off credit card issuers, about Khan's preparations to take a 'one-way ticket' to fight in Afghanistan and about Khyam's plan to start the fertiliser bombings in the next few weeks.

KHAN: 'Are you really a terrorist?'

OMAR KHYAM: 'They're working with us.'

KHAN: 'You're serious. You are, basically?'

OMAR KHYAM: 'I'm not a terrorist, but they're working through us.'

KHAN: 'Who are? There's no one higher than you.'

Omar Khyam did not mention Bluewater or the other targets, but he made it clear his group of bombers was ready to go.

OMAR KHYAM: 'I don't even live in Crawley any more. I moved out, yeah, because in the next month they're going to start raiding big time all over the UK.'

It was after this conversation, on 2 February 2004, that Khan and Tanweer were tailed back from Sussex to Yorkshire for the first time. It was always said that one of the intelligence failures that led to the 7/7 atrocities was the fact that MI5 did not contact the police about this connection. It has now been revealed that there were ten 'clusters' of secure emails between MI5 and West Yorkshire Police referring to Khan. The communication happened, but the opportunity to follow up and save more than fifty lives was missed.

Ever since 2005, there has been a great deal of misleading nonsense written about a terror simulation exercise in London, scheduled for 7 July, starting at 9.30 a.m. and run by a well-connected security company called Visor Consultants.

When Visor's MD, Peter Power, was interviewed that day on radio and TV news, he said he had run this exercise for a firm with 1,000 staff in Central London. This was quickly misquoted as being a 1,000-person exercise, supposedly involving actors, employees and security personnel spread out across the capital. The drill was actually run for Reed Elsevier, publisher of *Farmer's Weekly, New Scientist* and *Variety* magazine, which has a total of 1,000 staff in London.

But it involved just six people – the publisher's designated crisis-management team – sitting in a room and reacting to events, including firebombs on tube trains, outlined in a set of PowerPoint slides. The exercise was 'a table-top walkthrough' and the scenario also envisaged a bomb outside the offices of the *Jewish Chronicle*.

As Power said in 2009, Deutsche Bank had run a similar session a week earlier, and the 7 July exercise even started off with fictitious news clips about a terrorist attack, borrowed from an old BBC *Panorama* programme. You couldn't blame Peter Power for taking the opportunity to plug his firm and its crisis-planning services, while pointing out the real need for large organisations to devise contingency plans. But, as far as the tragic events of the day were concerned, this was a red herring.

SO MUCH EVIDENCE THAT DOESN'T ADD UP

The official UK Home Office report on the bombings, published in May 2006, seemed at first like a detailed, plausible piece of work, generally convincing despite its acknowledgement that there were still 'uncertainties'.

So it came as a shock when people pointed out straightforward factual errors that could have been eliminated with a minute's checking.

The report said the four bombers caught the 7.40 a.m. Thameslink train from Luton to London's King's Cross station, where they split up and went their separate ways.

They didn't. It seems they caught the train fifteen minutes earlier, at 7.25 a.m. Which was just as well, from their point of view, as Thameslink cancelled the 7.40 on that particular day and it did not run.

If they had banked on the 7.40, they would not have been able to get on a train until 7.56. And, if they had got on the delayed train that left Luton at 7.56 on that morning, then they would not have arrived at King's Cross until 8.42, too late (according to timings given by the Department for Transport) to board two of the three trains that were blown up.

Their 7.25 train was delayed and arrived at the King's Cross platform at 8.23, according to Thameslink. The bombers were then seen briefly on CCTV at King's Cross, apparently at 8.26.

Despite all the security cameras around this major London terminus, this was the last CCTV footage of the group. There were no more shots of the bombers on escalators, on the tube platforms or on the trains themselves, or of Hasib Hussain on either the number 91 or the number 30 bus.

Much of the police evidence around the 7 July bombings was infuriatingly gappy or contradictory. It was no consolation that a lot of the conspiracist theorising was even worse. One favourite item of evidence was the supposed clue in an article by ex-Mossad chief Efraim Halevy in the 7/7 edition of the *Jerusalem*

Post, with its glaring giveaway reference to the violence in London 'yesterday'.

This would indeed have been dynamite. But a simple check of the paper's 2005 files shows this article was published on 8 July, not 7 July. Advance knowledge would have been deeply incriminating. Knowledge of what you've just seen on BBC World News and CNN is not necessarily so significant.

But there were countless inconsistencies and loose ends in the official version of events that were never resolved. And a lot of them raised crucial issues.

There were awkward questions about the relative positions of the bombers, the blast sites in the carriages and the ID materials that were found, and about the apparent 'vaporisation' of one of the bombers, Shehzad Tanweer.

There was not a single survivor from the second carriage at Aldgate who had seen anyone looking like Tanweer. Identification was only possible via DNA from a foot-long section of vertebrae, which wasn't found for two days, and tiny bone and tissue remnants. Nothing else was left, so there were no fingerprints, no skull fragments and no chance to check dental records, for example.

Indeed, both the emergency doctor and the forensic medical examiner called in to check the number of victims at the Aldgate explosion identified seven bodies. The correct figure, including the bomber, Tanweer, ought to have been eight.

The main witness evidence for Hasib Hussain's presence on the bombed bus seemed to come from a survivor who claimed he was watching him fiddling in his rucksack. But the man was on the lower deck and the bomb went off upstairs.

Two victims of the Edgware Road tube blast were apparently, inexplicably, heading in the wrong direction, while at least eight victims on the number 30 bus were going to Old Street. This was not on the 30 route, though it was served by the 205, the bus in front, which can be seen in some of the photos from the scene.

On the tube, photos of blast damage that appeared to originate below the train floor raised other questions, including the suspicion, in some people's minds, that the bombs were actually outside the carriages, possibly on the track. And, if the bombs were on the track, the four British Muslims were not the bombers.

Any idea that the bombers might have been innocents who were conned or tricked into killing and maiming so many was hard to square with Mohammad Sidique Khan's final note to his wife, Hasina Patel, and the 'suicide videos' left behind by the two leaders of the group.

'You've been very patient with me, even though I never told you what I was doing and often lied to you,' Khan wrote in his farewell to Hasina. 'Please forgive me for the deceit, lies and absence. Raise our daughter well and try to understand what I did.'

Mohammad Sidique Khan's suicide video talked about 'forsaking everything for what we believe in', while Shehzad Tanweer's appeared to speak in terms directly related to the bombing: 'What you have witnessed now is only the beginning of a string of attacks that will continue and become stronger until you pull your forces out of Afghanistan and Iraq.'

The sad truth is that elements of secretive and evasive handling in the aftermath of these tragic events meant the British government, police and security services fuelled the fires of conspiracist thinking, inside the Muslim community and far beyond it. As the American embassy in London implied in mid-2006, in a candid report back to Washington revealed by WikiLeaks, this mistrust was never going to be easy to overcome.

'Since 7/7, HMG [Her Majesty's Government] has invested considerable time and resources in engaging the British Muslim community,' the secret US embassy cable said. 'The current tensions demonstrate just how little progress has been made.'

Many British Muslims still doubt the official version of what happened in London on 7 July 2005, despite the lengthy coroner's inquest that finally took place more than five years later. Many other observers still believe the public was only told as much as it was convenient for it to hear.

14

SECOND YORKSHIRE RIPPER

COULD THERE HAVE BEEN MORE THAN ONE?

Even those who were not alive in the late 1970s have heard of the Yorkshire Ripper, the cruel and elusive murderer who killed time after time and baffled some of Britain's finest detectives for more than five years.

When lorry driver Peter Sutcliffe was finally arrested in January 1981, the nation heaved a sigh of relief. Altogether, there had been at least thirteen murders – mainly of sex-trade workers in the West Yorkshire area – plus a number of vicious attacks on other women.

Sutcliffe was a violent paranoid schizophrenic, though he was deemed to be sane enough to stand trial. He attacked his victims with ball-peen hammers, knives and sharpened screwdrivers, killing and mutilating them because, he claimed later, he heard voices in his head telling him to kill prostitutes. The voices, he said, were the voice of God, and the former gravedigger claimed to believe they came to him from the headstone of a long-dead Polish immigrant.

Sutcliffe confessed and was tried on thirteen charges of

murder and seven of attempted murder. He was found guilty on all the charges and sentenced to life imprisonment.

Because he was held to be sane, Sutcliffe was sent to an ordinary prison to serve his life sentence. He was seriously assaulted by another prisoner and soon reassessed and sent to the secure psychiatric hospital at Broadmoor. In 2010, when a legal application that could have opened up the possibility of parole had been turned down, he was told he'd be spending the rest of his life in Broadmoor. After six years, though, it was ruled that Sutcliffe was mentally fit enough to be returned to prison. He was transferred to HM Prison Frankland in Durham and died in hospital in 2020 from COVID-related complications.

No one doubts that Peter Sutcliffe was rightly found guilty of committing a string of horrific murders. But did the numbers add up?

There were loud rumours that Sutcliffe knew all the macabre details of some of the murders, but couldn't say anything at all about some of the others. And there were claims that the forensic evidence clearly pointed to two different killers.

Forty years on, the questions remain. Were there two Yorkshire Rippers? And did the police, anxious to clear up a long-running, high-profile case, conspire to cover up the facts, even though it meant a ruthless serial killer was still at large?

During the years before Sutcliffe's arrest, the man leading the hunt, Assistant Chief Constable George Oldfield of West Yorkshire Police, had been taunted and teased by messages that claimed to be from the Yorkshire Ripper. These were taken seriously, as they seemed to include unpublished details only the killer could know, and they served to confuse the investigation. One message was on a cassette tape and the voice was quickly identified as having a distinctive Wearside accent, pinpointed as coming from the Castleton area of Sunderland. The recording became known as the Wearside Jack tape. Sutcliffe was eighty miles away and spoke very differently. While the police followed up the Sunderland connection, Sutcliffe went on killing.

In 2006, more than a quarter of a century later, an unemployed alcoholic called John Humble was convicted of perverting the course of justice, after a cold-case review had done some clever DNA matching with a saliva trace from one of the original envelopes. Humble was from Sunderland, within a mile of Castleton.

That finally dealt with the mystery of the Wearside Jack tape. But the bigger questions about the Yorkshire Ripper case still won't go away.

ONCE SUTCLIFFE WAS CAUGHT, THE KILLINGS STOPPED

There is one very simple reason to believe that, whatever the apparent inconsistencies, the police got it right.

The murders stopped, as far as we know, when Peter Sutcliffe was arrested, convicted and jailed.

That isn't conclusive proof, of course. If there was a second Yorkshire Ripper and he had been deliberately exploiting Sutcliffe's homicidal activities as a distraction and cover for his own crimes, you might expect that those would come to an end, too – assuming the second murderer was able to stop himself from killing again.

From a public safety point of view, the fact that the murders ceased was obviously a welcome development. But the ending of the long sequence of killings of prostitutes and other women in West Yorkshire didn't necessarily mean there was no longer a murderer to be brought to justice.

TWO BLOOD TYPES WOULD MEAN TWO RIPPERS

For the suspicious and the sceptical, the whole Yorkshire Ripper case has never been successfully solved.

Many of the witnesses and most of those who took part in the investigation are long dead. But one person who was deeply involved was Ron Warren, who was deputy chairman of the West Yorkshire Police Authority at the time of Sutcliffe's arrest. He never had any doubt that there were important aspects of the thirteen murders that were concealed from the public and the legal system.

'There were definitely two murderers involved in the thirteen,' Warren told the *Yorkshire Post* in 2005. 'It was well known in the operations room that there had to be two, because of the blood evidence. I do believe Sutcliffe was found guilty of more murders than he could possibly have committed.

'I suppose the police were more interested in getting it all wrapped up than in getting at the whole truth.'

Right at the end of his life, at the age of eighty-nine, Warren was asked if the police had really been aware that Sutcliffe was not the only killer.

'All the police knew there were two men involved,' he said. 'It was fairly obvious from the forensic evidence that there were two, because there were two different blood groups involved.'

There has been an argument for many years about Peter Sutcliffe's blood type. The police stated he was blood type B, while others have claimed that his father insisted it was type O, which might seem to be supported by Warren's comment.

But this issue is not as critical as it might seem. Physical evidence from several of the Ripper murders pointed to a killer who was not just type B, but a B secretor. This means that the B antigens are secreted and show up in body fluids. Those who stated Sutcliffe was type B also said that he was a non-secretor, which would mean that the body fluids found at those crime scenes were not from him. Whether he was identified as a type B non-secretor or as a type O, either way he could not be linked to those particular murders.

And, since there is no way of changing or disguising your blood group, that would appear to be decisive, damning evidence that there were two killers, two Yorkshire Rippers.

In fact, not long before Sutcliffe's arrest and confession, George Oldfield, the man leading the police inquiry, was quoted by *Sunday Times* journalists as conceding the point: 'There is not one Ripper, but at least two.'

No one doubts that Peter Sutcliffe committed at least some of the murders. But it took a long time for even that to be established.

Between November 1977 and February 1980, Peter Sutcliffe was interviewed and eliminated from police inquiries nine times.

Over and over again, inquiries about his cars, his movements, sightings of his vehicles in the red-light districts – even about a brand new £5 note from his pay packet that was found in the handbag of one of his early victims – were apparently contradicted by alibis or because his accent and handwriting did not match the misleading messages from the Sunderland hoaxer.

One bright policeman, Detective Constable Andrew Laptew, had a strong hunch that there was something not quite right about Sutcliffe. DC Laptew and his colleague DC Graham Greenwood didn't know Sutcliffe had already been questioned about the £5 note. But, as they interviewed him, they realised that he fitted almost everything the police knew about the man they were looking for. He was the right height and build, with dark hair and complexion, a beard and a walrus moustache. He had small feet and the odd gap between his front teeth that one of the attack victims had mentioned. He also worked as a lorry driver.

If Laptew had talked to Sutcliffe's workmates, he'd have found out his topical, ironic nickname. With his dark, brooding presence, they called him 'The Ripper'.

'He stuck in my mind,' Laptew said. 'He was the best I had seen so far and I had seen hundreds. The gap in his teeth struck me as significant. He fitted the frame and could not really be taken out of it.'

This was the fifth interview with Sutcliffe. When DC Laptew followed up afterwards and found Peter Sutcliffe was one of the possible recipients of the telltale £5 note, he wrote an urgent two-page report, recommending Sutcliffe should be re-interviewed by senior detectives. The report was passed on, left in a pile, considered and dismissed nine months later and eventually marked 'to file'.

The police have always avoided going into too much detail about how and why they repeatedly eliminated Sutcliffe from the investigation. But the answer is straightforward. He was ruled out, time after time, because he didn't appear to fit the evidence. Despite all the witness descriptions and evidence about £5 notes, vehicles, tyre tracks and boot prints that could have incriminated him, his alibis, mainly provided by his wife, seemed to put him in the clear.

And, of course, if you accept the forensic evidence that there were two Yorkshire Rippers at work, it's not surprising that the clues didn't all point the same way.

By early 1981, the pressure on the police to get a result was almost intolerable. The build-up of public anxiety and negative publicity over more than five years of failure blighted the careers of all the senior officers involved. After Peter Sutcliffe was finally arrested in Sheffield – for having false number plates on his car – it was a huge relief to West Yorkshire Police when Detective Superintendent Dick Holland persuaded him to confess to all thirteen murders.

Holland, it later turned out, had form. He was the officer who had suppressed forensic evidence five years earlier leading to Stefan Kiszko's wrongful conviction for the murder of eleven-year-old Lesley Molseed. Kiszko spent sixteen years in prison for a crime he didn't commit and died a year after being released.

There has been no serious legal attempt to establish the identity of the second Yorkshire Ripper, despite occasional complaints by some relatives of the murder victims, who have become increasingly convinced that there was a cover-up.

At present, no one knows whether the second killer, who was presumably a good deal smarter than Sutcliffe, actually ended his murderous career or carried on killing in less obviously connected ways and places. There is one extraordinary, impassioned and controversial book, *The Real Yorkshire Ripper*, by Noel O'Gara, that denounces the whole conspiracy of silence and names the man O'Gara believes was the killer who got away with it. O'Gara says this man was the 'real' Yorkshire Ripper and killed a total of ten women, while Sutcliffe was a copycat, used and manipulated by the first killer and only responsible for four deaths.

Others have given up on trying to do the criminal detective work but still hope for answers about why the police were allowed to pretend Peter Sutcliffe's conviction tied up all the loose ends.

The conspiracy to declare the case closed, in defiance of the evidence and only a matter of months after detectives were telling national newspaper reporters there were two Yorkshire Rippers on the loose, still leaves a nasty taste. And there must, surely, be big questions about how high the tentacles of such a cover-up would reach.

15

JEFFREY EPSTEIN

The strange death of the man who
knew too much

Until his long and shameful catalogue of sex crimes finally caught up with him, Jeffrey Epstein appeared to have it all. The New York-based hedge fund manager was worth more than $500 million. He owned a private island in the Caribbean. He lived in the largest single-family home in Manhattan and he knocked around with famous friends like Bill Gates, Donald Trump, Bill Clinton and Prince Andrew. 'I've known Jeff for fifteen years,' Trump said in 2002. 'Terrific guy. He's a lot of fun to be with. It is even said that he likes beautiful women as much as I do, and many of them are on the younger side.'

How young, exactly? In March 2005, a fourteen-year-old Florida girl told local police that Epstein had lured her to his Palm Beach mansion to give him a massage, promising her $300 in return. Wearing only a towel, Epstein had ordered the girl to strip and had proceeded to pleasure himself.

The girl's formal complaint prompted Palm Beach police and prosecutors to take a closer look at Epstein's seedy local activities. Within a year, they had identified forty young Florida women who claimed to have been illegally procured by the secretive multi-millionaire. The FBI became involved in the case, and federal authorities believed they had enough evidence to lay multiple sex trafficking charges against Epstein, which would have carried a maximum sentence of ten years' imprisonment.

Epstein replied by assembling a high-powered defence team that featured such legal luminaries as Alan Dershowitz and Kenneth Starr, who had led the impeachment case against Bill Clinton. Negotiating with prosecutors, Epstein's team succeeded in thrashing out a plea bargain that was called the 'deal of a lifetime'. In exchange for pleading guilty to one count of soliciting a minor, Epstein received an eighteen-month sentence in a cushy private wing of the Palm Beach County Jail. Under the terms of a so-called 'work-release agreement', Epstein was permitted to leave the jail for up to twelve hours a day, six days a week.

A decade later, when the full scale of Epstein's crimes had come to light, the *Miami Herald* took a fresh look at the cosy deal that Epstein had received in 2008, noting that the plea arrangement had 'essentially shut down' the ongoing FBI probe into Epstein's activities.

As it happened, the prosecutor who had approved the plea deal, a US attorney named Alexander Acosta, had since become Secretary of Labor in the Trump administration. He was obliged to resign from that position in 2019, after a federal judge ruled that Acosta and his team had broken the law in the Epstein case by concealing details of the plea agreement from Epstein's victims.

In the end, Epstein served only thirteen months of his 2008 prison sentence. It's since been alleged that he molested further victims while availing himself of the generous terms of his work-release arrangement. If he didn't, he certainly resumed his criminal lifestyle very shortly after completing his sentence.

Scandalised by Epstein's apparent cheating of the criminal justice system, his victims pursued him in the civil courts. In the final decade of his life, Epstein was bombarded with a seemingly endless series of civil lawsuits. One document filed during one of these cases accused him of running a 'sexual abuse ring' that systematically lent out under-age women to 'prominent American politicians, powerful business executives, foreign presidents' and other world leaders.

Several of the lawsuits filed against Epstein alleged that his crimes had been facilitated by an accomplice – the glamorous Ghislaine Maxwell, an Oxford-educated socialite and daughter of infamous media mogul Robert Maxwell, who'd met Epstein in the early 1990s. Epstein variously described Ghislaine Maxwell as his 'best friend' and his 'main girlfriend'. According to some of Epstein's victims, Maxwell had served as his chief 'groomer' and 'procurer'.

In 2014, the Epstein affair took another sensational turn. An American woman, Virginia Roberts, later known as Virginia Giuffre, filed a suit alleging that when she was seventeen and working as a spa attendant at Donald Trump's Mar-a-Lago resort, Ghislaine Maxwell had recruited her into Epstein's sex ring.

Among other allegations, Roberts charged that Epstein had paid her $15,000 to have sex with Prince Andrew, Duke of York. In 2017, the prince went on TV, in a long *Newsnight* interview with the BBC's Emily Maitlis, to rebut this claim. His performance raised more questions than it answered and was ridiculed in the media as a PR disaster, 'a nightmare' and 'a national joke'.

In February 2022, after months of sabre-rattling and legal skirmishes, Prince Andrew reached a settlement in a civil sexual assault suit brought against him by Giuffre. He agreed to pay her an undisclosed sum and to make a donation to her charity, which supports victims of sexual abuse. The settlement terms remain confidential, but some reports claim the exercise may have cost Prince Andrew up to £12 million.

In July 2019, the American justice system had a second crack at Jeffrey Epstein. Arrested by the FBI on conspiracy and sex trafficking charges, he was taken into custody at New York's Metropolitan Correctional Center, where he was assigned to a special housing unit reserved for inmates deemed unfit to be held alongside the facility's general population.

Epstein pleaded not guilty to all charges. At a bail hearing on 18 July, he went to extraordinary lengths to persuade the judge to let him post his own bail. He offered to put up his $56 million Manhattan mansion as collateral, along with his private jet. He promised to hire round-the-clock private security guards to supervise his house arrest.

But Epstein's bail offer was rejected and he was returned to the special housing unit. Five days later, on 23 July, he was found unconscious on the floor of his cell. His face was blue and there were visible injuries on his neck. Epstein survived, but claimed, at first, to have no recollection of how he sustained his wounds. Later he accused his cellmate, a burly former New York police officer who was awaiting trial on four counts of murder, of having assaulted him.

The prison authorities didn't buy Epstein's stories, and they investigated the incident as a suicide attempt. Despite his claims that he wasn't suicidal, Epstein was placed in the jail's suicide prevention unit. But his stay there turned out to be brief. After spending less than a week on suicide watch, Epstein was moved back to his cell.

Days later, on the morning of 10 August 2019, Epstein was found hanging from a strut of his metal bunk. A noose fashioned from a bedsheet was tightened around his throat. Guards cut him down and tried to resuscitate him, but Epstein was dead. Officially the death was ruled a suicide – the first official suicide at the Metropolitan Correctional Center in fourteen years.

Even before that verdict was reached, though, sceptics were taking the opposite view. Epstein's death, they believed, had all the hallmarks of a murder.

EPSTEIN'S PAST HAD CAUGHT UP WITH HIM

Jeffrey Epstein had ample reason to kill himself. The man who had once relaxed on his own private island, rubbing shoulders with princes and presidents, was now locked up in a fetid, vermin-infested cell.

Epstein must have known for years that he'd been living on borrowed time. But even he must have realised that this time the game was up. The case against him was watertight. Dozens of victims who had waited for years to tell their stories now stood ready to confront him in court. If convicted, he would face up to forty-five years in prison. At the age of sixty-six, Epstein was going to spend the rest of his life behind bars.

So surely there's no need here for conspiracy theories. The story of Epstein's death looks perfectly straightforward. He tried to kill himself once, and failed. The second time, he nailed it.

NO CCTV – AND NO CELL CHECK FOR EIGHT HOURS

Was Jeffrey Epstein suicidal? His brother Mark didn't think so. 'If he got a life sentence, I could then see him taking himself out,' he told a newspaper. 'But he had [another] bail hearing coming up in two days.'

Mark Epstein wasn't alone in smelling a rat. 'It's just too convenient,' said New York's mayor, Bill de Blasio. 'A lot of times, folks fall into conspiracy theories that instantly fall apart and sound extreme. But in this case, the facts themselves don't make sense on their face.'

Mayor de Blasio had a point. The facts surrounding Epstein's death were bizarre, to say the least. Let's start with the strange goings-on in the special housing unit. It was a condition of Epstein's incarceration there that he had to have a cellmate at all times. But his cellmate was transferred out of the facility on 9 August, the day before Epstein's death, and no replacement cellmate was assigned.

'What observer of news doesn't think that Epstein being left alone in a cell was not a bizarre choice for somebody to make?' thundered US TV host and political commentator Joe Scarborough. 'It sounds like something that you read in the past about mob informants who were under heavy guard but still somehow managed to find a way to kill themselves so they didn't have to testify.'

Then again, Epstein was being held in a twenty-first-century jail, well equipped with CCTV cameras. Surely the footage from all these cameras must have provided some clear evidence about the circumstances of Epstein's death?

Well…no. When lawyers for Epstein's former cellmate had

attempted to obtain footage relating to Epstein's first suicide attempt, they'd been given a series of contradictory replies by the jail's administrators. First they were told the relevant footage had gone missing. Then they were told it had turned up. Finally they were informed that 'the footage contained on the preserved video was for the correct date and time, but captured a different tier than the one where Cell-1 was located'.

In other words, jail authorities had erased the CCTV footage of whatever had happened in Epstein's cell on 23 July, while carefully preserving video from a camera pointed at a different cell at the same time.

As for the night of 9/10 August, the night of Epstein's death, Reuters reported that two cameras positioned outside his cell had 'malfunctioned' during the key hours, and had been sent to an FBI crime lab for examination.

On the whole, the camera evidence, or the lack of it, brings to mind a line of Lady Bracknell's. To lose one night's worth of CCTV footage may be regarded as a misfortune. To lose two nights' worth looks like carelessness – at the very best.

Speaking of carelessness, it was another condition of Epstein's incarceration that he would be checked on by his guards every half hour.

Did Epstein's guards adhere to that regulation? They did not. After some early attempts to cover the matter up, it turned out that when Epstein was found dead, no check had been carried out for a full eight hours.

'We messed up,' one of the guards admitted. An investigation found that instead of making their rounds, the guards on Epstein's wing had spent their shift sleeping and surfing the internet. They had then falsified their work logs in an effort to cover their tracks. Charged with conspiracy and filing false records, they avoided jail time by agreeing to do one hundred hours of community service.

The cavalcade of cock-ups surrounding Epstein's incarceration would be easier to dismiss as an irrelevance, if the physical evidence suggested that his death was a straightforward suicide. But it turns out that there are grounds for suspicion on that front too.

In the wake of Epstein's death, his brother hired a forensic pathologist, Dr Michael Baden, to assess the official verdict of suicide. Baden found that there were several good reasons to doubt that verdict. The noose around Epstein's neck was tied to his bunk at a point four feet from the floor, suggesting that he must have killed himself by kneeling forward into the noose. Pathologists call this a 'soft hanging', to distinguish it from the more normal kind of hanging in which asphyxiation is preceded by a violent fall.

But Epstein's injuries suggested that his hanging had been far from soft. As Baden pointed out, the autopsy revealed that his throat had been fractured in three separate places: twice in the thyroid cartilage, and once in the hyoid bone just above this cartilage.

In fifty years as a medical examiner in New York, Baden had never seen such injuries in a suicide. 'To have one fracture is unusual,' he said. 'To have two is rare. I have never seen three fractures in a suicidal hanging.'

Conceivably, Epstein might have sustained such injuries if he'd hanged himself violently, by hurling himself from the top bunk. But crime-scene photographs of his cell showed that items on the top bunk, including several pill bottles, were standing upright and undisturbed when Epstein's body was found.

Those photographs were widely circulated online after

Epstein's death, along with disturbing photographs of his autopsy. One post-mortem photo showed that Epstein's throat was marked with an angry red wound. But although Epstein's skin appeared to have been broken in several places, Baden pointed out that no blood was found on the sheet he supposedly hanged himself with.

Michael Baden's conclusion was that Epstein had probably been manually strangled with a ligature, possibly a rope. Injuries like his 'occur much more commonly in homicidal strangulations', said Baden. 'I think the evidence points to homicide rather than suicide.'

Who would want Epstein dead, though? Considering his backstory, we might be better off putting the question a different way. Who *wouldn't* want him dead?

'Jeffrey knew a lot of stuff about a lot of people,' his brother told one newspaper reporter. Indeed, Epstein himself had often made the same point. His Palm Beach and New York homes were known to be riddled with hidden cameras, strategically positioned to record the private activities of his rich and famous friends. A year before his death, Epstein told a *New York Times* reporter, off the record, that he had 'dirt' on a lot of famous and influential people, including photographs documenting both drug use and sexual transgressions.

Quite apart from the huge pile of potential blackmail material that Epstein claimed to be sitting on, we also need to consider the strange but tenacious rumour that he was some kind of spy. During his lifetime, Epstein often boasted to friends that he worked for the CIA.

Remember Alexander Acosta, the US attorney who cut Epstein the 'deal of a lifetime' in 2008? In 2019, the *Daily Beast* reported that Acosta had been quizzed about the Epstein plea deal when the Trump transition team was vetting him for a cabinet position. According to the *Beast*, Acosta told Trump's vetters that he'd 'been told' to back off Epstein. 'I was told Epstein "belonged to intelligence" and to leave it alone,' Acosta reportedly said.

The Epstein-as-spy rumours intensified when it emerged that during a search of his New York mansion, investigators found an expired Austrian passport in a locked safe. The passport had Epstein's photograph on it, but bore a false name and listed a residential address in Saudi Arabia. During the 1980s the passport had been used to enter Spain, France, Saudi Arabia and the United Kingdom.

In 2021, *Rolling Stone* reported allegations that Epstein had worked as an arms dealer during the 1980s. In that capacity, Epstein had allegedly met the larger-than-life British politician and media tycoon Robert Maxwell, who had then introduced him to certain Israeli politicians – and also to his daughter, Ghislaine.

For students of conspiracy, Robert Maxwell represents a large can of worms in his own right. In 1991, Robert Maxwell died mysteriously after falling, or jumping, from his yacht – the *Lady Ghislaine*. After his death, it was established that £460 million was missing from his newspaper companies' pension funds.

Rumours have abounded for years that Maxwell worked for Mossad, Israel's national intelligence agency. In 1959, a report submitted by a covert unit of the British Foreign Office claimed that Maxwell was 'a thoroughly bad character and almost certainly financed by Russia'.

Was Maxwell a double agent, then? Upping the ante, some believe he might have been a *triple* agent. 'My feeling is that he was probably an agent to the Russians, the Israelis, and the British,' a Maxwell family friend named Laura Goldman has said.

After a lengthy investigation into Jeffrey Epstein's death by the Justice Department, Donald Trump's Attorney General, William Barr, sought to reassure the American public that there had been no conspiracy. The whole thing, said Barr, was simply 'a perfect storm of screw-ups'.

Tempting as it may be to let Barr have the final word, we should probably note that Barr's father Donald, back in the 1970s, was headmaster of New York's elite Dalton School – the same institution that gave a young go-getter named Jeffrey Epstein his first big break. Barr was headmaster at Dalton from 1964 to 1974. In 1974, the twenty-one-year-old Epstein was hired to teach mathematics there, despite the fact that he was a college dropout with no teaching credentials.

Accounts vary as to whether Donald Barr played an active role in Epstein's hiring. But the Barr connection should serve as a final warning that the Epstein story is like an endless onion. Just when you think you've got to the bottom of it, you find there's another story underneath.

16

THE ILLUMINATI

EVERYBODY WANTS TO RULE THE WORLD

When it comes to world-domination conspiracy theories, the Illuminati are both the oldest and the newest thing.

Nothing else could possibly connect twenty-first-century hip-hop icons like Jay-Z, Kanye West, Rihanna, Lil Wayne and Beyoncé with an obscure bunch of eighteenth-century German academics and Freemasons with revolutionary beliefs, devil-worshipping tendencies and a taste for weird signs and symbols.

The original Illuminati were a flop. The group disbanded in 1785, after less than ten years, though it did attract the attention of a few big names, like Goethe, Germany's greatest poet and playwright. But Europe's rulers were so scared of subversives, Freemasons, secret societies and conspirators that the non-existent Illuminati got blamed for all sorts of revolutions, plots and accidents. America's third president, Thomas Jefferson, was accused of being an Illuminati puppet, which was a bit harsh, as, unlike many of the others, he wasn't even a Freemason.

Illuminati, of course, would claim to be enlightened, though the illumination would be provided by Lucifer (literally, the light-bearing one). Once the publication of a bestselling 1920s conspiracy theory round-up called *Secret Societies and Subversive Movements* had rekindled interest in the half-forgotten rumours of the previous century or so, the Illuminati started to get the blame for everything all over again. Few people claimed to be, or even know, Illuminati – or even to know what they stood for. But as time went on the name got tagged on to every kind of plot and secret conspiracy, and the bigger the better. World domination was on its way because the Illuminati were manipulating the Freemasons, the Communists, the British royal family, the drugs trade – and probably the United Nations, the MCC, the Sex Pistols and the Vatican – into doing their bidding.

The bestselling *Illuminatus!* trilogy was written as a fun project by Robert Shea and Robert Anton Wilson, two bored and faintly anarchistic junior editors in the offices of *Playboy* magazine. It was made up of three none-too-serious novels exploring every conspiracy theory the authors could think of and depicting the Illuminati as a sinister neo-Nazi force.

There was, however, little chance that it would be taken as lightly as its writers intended. The trilogy was a major publishing success in the mid-1970s and it unleashed a stream of books and films over the next twenty-five years, from respectable writers like Umberto Eco, assorted hysterical conspiracy freaks and others with an eye to the main chance, like *Da Vinci Code* author Dan Brown. But it was the arrival of the internet that finally threw the floodgates open and provided the platform that let hundreds of different theories and allegations bring the idea of the Illuminati right into the public eye.

In particular, the symbols, the mysticism and the theme of a battle for world domination were picked up from the mid-nineties onwards and thrown backwards and forwards by rival groups of East and West Coast hip-hop artists. Accusations and counter-accusations about Illuminati links and membership helped fuel the noisy and sometimes deadly feuds within the rapper community.

Certainly, this is a world with its own superstars and manipulators, armed power struggles and wanton assassinations. There are plenty of unresolved questions around the gunning down of rapper Tupac Shakur in 1996, for example, and of Biggie Smalls (The Notorious B.I.G.) early the following year. 2Pac – who also called himself Makaveli and made an album called *The Don Killuminati* – and Biggie were folk heroes to many young blacks, but both had many enemies as well as friends. Neither of these murders ever resulted in any convictions and both led to suspicions of conspiracies involving gangsters, Illuminati members and the police.

It's a while now since a top hip-hop star has been shot down. But still the Illuminati claims and counterclaims rattle around. Rapper Prodigy, writing from jail, constantly accuses Jay-Z and Kanye of devil-worshipping and involvement with Illuminati plans to enslave the world.

At the same time, it's not uncommon these days to see shopping trolleys in English suburban supermarkets with Beyoncé and Jay-Z T-shirts sporting flamboyant Illuminati symbols piled in alongside the soap powder and the ready meals. Pyramids, pentagrams, devil horns and all-seeing eyes are everywhere and Jay-Z's favourite sweatshirt slogan seems to be 'Do what thou wilt', once the rallying cry of early-twentieth-century occultist and self-proclaimed 'wickedest man in the world' Aleister Crowley.

However important these signs and signals are to some parts

of the hip-hop community, their significance is probably lost on most of those who just like the music. And, to look at it another way, if world domination is our fate, it might be more fun to be ruled by Beyoncé than by the more usual suspects – the CIA, the mafia and the US military/industrial complex.

DO THEY REALLY BELIEVE ALL THIS?

All the big world-domination mega-conspiracy theories tend to blur into one after a while. And at least some of the people who openly declare themselves as Illuminati don't seem to be particularly interested in that stuff. Check out www.illuminati-order.com. It's just the most polite, understated website you can find, expressing mildly (small-R) republican views about protecting individual rights and recommending people to read the rather boring writings of the Russian-born freethinker Ayn Rand.

It's enough to send you straight on to www.illuminati-news. com for the kind of full-on, ultra-paranoid, puppet-masters-and-pawns, Madonna-is-a-devil-worshipper, thirteen-chosen-families-control-everything stuff every internet user has come across, full of Royal Bloodlines, Shadow Governments and byzantine plots. As always, the main reason to disbelieve is the sheer difficulty of organising all this efficiently. Now we've seen how obviously inept the world's generals, bankers, oil barons and politicians have been in the last few years in the face of pandemics, climate threats and invasions, the big question is whether you really believe they could rule the world for more than a day without everything collapsing into chaos.

SUSPICIOUS MINDS IN A POST-TRUTH WORLD

There's no mistaking the evidence that some people – and the rappers are just the most visible example – are convinced that they, or their enemies, are part of a big, international movement or conspiracy.

The claims, counterclaims and accusations that go along with this have certainly played a part in the background to some high-profile murders and influenced millions of young people in America and around the world. Signs and symbols associated with the Illuminati, such as the familiar design of an all-seeing eye within a pyramid, can be found everywhere, though it's often unclear whether they are meant to be viewed as positive or negative images.

From the outside, this appropriation of long-established icons and graphic devices looks vaguely familiar. For those who have studied the 1970s, it is reminiscent of the way many young punks, including Johnny Rotten and Siouxsie Sioux, were irresistibly drawn to the swastika and other Nazi symbols, simply because of their graphic power and shock value. Most of those kids were anti-racist and left-leaning, but their desire to provoke and scandalise the parental generation outweighed any thoughts about the grim historical significance of their chosen emblems.

So the ragbag of symbols and ill-defined resentments associated with songs and writings about the Illuminati doesn't necessarily add up to much. The most well-known symbol, that eye-in-a-pyramid, known as the Eye of Providence, is especially ambiguous as it appears in so many different contexts, from the doorways of Masonic buildings to the reverse of every single US dollar bill. Is that a symbolic reminder, perhaps, that every buck you make is ultimately under the control of the Illuminati overlords?

It's certainly true that interest in the Illuminati has grown hand in hand with the spread of conspiracy theories and distrust of government and authority over the last few years, especially among the have-nots who feel the way society works is stacked against them. For the underdogs, those who are born in the wrong place, with the wrong parents, accent, religion or skin colour, it must feel as if there really is a conspiracy to do them down and limit their opportunities. Whether this is blamed on the Illuminati or the pitiless workings of Western capitalism – a lousy system, but probably the best we've got – is just a matter of personal choice.

But the sense of distrust and suspicion that goes with these feelings is definitely starting to have real political consequences now, in a post-truth world where even the existence of a global pandemic or the result of a presidential election can be called into question by millions of ordinary people. Whether or not there's any truth in the idea that the stars and politicians and power brokers and secret societies are all united in one big conspiratorial plot against us, any idea that changes what happens in the world like this cannot be completely ignored.

17

MARILYN MONROE

GOODBYE, NORMA JEANE

The death of Marilyn Monroe is the one they just can't leave alone. Everyone knows the stories. Everyone's read books and articles. Sometimes it seems everyone's written books and articles. Yet sixty years on, the suspicions and conspiracy theories just won't go away.

So here are four things about the background to Marilyn Monroe's death that you don't often see emphasised.

1) Marilyn died three days before she was due to remarry her baseball star second husband, the devoted Joe DiMaggio, after seeing a lot of him throughout 1961 and 1962.

2) It's true she's been fired from her last movie, the seemingly jinxed *Something's Got to Give*. It's also true that she had survived that battle, won herself a new contract from 20th Century-Fox, at a higher fee, and been re-signed to the movie four days before her death.

3) On the evening before her death, she had talked to Joe's son, Joe DiMaggio Jr, at around 7.15 p.m. and had then received

a phone call from actor Peter Lawford, brother-in-law of Jack and Robert Kennedy, inviting her to a party.

4) Despite her problems with drugs and alcohol, and claims that her looks were shot and she could no longer act, the substantial out-takes from *Something's Got to Give*, available on YouTube, show a comedy actress who could still dazzle and delight.

People's moods can crash quickly, so these positive factors do not prove the coroner's suicide verdict was wrong. But they do lend weight to the suspicion that the death of Hollywood's most lasting sex symbol was likely to have been either accident or murder.

The official version of Marilyn Monroe's death says she committed suicide by deliberately taking a huge drug overdose – a mixture of chloral hydrate and Nembutal, in a quantity that would have been enough to kill three or four people. There were empty Nembutal bottles beside the bed and a massive amount of the barbiturate in her bloodstream, but the post-mortem showed no sign of the capsules in her stomach.

The first call to the LA Police Department came at 4.25 a.m. on Sunday, 5 August 1962. It was answered by Sergeant Jack Clemmons, who arrived at the star's home to find the thirty-six-year-old actress lying naked, face down on the bed, arms by her sides, covered by a sheet, and dead. Clemmons had seen overdose victims before. He was immediately convinced that the body had been arranged in that position after death. There were three people present – Dr Hyman Engelberg, the star's personal physician, Dr Ralph Greenson, her friend and psychiatrist, and Mrs Eunice Murray, her maid. Clemmons noted at the time that there was no glass in the room, so Monroe could not have taken a drink to wash down the capsules.

WAS MARILYN KILLED BY HER DOCTORS' MISTAKES?

Even assuming Marilyn Monroe did not deliberately kill herself, we shouldn't necessarily jump straight away to the conclusion that she was murdered.

It is easy to imagine how two well-intentioned doctors, the physician and the psychiatrist, could have got their wires crossed and accidentally given her two separate drugs that would have combined to fatal effect.

Nembutal and chloral hydrate do not interact with each other. But both affect the body in similar ways, so ingesting both together means adding the effects of one on top of the other. Marilyn was addicted to Nembutal (pentobarbital) and had been taking it to help with her insomnia for many months. She had built up a very high tolerance to the drug, so the doses involved were bound to be far larger than any normal person could survive.

THE FACTS SAY MARILYN WAS MURDERED

All the obvious evidence seemed to point to the conclusion that the death of Marilyn Monroe was suicide.

The empty Nembutal bottles, the huge doses of barbiturates and sedatives in her bloodstream, her known emotional instability, the history of repeated 'cry-for-help' suicide attempts – they all added up.

It's true that the witness statements were so violently contradictory that no one's testimony should be taken at face value.

It's true that there were those who swore Bobby Kennedy was at Marilyn's home that night, or that they were on the phone to her when someone suddenly came into the room, or that they were called to bring an ambulance to pick up the body hours before the official time of death. But this is a case where it's best to assume everyone has a reason to lie or bend the truth.

The three people who were at the house when the police arrived – Dr Engelberg, Dr Greenson and the maid, Eunice Murray – all lied, or, at the very least, gave changing, inconsistent and contradictory accounts of what happened.

So it is hard to know what to believe.

Except that Marilyn died from a massive overdose – and that she did not take the drugs herself.

The autopsy report is absolutely clear in its implications. Despite the large amounts of Nembutal and chloral hydrate in her bloodstream, there was no trace of the drugs in her digestive system. They were not taken by mouth.

You can find part of the original typewritten autopsy report easily enough on the web. The autopsy also indicated that there was extensive bruising, including one large bruise to the hip, and skin discoloration that indicated she had died on her back. The policeman called to the scene was quite right to think she had been placed in the face-down position by someone else, after her death.

There was no evidence in the post-mortem examination report that the drugs in Marilyn's body had been injected. The pathologist stated that was one of the first things he looked for. No needle mark or associated bruising was found, yet, as we already know, she did not swallow the fifty or more capsules that would have delivered these doses.

One suggestion that fits with this strange jigsaw of forensic evidence is the idea that she may have been given the drugs by way of a suppository. And, no, there is no way on earth that she could have taken in the relevant quantities of Nembutal and chloral hydrate through the use of normal medicated suppositories.

If this was the route by which the drugs entered her body, it was neither suicide nor accident. It would have taken a carefully doctored suppository, deliberately loaded with a vast overdose, to deliver the levels found in Marilyn's bloodstream.

At this point, the swirling mass of rumours and murder accusations becomes hard for anyone to follow.

The mafia had a long tradition of anally administered hits in the 1950s and 1960s and even employed a highly qualified pharmacist, based in Chicago, who specialised in preparing the necessary items.

But the people with the most pressing need to ensure that Marilyn Monroe did not carry out her recent unwise threat to 'blow the lid off Washington' were the two Kennedy brothers, JFK and RFK. Marilyn had convinced herself, during her passionate affair with Jack, that he would eventually divorce Jackie and marry her. As the relationship wound down, in tears and recriminations, Bobby became involved, first as a comforter, then as a lover.

The issue was getting urgent, as one of America's most-read gossip columnists had just, the previous day, made the first breach in the wall of silence around Marilyn's affairs with the Kennedy husbands.

'She's cooking in the sex-appeal department, too,' said Dorothy Kilgallen's piece. 'She's proved vastly alluring to a handsome gentleman who is a bigger name than Joe DiMaggio in his heyday.'

The article was heavy with hints, though it wasn't wholly obvious whether it was referring to Jack or Bobby. Either way, though, the pressure on the Kennedy brothers was ratcheting up.

The declassified FBI files on Marilyn make many references to her 'romantic and sex affair' with Robert Kennedy, her time spent with the president, JFK, and, incidentally, 'an intermittent lesbian affair' with someone whose name is blacked out.

These FBI files note that Bobby Kennedy was staying at the Beverly Hills Hotel on the night of Marilyn's death but checked out very early the next day and flew to San Francisco. Several witnesses say he went to Marilyn's home, either once or twice, on the evening she died, and a policewoman claims to have stopped Peter Lawford's car for speeding and seen RFK and Dr Ralph Greenson in the back.

If the mafia killed Marilyn, we will probably never know why. Was it aimed at spiting the Kennedy brothers, framing them or doing them a favour?

For that matter, it could have been done by mafia hitmen on behalf of the CIA, as a way of getting back at the two politicians who kept seeking to curb the agency's powers and destroy its too-cosy relationship with organised crime.

Joe DiMaggio was heartbroken when Marilyn died and never married again. He was convinced it was Bobby Kennedy who was ultimately responsible for her death. The baseball star's son, Joe Jr, who adored Marilyn, once vowed in public that one day he would kill RFK. But that, as it turned out, was something that could be left to others.

18

FIRST GULF WAR

DID AMERICA TRAP SADDAM INTO
WALKING INTO A NOOSE?

The world gasped in horror in 1990, as Iraq's megalomaniac president, Saddam Hussein, sent his tanks across the border to invade the tiny oil-rich state of Kuwait.

By his own lights, Saddam had several reasons for invading and annexing his wealthy neighbour.

Kuwait had bankrolled Iraq's eight-year war against Iran to the tune of $15 billion and then stubbornly refused to write off the debt.

It had also started pumping more oil, driving the world price down and slashing Iraq's oil income, an act Saddam called 'economic warfare'. The Kuwaitis were even, according to Saddam, using sneaky slant drilling techniques to dip into Iraq's giant Rumaila oilfield, just across the Kuwait border, and steal Iraqi oil.

But how could Saddam Hussein ever have thought he could march in and take over a neighbouring state without opposition from other countries – and particularly other, big countries with major oil interests in the region?

The answer, it seems, is that the Americans told him it would be all right.

When the US ambassador to Baghdad, April C Glaspie, was suddenly called to a surprise meeting with Saddam, a week before the invasion, it was an unexpected chance to pass on a high-level warning not to use force against Kuwait.

Glaspie said she did this and parts of the transcript of the meeting issued later by the Iraqis show that there were some diplomatic words to that effect. But the remarks that stuck in Saddam's mind pointed the other way.

In particular, one comment stood out loud and clear: 'We have no opinion on the Arab-Arab conflicts, like your border disagreement with Kuwait.'

That seemed clear enough. And, like so many people, Saddam was good at hearing what he wanted to hear.

He had already noted the cautious comments from the US State Department and the Department of Defense the day before. Spokesmen for both departments had intoned, with robot-like precision, identical statements that read: 'We remain strongly committed to supporting the individual and collective self-defence of our friends in the Gulf, with whom we have deep and long-standing ties.'

This was a deliberately vague alternative to saying, 'If Saddam invades Kuwait, we'll bomb Iraq till the rocks bounce.' And it had encouraged the dictator in his belief that America did not have the will, or the guts, to fight on Kuwait's behalf.

SADDAM THOUGHT HE'D HAD THE GREEN LIGHT

There is some evidence that America did make an effort to explain to Iraq that it was not joking about standing up for Kuwait. After he received Ambassador Glaspie's report, President George Bush Sr apparently sent Saddam a personal message warning against the use of force to solve problems in the Gulf, while carefully not mentioning the word 'Kuwait'.

Nevertheless, within two days, John Kelly, Assistant US Secretary of State for European and Near Eastern affairs, was emphasising to Congress that the US had 'historically avoided taking a position on border disputes' in the Arab world.

'We have no defence treaty with any Gulf country,' he said, with one eye on the massed forces along the Iraqi border. If Saddam was looking for a hint that the US would not feel bound to intervene, this must have seemed like it.

When the storm broke and Saddam's tanks, commando units and helicopters moved in, America objected loudly but did not race to defend Kuwait. This came as a shock to senior Kuwaitis, who had believed the job of their armed forces was just to hold out for twenty-four hours until the Americans rode to the rescue. Instead, they became prisoners of Saddam for more than six months.

And though the twenty-eight-nation US-led coalition began bombing Iraq mercilessly in January 1991 and threw the Iraqis out of Kuwait the following month, it was rumoured that it took some bullying from the British prime minister, Margaret Thatcher, to persuade President Bush to grasp the military option.

DID SOMEONE SAY 'ALL OF KUWAIT'?

Ambassador April Glaspie's own reported summary of what had gone on in her two hours with Saddam was not backed up by publicly available evidence until January 2011, when WikiLeaks revealed the full text of the secret 2,000-word cable she had sent to the State Department on the day of the meeting.

This cable throws new light on an important turning point in the modern history of the Middle East. It's full of surprises.

For example, there's Saddam making an unexpected joke about US trade sanctions, which had been extended to cover many products that could have both civil and military uses. 'There is nothing left for Iraq to buy in the US,' says Saddam. 'Everything is prohibited, except for wheat – and no doubt that will soon be declared a dual-use item.'

Then there is his comment that Iraq is so poor that pensions for widows and orphans will have to be cut, at which the interpreter and a note-taker burst into tears and the meeting is held up for a minute or two. And there is a slightly different account of the key exchange about the US having 'no opinion on Arab-Arab conflicts', which makes the supposed 'green light' for Saddam Hussein's invasion plans less clear-cut.

The cable says: 'On the border question, Saddam referred to the 1961 agreement and a "Line of Patrol" it had established. The Kuwaitis, he said, had told Mubarak [the Egyptian president] Iraq was 20km "in front" of this line. The ambassador said that she had served in Kuwait twenty years before. Then, as now, we took no position on these Arab affairs.'

One person who always believed Saddam Hussein had been deliberately tempted and tricked into launching the invasion of

Kuwait was Jordan's King Hussein.

The king had had a conversation with Kuwait's foreign minister just before the tanks rolled in, in which the Kuwaiti said, 'We are not going to respond. If they don't like it, let them occupy our territory. We are going to bring in the Americans.'

The Kuwaiti minister may have assumed, just as many Americans did, that any attack by Saddam would only involve an attempt to capture an extra slice of the oil-rich territory along the border, and, perhaps, one or two islands in the Gulf that Iraq had long coveted.

'Let them occupy our territory' was probably not intended to mean: 'Let them occupy every inch of Kuwait, loot our treasury, take our oil, terrorise and mistreat our people and wipe the name of Kuwait off the map.'

Even the US government may have miscalculated on this point. April Glaspie, the ambassador who had met Saddam, was buttonholed by two reporters from the *Independent* newspaper in London a few weeks later and asked about the Iraqi reports of the meeting. Caught off guard, Glaspie blurted out an extraordinary reply: 'Obviously, I didn't think, and nobody else did, that the Iraqis were going to take all of Kuwait.'

'All of Kuwait'? The implications of this sentence have reverberated down the years. On the face of it, this certainly seemed like an admission that Glaspie, representing the US government, was at least half-expecting the Iraqis to take some of Kuwait.

This ties in with a secret offer made by Iraq three weeks after the invasion, in which it said it would leave Kuwait as long as UN sanctions were lifted and it was given two key islands in the Gulf and the Kuwaiti section of the Rumaila oilfield.

But King Hussein of Jordan believed the Americans expected

far more. He thought they fully expected the Iraqis to launch an all-out invasion – and that this was what they had wanted all along.

The king later told an American interviewer the whole Arab world believed Saddam had been tempted into 'stepping into a noose that had been prepared for him'.

If Saddam did walk into a trap, it is not surprising that he did not sense the danger. Right through the long war with Iran, both Kuwait and America had strongly backed Iraq. Kuwait gave money and political support and was bombed by Iran for its pains. The US provided weapons, intelligence reports and some very substantial loans.

The American motive for doing this was to curb the power of fundamentalist and militant Iran. But once Iran was stopped in its tracks, the next priority became dealing with Saddam Hussein.

Those who believe the US and its allies conspired to engineer the first Gulf War say destroying Iraq's army, undermining its political and economic influence in the Gulf region, stopping its nuclear, gas and germ warfare programmes and getting rid of Saddam were the four main objectives.

Three of these were successfully crossed off the shopping list by spring 1991, but it took another decade and another Gulf War before the regime change America wanted could be achieved.

19

PORTON DOWN

NERVE GAS AND GERM WEAPONS IN
THE HOME COUNTIES

They sprayed germs and chemicals from boats and planes on the people of Dorset, Devon, Wiltshire and Hampshire, experimented with sarin nerve gas on young servicemen who were told it was a cold cure, gave youngsters LSD to drink and tried out unknown Nazi chemical weapons to see what effects they had.

They let *E. coli* bacteria drift across Southampton and Swindon to see how germ warfare agents would react with pollution in large towns. And they tested chemical weapons on 3,500 volunteers without telling them what they were doing.

This is just the list of activities the UK Ministry of Defence (MoD) will now admit to, after several years of reluctantly declassifying secret documents and fighting in court to deny any responsibility for the victims' subsequent health problems.

The MoD's centre for all these operations was Porton Down, set in the green and gently rolling countryside of Wiltshire, on the edge of Salisbury Plain.

Porton has long been Britain's main centre for testing chemical weapons and germ warfare agents. It was set up to experiment with poison gas during the First World War, when both sides (not just the Germans, as most people think) used gas to try to break the deadlock of trench warfare.

But it was in the 1950s that Porton was involved in some of the nastiest experiments in peacetime history.

Several thousand young British servicemen – at a time when conscription meant every boy must do National Service in the armed forces – were used as human guinea pigs to test the effectiveness of newly developed chemical weapons, including two deadly nerve agents, tabun and sarin.

The lads who volunteered to help with the sarin tests, in 1953, got fifteen shillings each and an extra three-day leave pass.

Many fell ill, and one, a twenty-year-old RAF engineer called Ronald Maddison, died in agony in May 1953, within forty-five minutes of having twenty drops of sarin solution dripped on to a patch of cloth taped to his arm. An inquest was held at the time, under conditions of military secrecy, and recorded a shameful verdict of 'misadventure'.

It took just over fifty years before the inquest was reopened, in 2004, in front of a jury. The case followed Operation Antler, a four-year police investigation that looked at half a century of experiments at Porton Down from 1939 to 1989, involving over 20,000 volunteers. This time, there was a unanimous inquest verdict of 'unlawful killing', leading, after an expensive and unsuccessful appeal by the UK government, to a compensation award in 2006 of £100,000 to Maddison's family.

The shrinking band of survivors of Porton's in-house testing programmes all have vivid memories of what happened to them. They recall being asked to inhale mustard gas, drink the clear liquid that turned out to be terrifyingly hallucinogenic LSD or hold out an arm while the tiny drops of sarin were dripped onto their skin.

And they all seem adamant, despite emphatic denials from Porton, that they were told the same stupid story: 'You're helping with an important task. You're helping us find a cure for the common cold.'

Both sarin and LSD victims have confirmed exactly this tale in recent years, though the MoD still tries to insist that no one was tricked or lied to about the trials.

In fact, many of the survivors have independently described the same printed poster asking for volunteers for cold-cure research, though no one seems to be able to unearth a copy of this crucial piece of evidence.

Another of the sarin guinea pigs was Ken Earl, an RAF medic. He believed finding a cold cure was an important, worthwhile goal, though he was also impressed by the other tempting incentives he was offered – an extra two shillings a day, plus a weekend leave pass to see his girlfriend. He later suffered from immune system problems, starting in his thirties, which he attributed to his experiences at Porton Down.

So the cover-up has gone on, with an official report from 2006 saying there was 'no evidence to justify a conclusion that the conduct of the trials at any point went beyond the limits of what should ever be contemplated, far less tolerated, in a civilised society'.

Despite this denial, the report did admit, unblushingly, that some of the tests carried out in the 1940s and 1950s involved 'serious departures' from ethical standards. But its 'independent ethical assessor', Professor Sir Ian Kennedy, asserted these were only a few, so they presumably do not count.

What else went on at Porton? Why is there still an effort to hush up and deny even the facts that have been proved in court? How many volunteers, already dead, had their health ruined by experiments that were kept under wraps for half a century or more? Why did the sarin testing experiments carry on after Ronald Maddison's death, despite the public announcement of a government ban on them?

And how many residents of Dorset and Wiltshire, Southampton and Swindon are still unaware, to this day, that they, too, played more of a role than they think they did in Britain's Cold War chemical and biological warfare arms race?

A GRUDGING ADMISSION OF 'GROSS NEGLIGENCE'

During the period of World War Two and the Cold War years that followed, the fear of attacks by poison gas or, later, biological weapons was very powerful.

In fact, strangely enough, Britain was unlikely to be attacked with gas by the Nazis, because Hitler, who had been gassed in the trenches in World War One, hated gas as a weapon and vetoed suggestions from his generals that his armies should use it. But in the 1950s and after, in the Cold War era of H-bombs and genuine weapons of mass destruction, the threat of chemical and germ warfare was a recurrent nightmare.

Even the countries least likely to use these weapons had to know about them. They needed to know what defences, if any, would work. And the best deterrent seemed to be to have a counter-threat of your own. That's what Porton Down was there for. Testing had to be done and tests on animals never accurately explained how these chemical and biological warfare agents would work on humans. So volunteers were used, drawn from the armed forces and given as much information as they could be given about what was being tested, the MoD would claim.

After the Wiltshire Police finally became involved, in 1999, following a complaint from one of the volunteers, Gordon Bell, the survivors' stories were followed up and over three hundred people were interviewed.

It soon became clear that many records of the tests and the individuals involved had been lost or deliberately destroyed, so the truth was sometimes hard to prove. But, while the cause of Ronald Maddison's death was finally established, the four-year £2 million police investigation produced no revelations that could lead to prosecutions. When its appeal against the Maddison verdict was lost in the High Court, the MoD grudgingly accepted its liability and admitted 'gross negligence'.

AS THE VETERANS DIE OFF, THE MOD WON'T BUDGE

In 2008, the 360 victims of the Porton Down experiments who were still alive were granted compensation for their pain and subsequent ill-health. The total payout was £3 million, or about £8,330 each, and it came after the MoD conceded that there had been some 'shortcomings' in connection with the experiments. The lawyers and the MoD faced both ways at once, emphasising that the money was being paid without admission of liability and saying, at the same time, that the government sincerely apologised to those who 'may' have been affected.

In a separate award, also in 2008, three of the guinea pigs involved in LSD experiments in 1953 and 1954 were given similar out-of-court compensation payments by MI6, the secret intelligence service. The MoD again made no admission of liability, and it refused a request to put relevant documents from the case into the public domain.

One of these pioneering trippers, Don Webb, a nineteen-year-old airman at the time, was disappointed, but not surprised. 'They stick to the old maxim "Never explain; never apologise",' he said. 'I think this is as near to an apology or explanation as I'll get.'

The Porton Down Veterans Support Group once had 500 members, though age and ill-health have whittled the numbers down. The remaining veterans pulled out of a government research study looking at cancer and mortality rates among Porton old boys, because they felt its terms of reference were too narrow and that it was determined to ignore other serious health issues, such as eye, kidney and heart problems, dizziness and early memory loss.

They believe there are still more ugly secrets to uncover, but it seems clear that nothing new is going to be revealed without a fight.

The Crown Prosecution Service has said, even after the 'unlawful killing' verdict on Ronald Maddison, that there is not enough evidence to charge any individual. There are still at least twenty-five families that believe the premature deaths of their ex-guinea pig relatives were caused by what was done to them at Porton. But, as time ticks away, they may never get the answers to their questions.

20

SANDY HOOK

A CONSPIRACY PROFITEER GETS
HIS COMEUPPANCE

In Newtown, Connecticut, on the morning of 14 December 2012, a troubled twenty-year-old named Adam Lanza carried out the second-deadliest school shooting in American history. Having shot dead his gun-enthusiast mother while she lay in her bed, Lanza armed himself with a semi-automatic assault rifle and two pistols and drove five miles to Sandy Hook Elementary School, the school where he had learned to read and write. Once there, he blasted his way through a locked entrance door and, in the space of five nightmare minutes, fired a total of 156 rounds, murdering twenty children aged six and seven and six female members of staff. He then shot and killed himself.

As America reeled and the press scrambled to understand and report what had happened at Sandy Hook, a certain amount of error and confusion crept into the coverage. For example, some of the first reports suggested that a potential second shooter had been apprehended in the woods near the school. Other early bulletins gave incorrect details of the weapons Lanza had used in the attack.

Before long, these early reporting errors were put right. The man stopped in the woods turned out to be an off-duty police officer who had nothing to do with the terrible events inside the school. Confusion about the murder weapon was also resolved, as the full, horrifying truth about the Sandy Hook massacre came into focus.

Conspiracy theorists, however, detected a pattern in the media's early mistakes. Indeed, they refused to accept them as mistakes. They viewed them as accidental revelations of the hidden truth – clues that proved the official story of what happened at Sandy Hook was a fabrication.

According to the conspiracy theorists, the supposed shootings at the school were an elaborate false flag operation, staged by a federal government that was hell-bent on taking away the American citizen's sacred constitutional right to bear arms.

One conspiracy story claimed that the Sandy Hook shootings had actually been perpetrated by multiple gunmen.

Another, more popular, conspiracy theory had it that there had been no real massacre at all, and that the whole thing was a sham, a staged performance. According to this version of events, the grieving parents filmed at the scene were merely actors, professional stooges employed to lend authenticity to the charade.

Conspiracy theorists were spurred on in their suspicions by a communications professor at Florida Atlantic University, James Tracy. Within days, he was pumping out a series of blog posts introducing them to the term 'crisis actor'. Tracy's explanation was that the government had faked the Sandy Hook slaughter with the help of 'crisis actors' hired from a theatrical agency in Denver, Colorado. The reactions of bereaved and traumatised parents did not convince him.

'After such a harrowing event, why are select would-be family members and students lingering in the area and repeatedly offering themselves for interviews?' he wrote. 'A possible reason is that they are trained actors working under the direction of state and federal authorities and in coordination with cable and broadcast network talent to provide tailor-made crisis acting that realistically drives home the event's tragic features.'

While President Obama went on television, expressed his horror and vowed to make gun control a central theme of his second term in office, a growing minority of conspiracy theory addicts simply refused to believe anyone at all had died at Sandy Hook.

But were there any good reasons to believe that these conspiracy stories might be true?

'NO ONE DIED,' JONES CLAIMED. 'IT WAS A GIANT HOAX'

The short answer is no. To know what happened at Sandy Hook, there is no need to look to any conspiracy theories. They do not merit serious attention. They merely demonstrate that there is nothing – nothing at all – that certain people will not say or think in order to keep believing that the US government is coming after their guns. For the student of conspiracy theory, though, Sandy Hook is of interest for another reason. It may well be the case that brings about the downfall of Alex Jones, the long-time king of American conspiracism.

Jones sits at the centre of a vast commercial empire, based

on *The Alex Jones Show*, which is syndicated to a hundred radio stations, and his Infowars website, which has claimed up to ten million monthly visits. He has made a profitable industry out of fake news and conspiracy theories for twenty years. He uses Infowars as a platform to sell diet supplements, toothpaste and bulletproof vests and was warned off by the US Food and Drug Administration and New York's attorney general in April 2020 after claiming that some of his products were effective treatments for COVID-19. At a rally at the Capitol that same month, he told unmasked supporters that COVID was 'a hoax'.

Jones's irresponsible false flag claims about Sandy Hook ('No one died!'), and about the subsequent massacre at the Marjory Stoneman Douglas High School in Florida, where seventeen people were killed, caused widespread revulsion. They proved to be the last straw for social media companies like YouTube, Facebook, Apple, Spotify and Vimeo – all of which finally moved to banish Alex Jones from their platforms, costing him millions of followers and playing havoc with his income streams.

Moreover, Jones crossed the line so egregiously in relation to Sandy Hook that several relatives of the victims ended up suing him for defamation and for the infliction of emotional distress. As a consequence, he was obliged to defend his pronouncements in court – a rare case of a conspiracy theorist being forced to put up or shut up in a fact-respecting forum.

When it came to it, Jones performed abysmally. The judges ruled against him in every single case. At the time of writing, the juries involved have not yet delivered their verdicts about damages. But their decisions have the potential to bring about Jones's financial ruin.

Ironically, Jones was not an early adopter of the Sandy Hook conspiracy theory. By his own admission, it took him a while to get on board.

'It took me about a year with Sandy Hook to come to grips with the fact that the whole thing was fake,' he said in 2014. 'I mean, even I couldn't believe it… But then I did deep research – and, my gosh, it just pretty much didn't happen.'

Jones may have come to the case relatively late, but he compensated by going in very hard.

Sandy Hook was a 'giant hoax', he declared. It was 'synthetic, completely fake, with actors – in my view, manufactured'. The people at the scene 'were patsy provocateurs', he said, getting his conspiratorial clichés a bit mixed up. 'I couldn't believe it at first. I knew they had actors there, clearly, but I thought they killed some real kids. And it just shows how bold they are that they clearly used actors.'

Nor did Jones stop there. On his Infowars website, he showed video clips of several of the Sandy Hook parents in tears. To underline his belief that they were merely actors, Jones mocked and taunted them by pretending to cry himself.

Oddly enough, these contemptible antics did not seem to hinder Jones's ability to win friends and influence people. Far from it. At the same time as he was saying these things, Jones acquired a very influential friend indeed – Donald J Trump, the next president of the United States. Jones and Trump were introduced by their mutual friend, Republican fixer Roger Stone. In December 2015, by which time Trump had established himself as the front-runner in his party's primaries, he made a notorious thirty-minute appearance on *The Alex Jones Show*. 'Your reputation is amazing,' Trump gushingly told Jones. 'I will not let you down. You will be very, very impressed, I hope. And I think we'll be speaking a lot.'

When Trump became president, Jones's immediate reaction was instructive. On election night, as the count began to swing in Trump's favour, an Infowars staffer claims Jones looked depressed. 'You could see his mood change,' the anonymous staffer told *Buzzfeed News*. But why wasn't Jones happy to see his friend heading for the White House? Because his business model was based on fear, the staffer explained. 'He has to have that power of fear – that idea that "They're gonna take your guns." Trump winning put it all in jeopardy.'

As it turned out, Jones was right to fear that Trump's victory would be bad for business. A week after the election, a young woman named Erica Lafferty, whose mother had been gunned down by Adam Lanza at Sandy Hook, composed an open letter to the president-elect and published it online. Lafferty urged Trump to distance himself from Jones and repudiate his allegations about Sandy Hook.

'Alex Jones has fanned the flames of a hateful conspiracy theory claiming that the shooting that took my mother *never happened*,' Lafferty wrote. 'It's unthinkable. It's unacceptable. I'm asking you to denounce it immediately and cut ties with Alex Jones and anyone who subscribes to these dangerous ideas.'

Ms Lafferty's public plea elicited an instant response – not from the president, but from Jones himself.

The day after Lafferty's letter appeared online, Jones made a panicked on-air attempt to distance himself from his own theories.

He claimed, falsely, to have been misquoted on the subject of Sandy Hook. 'So they take it out of context and say, "Look, he says no children ever died from mass shooting." I never said that,' Jones lied.

If these squirming feats of positional contortionism were

meant to show Trump that he wasn't toxic company, the attempt didn't work. The incoming president didn't explicitly disavow Jones, but he never appeared on Infowars again.

After that, the bad news for Alex Jones kept on coming. In early 2018, he was booted off YouTube for repeatedly violating the company's terms of service. A host of other tech platforms swiftly followed suit, drastically weakening his social media profile and crippling his ability to broadcast and monetise his ideology.

Then the Sandy Hook lawsuits began. The first of these was a civil case brought in April 2018 by Lenny Pozner, whose son Noah had been the youngest child killed at Sandy Hook. As a consequence of Jones's repeated claim that the Sandy Hook parents were government stooges, Pozner and his wife had been subjected to a sustained and vicious campaign of harassment by Alex Jones fans. By 2018, Pozner and his wife had been menaced into moving house seven times in five years. At one point an Infowars 'reporter' revealed the Pozners' new address on the air, forcing the couple to move yet again. By 2019, the Pozners were divorced and living hundreds of miles from their son's grave.

After Pozner's lawsuit came the deluge. At one point Jones was the subject of four separate Sandy Hook cases, involving a total of nine plaintiffs.

In March 2019, a video appeared online of a rambling three-hour deposition that Jones had delivered during one of the court cases. It proved to be a predictable disaster for Jones. Under questioning from the plaintiff's attorney, Jones proved completely unable to defend his claims about Sandy Hook.

'What you said is not real,' the plaintiff's attorney told Jones. Remarkably, Jones did not seem to disagree. He admitted that he was merely a pundit, just 'someone giving an opinion'. Moreover, Jones testified under oath that he was mentally ill, or had been. He claimed that he had suffered, in the past, from a form of psychosis 'where I basically thought everything was staged, even though I'm now learning a lot of times things aren't staged'.

In November 2019, Jones sat down to give another Sandy Hook deposition, and once more the video was posted online. During three hours of testimony, he said 'I don't remember' forty-four times and 'I don't know' fifty-one times.

In September 2021, a judge presiding over two of the Sandy Hook lawsuits issued default findings against Jones, making him liable for damages and legal costs in both cases. The judge ruled that Jones and his team had acted in flagrant bad faith by repeatedly failing to comply with court orders.

Two months later, a Connecticut judge presiding over the remaining Sandy Hook lawsuit also issued a default finding against Jones, completing a clean sweep of rulings against him.

Jones and his attorneys have vowed to appeal against the judgments. Assuming the appeals fail, it is now in the hands of the juries to determine the scale of the damages he must pay. Their verdicts have the potential to inflict financial ruin on the one-time king of conspiracy theory.

A PATHETIC ATTEMPT TO DEFEND THE INDEFENSIBLE

After all that, can there be any reason – any reason at all – to believe that the Sandy Hook shootings were a hoax?

No.

If there were any reasons to believe, Alex Jones would have

brought them out in his defence. Instead he offered nothing but hot air – which, we may fairly conclude, is all that these sad and cynical conspiracy theories were made of in the first place.

The worst massacre of children in America's history was carried out by one deranged and death-obsessed individual, acting alone. There was no plot, no conspiracy by the government or the liberal anti-gun lobby to create martyrs. They don't need to fake children's deaths to make their arguments. In 2021, more than 300 American girls and boys under the age of twelve died of gunshot wounds.

The only conspiracy around the Sandy Hook Elementary School tragedy was the wilful attempt to misrepresent what had happened by a noisy group of paranoid fantasists and anti-gun control activists – and by one man whose conspiracy factory was the key to a personal fortune.

21

POPE JOHN PAUL I

VICTIM OF A TRIPLE CONSPIRACY?

The 1970s were a dreadful time for the Roman Catholic Church. Many of the awful crimes against children that have only recently been exposed took place during this dark decade, while the Vatican's finances were being abused and manipulated under the control of 'God's Godfather', the chain-smoking, mafia-connected Bishop Paul Marcinkus.

Yet the darkest secret of all may still be the unexplained death of Pope John Paul I, 'The Smiling Pope', just thirty-three days after his election to the papacy on 26 August 1978.

Pope John Paul I was sixty-five, much younger than most Popes, and almost handsome, with a modern, charismatic appeal that hinted at a major generational change in the Church of Rome. Parallels were drawn with the new era in America that had been heralded by the election of John F Kennedy.

Yet, within weeks, he was gone. Pope John Paul I died alone, supposedly while reading, sitting up in bed, in the middle of the night. His death was sudden and obviously unexpected and the official statements about the circumstances immediately struck observers as inaccurate and contradictory.

There seemed to be confusion about the basic facts, such as when he died, who found him and when that was, and what he was reading at the time he passed away. There was no post-mortem to establish the cause of death and there was even a bureaucratic muddle about whether a proper death certificate had been issued.

As Catholics everywhere reeled at the news that their new Pope was already dead, rumours sprang up of a murderous conspiracy. Little serious effort was made to dispel them and they remain just as strong today.

Albino Luciani had not been everyone's choice as Pope. He was elected at the fourth ballot, after a split had emerged in the College of Cardinals between the conservatives, who thought the church was already moving too fast towards the modern world, and the moderates and reformers.

But John Paul I had made an immediate impression in his first few days as Pope, showing a relaxed, human side that won him an enthusiastic reception from the general public. He chose not to have the usual coronation after his election, breaking a thousand-year-old tradition, and he refused to say 'we' all the time, preferring to say 'I', though Vatican officials hurried to rewrite his speeches and press comments with the traditional 'we'.

This warm, conversational informality wasn't everyone's idea of what a Pope should be. One Vatican insider dismissed him as a joke, saying, 'They have elected Peter Sellers.'

The remark was shrewd, as well as bitter, as John Paul I, with his quick, wry smile, did sometimes look a bit like the man who played Bluebottle in *The Goon Show* and Inspector Clouseau in the *Pink Panther* movies.

Other critics felt he was weak and intellectually lightweight. But when the Argentinian dictator, General Jorge Videla, came to the Vatican on a prearranged visit, Pope John Paul I sternly condemned his regime's pitiless cruelty and large-scale human rights violations.

TIDYING UP THE DEATHBED SCENE

Though he was one of the youngest Popes ever elected, John Paul I was still sixty-five years old. He looked younger, but he did have health problems, including serious swelling of the feet and ankles, which may have played a part in his sudden death.

The papal doctor said he died of a heart attack and later researchers have narrowed the likely cause down to a pulmonary embolism. Albino Luciani had already suffered a retinal embolism, two years before. The time of the heart attack was said to be about 11 p.m.

The fact that the Vatican was caught lying about how the Pope was found, after his death, may well signify window-dressing rather than conspiracy.

It was originally claimed that the deceased Pope was discovered by his two private secretaries, John Magee and Don Diego Lorenzi, propped up in bed, wearing his glasses and reading *The Imitation of Christ* by the fifteenth-century German-Dutch mystic Thomas à Kempis (the monk who coined the saying 'Man proposes, God disposes'). A later official version of events contradicted this and said he was found lying on the floor, after 5 a.m., by the nun who brought him his morning coffee.

While the picture of two anxious Vatican flunkeys grappling

with the body to position it in a more piously papal pose is bizarre and unsettling, it isn't necessarily sinister.

John Magee, later Bishop of Cloyne, always knew suspicion would fall on him. In an interview nearly thirty years later, he said he had been accused of poisoning the Pope and had even been questioned by Interpol. He claimed the death of John Paul I was the result of stress and exhaustion in the hectic period following his election. Magee admitted that the nun with the coffee, Sister Vicenza, was the first to find the Pope's body, though he had been the first to raise the alarm. And he continued to insist that the Pope was discovered in bed.

WHO MIGHT HAVE WANTED THE POPE DEAD?

The big surprise about John Magee's version of events is that it makes Pope John Paul I's death seem no surprise at all.

Bishop Magee, who was later heavily criticised for his handling of child sex-abuse cases involving priests in his Irish diocese, argued that Luciani had already been ill when he was elected. He claimed the pontiff was uneasy and agitated throughout the thirty-three days and had complained of serious chest pains before going to bed.

Magee said the Pope had even spoken of being close to death and had mentioned that he would probably be succeeded by 'the foreigner', the Polish-born Cardinal Wojtyla, who became Pope John Paul II.

But suspicion still swirls around the death of Pope John Paul I. One of the best-known books on the subject, David Yallop's *In God's Name*, claimed he was poisoned with a heart drug, digitalis, by a conspiracy involving religious conservatives, mafia money-men and a secret network of Freemasons (including, inevitably, Bishop Marcinkus) inside the Vatican.

Whether or not there was any such super-conspiracy, it is easy to see why any one of these groups might have wanted the Pope out of the way.

Vatican reactionaries certainly feared that Luciani might go beyond the reforms of Vatican II and lift the ban on birth control, though he had always toed the official line on this before.

Everyone involved in the Vatican's finances must have dreaded a new broom sweeping aside the lies and hypocrisy around the Istituto per le Opere di Religione, the Vatican Bank, and its far-too-cosy dealings with mafia money-launderers and Roberto Calvi's crooked Banco Ambrosiano.

Bishop (later Archbishop) Marcinkus, who ran the Vatican Bank from 1971 to 1989, was deeply involved in all this and chose to play golf regularly with Calvi and Sicilian tax expert Michele 'The Shark' Sindona, both of whom went on to meet spectacularly sticky ends. Marcinkus, who was a director of Ambrosiano Overseas, based in the Bahamas, had been indicted in the US on fraud charges in 1973, but had refused to open the Vatican's books and defend himself. He was later granted special immunity from prosecution by Pope John Paul II.

The Freemasons who are said to have virtually taken control of the Vatican supposedly belonged to a violently neo-Fascist secret Masonic lodge, known as P2 or Propaganda Due.

P2 certainly seems to have brought together an unholy alliance of politicians, police chiefs, mafiosi and media figures – including, according to one membership list, the young Silvio Berlusconi. There is less hard evidence of priestly involvement, but many people in Italy take that as read. One ex-P2 member claimed that both Cardinal Villot, the Pope's second-in-command, and Marcinkus were deeply implicated. This informer, a journalist called Carmine Pecorelli, was unable to offer any convincing proof of an evil conspiracy before he met with an untimely end, shot dead in his car in Rome, by a person or persons unknown, in early 1979.

22

ROBERTO CALVI

'WHO "SUICIDED" CALVI?'

According to the London inquest jury in 1982, Italian banker Roberto Calvi committed suicide.

The next inquest, the following year, recorded an open verdict, meaning that the cause of death could not be established. In 1997, Italian police accused two people of killing him. In 2002, forensic experts appointed by Italian judges said it was homicide. In 2007, five people accused of Calvi's murder were cleared. In 2010, the acquittals were confirmed after three of the five had been tried again.

For nearly thirty years, it had been generally accepted that Roberto Calvi was murdered. He was the head of the notorious Banco Ambrosiano, which had collapsed owing roughly £800 million to the sort of people you don't want to owe a penny to. He was out on bail pending an appeal against a four-year sentence for illegally exporting $27 million, and he had apparently already tried to take his own life while in jail.

This time, however, he had had help. Calvi was found hanging by the neck from a length of orange nylon rope dangling from some scaffolding under Blackfriars Bridge, in the middle of London.

He had £10,000 in his pockets, and several heavy bricks, and lumps of concrete were stuffed down the front of his trousers. This macabre death made the news in England and in Italy, where one leading newspaper, *La Repubblica*, ran the memorable front-page headline 'WHO "SUICIDED" CALVI?'

There's no doubt things had not been going well for sixty-two-year-old Calvi in the last weeks of his life. He had been known for some years as 'God's Banker' because of the close and sometimes dubious connections between Banco Ambrosiano and the Institute for Religious Works, better known as the Vatican Bank. Twelve days before his death, he'd written a private letter to the Pope, John Paul II, saying he felt 'betrayed and abandoned' by the Vatican and threatening that, if Banco Ambrosiano folded, it would trigger 'a catastrophe of unimaginable proportions, in which the Church will suffer the gravest damage'.

A few days later, he'd fled from his flat in Rome. Carrying a false passport, and having shaved off his moustache to avoid recognition, he hired a private plane in Venice to bring him to London. On 16 June 1982, the day before his death, he had been stripped of his position at Banco Ambrosiano by the Italian Treasury.

NOT HANGED, BUT STRANGLED

For conspiracy connoisseurs, the big question about Roberto Calvi's death is whether it was a simple murder or part of a bigger plot.

The defendants in the Italian trial that ran from 2005 to

2007 claimed Calvi really had committed suicide, feeling he had nowhere to go after Vatican financiers backed down on promises to bail him out.

That part of their story was plausible in itself, but it came too late. Calvi's body had been exhumed in the late 1990s and forensic examination of the neck injuries had proved that he had been strangled, rather than hanged.

It had also been pointed out that what looked like a hanging on the morning of 17 June 1982 had been seen that way because the tide was out and the River Thames was low. Calvi's clothes were wet through and he had died during the night, at a time when the water level was up to within a few feet of the scaffolding, making suicide by hanging an impossible feat. He could have drowned, but there was no water in his lungs.

There were plenty of people who might have wanted to kill him, however, including some very senior mafia figures who felt he really should have returned several million pounds of dirty money he had promised to launder for them.

THE ULTIMATE ITALIAN JOB

The background to Roberto Calvi's death was Italy – and, in Italy, everything is interconnected.

Banco Ambrosiano had almost certainly laundered mafia heroin money. Calvi and his bank had done a lot of business with the Vatican Bank, which was a major shareholder in several Banco Ambrosiano companies, and specifically with the powerful and cynical Archbishop Paul Marcinkus.

Marcinkus – also known as 'God's Godfather' or 'the Pope's Gorilla' – was the Pope's bodyguard, a governor of the Vatican and head of the Vatican Bank for eighteen years. He was accused of a number of serious irregularities during his time in charge of the Vatican's finances and was thought to have worked with Calvi to launder and recycle mafia funds on a large scale.

At the time of Calvi's death, Banco Ambrosiano was owed billions of lire by Panamanian companies linked to the Vatican Bank. The Church denied legal responsibility for the collapse of the bank but owned up to a moral involvement and paid out £138 million to creditors.

Apart from purely financial shenanigans, one of the other secrets the Vatican might not have wished to see aired in public was Calvi's part in the channelling of Catholic funds to political organisations and anti-Marxist groups in Europe and South America.

The most spectacular example of this was the Polish-born Pope John Paul II's alleged undercover support for Solidarity, the fledgling Polish trade union movement led by shipyard worker Lech Wałęsa.

The Pope's pioneering visit to Poland in 1979 had established contact with Polish dissidents and was credited with sowing the seeds of Solidarity. But supplying funds for the anti-Communist union was a highly sensitive issue and could have had serious international repercussions. When Licio Gelli, former grand master of Italy's illegal and influential Propaganda Due or P2 masonic lodge, was under investigation in 2005 over Calvi's death, he told the court the banker's murder was 'commissioned in Poland'. (P2 members, incidentally, wore rather theatrical black robes to their meetings and called themselves '*i frati neri*', 'the black friars'.)

In the court in Rome, Gelli and five other 2005 suspects were accused in the initial indictment of ordering Calvi's murder to stop him 'using blackmail power against his political and institutional sponsors from the world of Freemasonry, belonging to the P2 lodge, or from the Institute for Religious Works [Vatican Bank] with whom he had managed investments and financing with conspicuous sums of money, some of it coming from Cosa Nostra and public agencies'.

Licio Gelli was the ultimate in well-connected but unreliable witnesses. But he was not charged in connection with Calvi's murder. His name was dropped from the final indictment and he did not stand trial. The other defendants were eventually acquitted for lack of evidence, so no one has ever been convicted.

'Calvi's death was made to look like suicide,' Gelli told the investigating magistrates. 'One evening I was at dinner with Calvi. He told me that the next day he had to go and see "the most Holy One" in the Vatican to get $80 million he had to pay for bills relating to Poland – and that if he did not get the money "everything would blow up".'

Gelli's involvement sums up the peculiarly Italian nature of the Calvi affair. Before it was dissolved in 1981 for trying to plot a neo-Fascist coup, his Propaganda Due's thousand lodge members included politicians, judges, generals and civil servants, mafia leaders and, allegedly, a number of high-ranking Vatican priests.

Roberto Calvi's death was fairly obviously a mafia execution, delegated to the experts in managing these things. But how many of the usual suspects were really involved in the conspiracy behind the murder? Given the secrecy that surrounds the inner workings of Italian politics, organised crime, the banking industry and the Vatican, this is one plot that's guaranteed never to be disentangled.

23

WORLD WAR TWO

WHO REALLY STARTED IT?

'I have to tell you now that no such undertaking has been received and that, consequently, this country is at war with Germany.'

For the people of Britain, Prime Minister Neville Chamberlain's radio announcement on the morning of Sunday 3 September 1939 marked the beginning of nearly six years of war in Europe. Britain had asked Germany for assurances that it would withdraw its troops that were attacking Poland, and Hitler, of course, had refused. Britain and France were to come to the aid of Poland and the world was to be plunged into war for the second time in twenty-five years.

History is written by the winners and history says Germany started the war by invading Poland. But Hitler, the master of the big lie, had another version of what was happening that he was anxious to present to the German people.

Two days earlier, he had announced in a speech to the Reichstag in Berlin that Poland had attacked Germany and invaded German soil in the early hours of the morning.

The story was that Polish troops had crossed the border at

around 5.45 a.m. on 1 September 1939 in a surprise assault. German units had fought back bravely and a dozen Polish soldiers had been killed in the first battle. Polish radio signals had been intercepted, Hitler said, that showed this was not just a skirmish but the start of an invasion.

In fact, German SS troops dressed up in Polish uniforms had staged a phoney attack on a radio station near the town of Gleiwitz, pretending to be saboteurs, and had broadcast provocative anti-German messages calling on the Polish minority in eastern Germany to take up arms against Hitler. The trick was part of a plan called Operation Himmler that involved over forty of these small-scale false flag operations designed to provide excuses for invading Poland.

As Nazi forces surged across the border and his planes screamed in overhead, the Führer kept up the pretence that the Poles had started the war.

Hitler was a dedicated conspirator, with a cynical belief that trickery, plotting and deception were essential for success. Ten days before, he had told his generals he would give them a moral fig leaf to go ahead with '*Fall Weiss*' ('Case White'), the plan for the invasion of Poland.

'I will provide a propaganda reason for starting the war, whether it's believable or not,' he said. 'The victor won't be asked if he told the truth.'

A SECRET CONSPIRACY TO CARVE UP POLAND

The huge conspiracy that lay behind Hitler's smaller false flag deceits at the start of the war was the surprise Molotov-Ribbentrop Pact that had been agreed with the Soviet Union a week earlier, on 23 August 1939. The USSR had still been in treaty negotiations with Britain and France up to two days before this unholy alliance was signed.

The treaty claimed to be a non-aggression pact. But it included a top-secret protocol with plans to split northern Europe into two 'spheres of interest' in the event of potential 'territorial and political rearrangements'. This agreement involved dividing Poland down the middle and sharing it out between Germany and the Soviet Union.

The Soviets, who abruptly switched sides in 1941 when Hitler began to invade Russia, were not keen to burden their new allies in Britain and the US with all the little details of their previous arrangements and forgot to mention this deal to slice up Poland. It was only revealed to the rest of the world after the Nazis were defeated in 1945.

As far as the Molotov-Ribbentrop Pact was concerned, conspiracy did not apparently come into it. The Soviets had spent most of 1939 talking to Britain and France about an alliance and been unable to reach agreement.

When diplomatic discussions with London and Paris about a military alliance broke down, it was only natural that the USSR would try to find another treaty partner to help guarantee its security.

This was not quite how it happened, though, as backroom wheeling and dealing between Hitler's people and Stalin's officials had actually been going on for six weeks or so.

The news of a treaty between the Soviet Communists and the German Fascists was an unwelcome bombshell for the rest of Europe, but it was not thought of as a conspiracy. The only bit of secret plotting was the key protocol about dividing Poland, but that did not come to light for nearly six years.

THE FALSE FLAG OP THAT WENT OFF AT HALF-COCK

Once the deal with Russia was in place, Hitler was ready to start the war – or at least accuse Poland of starting it.

After he announced the faked Polish attack on Germany, neutral American journalists were driven to the radio station at Gleiwitz to be shown the bodies of twelve Polish soldiers. But the bodies they saw were not invaders shot in battle. They were eleven concentration camp prisoners who had been taken to the radio tower, plus one local Polish activist picked up by the Gestapo. In what was arguably the first war crime of WWII, they were ordered to put on Polish Army uniforms, murdered with lethal injections and then riddled with bullets by SS thugs.

Most of the detail that's available about the Gleiwitz incident comes from the statement of SS Major Alfred Naujocks at the Nuremberg War Trials in 1946.

Naujocks survived imprisonment to become a post-war businessman in Hamburg and eventually cashed in on the rights to his story under the title *The Man Who Started the War*. He claimed the Gleiwitz operation was carried out on direct orders from his boss, Heinrich Müller, head of the Gestapo.

Evidence from Naujocks is not necessarily reliable, as he was a slippery witness. Indeed, he was probably involved in running the secret Odessa Network that helped ex-SS war criminals escape from Germany to start new lives in South America. But his account matches well with the US press reports from Gleiwitz and what is known about Operation Himmler and the Führer's intentions.

Hitler's plan to shift the blame for starting hostilities onto Poland was important to him as a contribution to German morale. Operation Himmler was planned well in advance. In fact, it had even gone off at half-cock a few days earlier, on 26 August, the date he had originally chosen for the start of the war. This resulted in a scene of grim farce, as one undercover unit was not told the war had been postponed and went ahead with its attack, from the Polish side, on a German customs post.

The disguised SS troops, led by Obersturmbannführer Otfried Helwig, were surprised when they 'attacked' the customs officers and were met with enthusiastic live return fire. By the time the incident was over, several Germans on both sides had been killed. The first combat casualties of the war were therefore friendly fire victims, shot by their own side.

The Blitzkrieg strike that led to Poland's defeat in just over a month was followed by a seven-month lull in Europe when there was very little land fighting. This period – known as 'the Phoney War' in English and '*der Sitzkrieg*' ('the Sitting-Down War') in German – was followed by the German invasion of Belgium and Holland and the appointment of Winston Churchill as Britain's new prime minister on the same day, 10 May 1940.

Hitler's scheming had caught Britain and France on the hop and won him the flying start he wanted for his European war. His last-minute pact with Stalin's regime had intimidated his enemies, as the Western nations were appalled to see the Communist USSR and Nazi Germany standing shoulder to shoulder.

No one was to know, at that stage, that less than two years later Hitler would be turning the largest invasion force in history loose to attack the very same Soviet allies with whom he'd conspired to carve up Poland.

24

BOB WOOLMER

A CLEAR CONSPIRACY TO MURDER

Just how important is cricket? To players and supporters in England and Australia, South Africa, New Zealand and the West Indies, it provides some of the greatest, subtlest, most competitive sporting confrontations of all. To most of the rest of the world, it is an impenetrable ritual with all the interest and excitement of long-distance race walking.

But to hundreds of millions of fans in India, Pakistan, Sri Lanka and Bangladesh, it is a passion, an obsession, almost a religion. Cricket has an importance and patriotic significance that seems overwhelming, almost a matter of life and death.

And for Bob Woolmer, the former England batsman who was coach to the Pakistan team at the 2007 Cricket World Cup Finals in the West Indies, a matter of life and death was what it became.

Because Bob Woolmer was murdered.

Despite the Jamaican inquest jury's open verdict, which implied that it was impossible to tell whether or not death was by natural causes, he was undoubtedly killed.

Bob Woolmer's lifeless body was found slumped in the

bathroom of his hotel room at the Pegasus Hotel in Kingston, Jamaica, on 18 March 2007, the morning after his powerful Pakistan side had been dumped out of the World Cup one-day competition by the minnows of Ireland, most of them part-timers.

Pakistan's fans were incensed by the defeat and many seemed prepared to blame the manager, rather than the surprisingly inept performance of the players on the pitch. They burned effigies of Woolmer and team captain Inzamam-ul-Haq in the street and carried banners saying '*Woolmer murdabad, Woolmer murdabad*'. The slogan meant 'Death to Woolmer'.

The bathroom where Bob Woolmer collapsed was a mess, with blood, faeces and vomit everywhere, and there was a mysterious, unidentified 'straw-coloured liquid' on the floor near the bed. His body was naked and police said his face had a blue-ish tinge, which might point to asphyxiation. Early toxicology reports suggested he had been poisoned. Other sources said he might have died of a heart attack. Then there were suggestions that he could have committed suicide, in reaction to his team's shock exit from the World Cup.

After four days, the Jamaican police confidently announced that fifty-eight-year-old Bob Woolmer's death was murder 'by manual strangulation'. Three months later, the revised police opinion was that there was no crime to be solved and that he had died of natural causes.

None of this inspired confidence in the investigative and autopsy processes.

Rumours swirled around the town, the international cricketing community and the wider world.

Bob Woolmer had been killed in a robbery that went wrong, people said. He had been killed by furious Pakistani cricket fans who blamed him for the humiliating defeat, with or without the complicity of Pakistan's ISI security services. He had been executed under a *fatwa* for showing lack of respect for the fundamentalist Islamic beliefs espoused by five or six of his team and many millions of their fans. He had been murdered by Indian bookmakers for refusing to fix the result of a match. He had been murdered by Indian bookmakers for actually fixing the result of the St Patrick's Day match against Ireland. Or perhaps he had stumbled upon evidence of player involvement in match fixing and been silenced before he could name names.

Match fixing is the dark shadow behind these international competitions. In many ways, cricket is the easiest game in the world to fix. Players can drop catches or deliberately miss a ball and be bowled out. Captains or managers can make inscrutable tactical decisions that change the course of a match. But fixing games to suit the needs of illegal betting syndicates need not involve changing the result. Even a bowler delivering one technically illegal no-ball at a particular time can be enough to win the gambling syndicates huge sums. This is called spot fixing and it can be arranged and done in such a way that the cheating is almost impossible to detect.

Cricket's record in these matters has not been blameless. In the 1990s, former Pakistan captain Salim Malik was found guilty of match-fixing offences, though his lifetime ban was overturned by a local court in Pakistan in 2008.

In 2000, Hansie Cronje, South Africa's captain, was thrown out of the game in disgrace after being found guilty of fixing matches on behalf of gambling syndicates. That conviction shook world cricket and eyebrows were raised again when Cronje died, two years later, in a plane crash in which he was the only passenger. Bob Woolmer had been the South African national team's coach during most of the time that Cronje had been captain. Indian captain and batting hero Mohammad Azharuddin, who had been named by Cronje, was also banned for life in 2000.

Even since Bob Woolmer's death, Pakistan's summer 2010 tour to England was overshadowed by serious match-fixing allegations against two brilliant young fast bowlers, Mohammad Amir and Mohammad Asif, and the captain, batsman Salman Butt. All three Pakistani players were found guilty and jailed by the British courts in November 2011.

That same month, ex-Somerset captain turned cricket journalist and commentator Peter Roebuck died in Cape Town, while covering the Australian tour of South Africa.

Reports at the time said he appeared to have committed suicide by jumping from the window of his hotel, minutes after being questioned by police about allegations of sexual assault. Roebuck was known as a troubled soul, but he was also a renowned anti-corruption campaigner. Inevitably, those who had strong suspicions about Bob Woolmer's death wondered if this, too, might have some dark connection with match-fixing and betting syndicates.

The money changing hands in connection with illegal betting in India and elsewhere was not just millions but billions. Organised crime had become deeply involved in the bookmaking business and its match-fixing sideline, and some well-informed people believe there were links at the top to the al-Qaeda terrorist group. Those who know the background know there are powerful and well-funded organisations that could and would have murdered Bob Woolmer without a second thought, if it suited their interests.

TOO MANY LOOPHOLES FOR THE INQUEST JURY

There is no good reason to doubt that Bob Woolmer's death was murder and that there are conspirators somewhere who are very glad to know the case has been closed and pushed to one side.

But the chaotic and uncoordinated investigations appear to have been purely the result of cock-ups, rather than any conspiracy to suppress the truth.

Three eminent pathologists – in Britain, South Africa and Canada – had been asked to analyse forensic samples and had come up with conclusions that seemed to point to death by natural causes.

Yet even here, there was a great deal of chaos and confusion. The London pathologist, John Slaughter, testified that he had found no evidence of poison in the blood sample he was sent. But the director of the Jamaican forensics laboratory quoted Slaughter as telling her there was 'enough stomach content, but in regard to urine, blood and straw-coloured liquid, there was not enough for a tox-screen'.

By the time the inquest jury considered its verdict, in November 2007, the eleven jurors had been listening to discussion and argument about the details of the case for nearly six weeks. They had been subjected to such a barrage of circumstantial and contradictory evidence that there was little hope of reaching a sound conclusion.

'We had no choice,' the jury foreman said. 'We came to an open verdict because the evidence was too weak. There were too many what-ifs and loopholes.'

THE FAKED EMAIL PROVES IT WAS MURDER

In fact, although the guilty people were never identified, it only takes one or two pieces of clear-cut evidence to show that the Bob Woolmer case should have been reopened, rather than left to drift away into the mists of history.

Both the presence of an unexplained and powerful poison, cypermethrin, in some (though not all) of the post-mortem samples and the glaring inconsistencies between the two emails supposedly written by Bob Woolmer on the night he died underline the belief that he was murdered.

Who did it and why are more complicated questions. But they were never going to be answered without a more thorough and scrupulous criminal investigation. If this couldn't have been arranged or funded through normal law-enforcement channels, it should have been a high priority for the International Cricket Council (the ICC). For the sport to survive and thrive, it seemed vital that world cricket shouldn't leave the questions unanswered and the final story untold.

Part of that story seems to be that Bob Woolmer was poisoned with cockroach powder or ant killer. Cypermethrin is a synthetic pyrethroid neurotoxin that acts within ten minutes or so if swallowed. It is sold as an insecticide. A lethal dose for an adult could be anything from 10mg upwards. In humans, cypermethrin causes repeated vomiting, diarrhoea, breathing difficulties, convulsions and ultimately death.

Three samples of Bob Woolmer's blood were tested at different times by different toxicologists. Two of the blood samples were clear, but one contained evidence of cypermethrin. A urine sample also contained traces of the poison.

Cypermethrin was also reported in the mysterious 'straw-coloured liquid' that was found on the floor near the bed in the hotel room and in a stomach-contents sample tested at the government forensic laboratory in Kingston. Jamaica's acting chief forensic officer, Fitzmore Coates, whose methods were questioned at the inquest, told the court, 'The final calculation of cypermethrin in stomach content which I analysed would be significant. It could cause vomiting, diarrhoea, nausea – and death.'

Independent pathologists from the UK, Canada and South Africa criticised the Jamaican forensic unit's techniques and said the samples that showed cypermethrin could have been contaminated with the pesticide at the labs. But that is hard to square with the statement of Cheryl Corbin, director of the forensic sciences centre 1,200 miles away in Barbados. Corbin said that, in tests conducted at her laboratory, cypermethrin was found in both the straw-coloured liquid and the stomach content samples.

Yet, even if the poison in different parts of the body can somehow be explained away, there is one damning and overwhelming piece of evidence that proves someone was in Bob Woolmer's room in the middle of the night, around the time of his death. This person was pretending to be him and wrote the last email sent from his victim's laptop, at about 6 a.m.

To understand why this can be stated with such certainty, it is worth looking at the last email Bob Woolmer himself wrote. He was fed up, as any team manager would be, after the St Patrick's Day massacre, which had clearly made him consider resigning. Yet his tone, in writing to Gill, his wife, in Cape Town, was easy, light and smoothly articulate. The English is effortless, educated and informal.

'Hi, darling, feeling a little depressed currently as you might imagine… Our batting performance was abysmal and my worst fears were realised. I could tell the players were for some reason not able to fire themselves up.'

He rounded off the note affectionately and with a touch of rueful irony (in the phrase 'but I doubt it, as you were probably watching!').

'I hope your day was better, but I doubt it, as you were probably watching! Not much more to add, I am afraid, but I still love you lots.'

Now compare this with the email he is supposed to have written just a little later, at six in the morning, to Nasim Ashraf, chairman of the Pakistan Cricket Board.

'I would like to praise my association with the Pakistan team but now I would like to announce my retirement after the World Cup, to live the rest of my life in Cape Town.'

This makes no sense. 'I would like to praise my association with the Pakistan team' is virtually meaningless. It's certainly not normal, natural English.

The email continues: 'I have no lust for the job and I will not like others to make personal remarks at me. Professionally, I am open to criticism, I will be ready to continue the job if the president asks me for it.'

'I have no lust for the job' is strange wording. 'I will not like others' should be, perhaps, 'I would not like others'. No native English speaker with Woolmer's background would say or write, 'to make personal remarks at me', rather than 'to make personal remarks about me'. And the last sentence is not only extraordinarily cack-handed ('continue the job if the president asks me for it') but also contains an astonishing swerve of direction, as it suddenly moves from 'I'm retiring' to 'I will be ready to continue the job'.

This email is a fake. It should have been recognised as a forgery. No writer, editor or academic would be fooled by it for one minute.

And because this is a fake, we know Bob Woolmer was murdered. We know it wasn't by a random thief, because no casual intruder would bother to sit down, in mid-burglary, and write an email to the Pakistan Cricket Board. So it was written by someone with some direct interest in cricket, as part of some wider conspiracy. This is what the police needed to untangle. This is the unsolved, unquestioned murder that still hasn't been properly investigated more than fifteen years later. It remains a huge blot on cricket's conscience, but no one has ever taken it as seriously as they should.

The final word on the incriminating email goes to Neil Manthorp, a South African sports journalist and a long-time friend of Bob Woolmer.

'I have received hundreds of emails from him over the years,' Manthorp told the *Sunday Telegraph*. 'This is not his style – not the sort of words and phrases that he would use.'

25

SHAPE-SHIFTING LIZARDS AND THE DUKE OF EDINBURGH

No. Wait. I'll keep it brief.

By now, most people will have heard some mention of the ultra-conspiracists' theory that the senior members of the British royal family are actually twelve-foot-tall extra-terrestrial lizard-like beings with shape-shifting properties that enable them to appear in any form they wish.

The Windsors, as a family, are used to this sort of hurtful remark. They ended up having to change their family name in the middle of World War One, from the undiplomatically German 'Saxe-Coburg-Gotha' to something a little more, well, English. And, as we know, the more recent generations have also had to put up with a certain amount of sniping and criticism.

For many years, the particular target of conspiracy theorists was Prince Philip, Duke of Edinburgh, husband and consort of the Queen and breaker of many taboos and conventions, who died in April 2021. But the smiling nonagenarian monarch herself has been identified by some as the head of a worldwide drug-dealing cartel and leader of a transnational plot to impose world domination, accusations which, if true, would leave her open to the charge of rank hypocrisy.

According to New Age visionary and conspiracy spotter David Icke, a one-time Football League goalkeeper (with Hereford United) and popular television sports presenter, the shape-shifting lizards of Buckingham Palace have long been deeply involved in human blood sacrifices.

Icke, who was formerly a leading Green Party spokesman, once announced on the BBC's *Terry Wogan Show* that he was the Son of God. He has since written many bestselling books denouncing the Queen and Prince Philip, the Queen Mother, George W Bush, Al Gore, the Rothschild family, the Rockefellers and various country and western singers as megalomaniac lizards.

This reptilian elite is apparently descended from creatures originating from the constellation Draco. Their hybrid reptile/human DNA allows them to take on and maintain a human shape, as long as they have regular supplies of blood. They mostly live underground, in caverns and tunnels, and have been known about since Babylonian times. *Homo sapiens*, it turns out, is just the result of a huge breeding programme run by these reptilians.

The original astronauts came visiting in search of what David Icke calls 'mono-atomic gold'. Eating this supposedly gives them the power to process vast amounts of information, travel through different dimensions and change their shape from reptile to human forms. They have a nasty vested interest in stirring up human conflict, too, as they can absorb and gain power from the negative energy it generates, and they are responsible for black magic and ritual sacrifices on an unimagined scale.

TOO WEIRD EVEN FOR THE ARCH-CONSPIRACISTS

Many of the pronouncements of David Icke and the lizard conspiracists have been subject to review and amendment. And their theories are not always welcomed, even by those whose lives and careers revolve around warning people of the grand conspiracies that are supposedly moving us towards micro-chipped slavery under a single totalitarian world government.

Alex Jones, for example, is the outspoken Texan talk-show host who became one of America's best-known conspiracy theorists. But even he couldn't go along with the shape-shifting reptile stories. His complaint was that while Icke talked lucidly about many of the same things that concerned him, he then undermined everything with 'asinine' stuff about green lizards.

'It discredits all the reality we're talking about, and that's the problem with David Icke,' said Jones. 'He's got a good line to a point, and then he discredits it all. It's like a turd in the punchbowl.'

BUT AFTER ICKE HAS BACKED OFF, SOME STILL BELIEVE

Although his was the main voice warning the world about the reptilian powers behind the throne through the 1990s and beyond, some of what David Icke says today is surprisingly believable. Where his older ideas about the race of reptilian-mammalian hybrids involved a lot of talk about bloodlines, family influences and international conspiracies, he is very keen these days to build logical arguments and to fend off those critics who have accused him of coded anti-Semitism.

He now talks and writes at great length about the need for ordinary people ('of all religions, races, cultures and income levels') to get together and use their strength in numbers to fight back against the manipulators.

These are sometimes identified as the Illuminati and the Rothschild, Rockefeller and Windsor dynasties, but the enemy is largely seen as being greedy bankers and arrogant politicians, and the people in uniform and men in dark suits who do their bidding.

In other words, these days it's mainly a generic anti-conspiracy, anti-government libertarian agenda, with little mention of anything other-worldly or obviously screwball.

But you can't keep a good nut down. In April 2020, during the first terrifying months of the pandemic, David Icke put out an impassioned video on YouTube and Facebook claiming there was a direct link between the spread of COVID-19 and the 5G mobile networks. The video was deleted from both platforms, but not before telecom engineers had been abused in the streets and there had been several arson attacks on mobile phone masts. At an anti-lockdown protest in Trafalgar Square four months later, he changed tack. COVID was a complete myth, he told his followers. 'Anyone with a half a brain cell on active duty can see coronavirus is nonsense,' he said.

It's not always clear these days whether David Icke and the people around him still believe in the reptilian conspiracy at all.

But that doesn't matter now. You have only to look on the internet, and especially at all the video 'proof' uploaded on YouTube, to see that things have moved on. There are hundreds of conspiracy hunters whose self-appointed mission is to spot newsreaders and TV presenters with reptilian facial expressions or tell-tale membrane films across their eyes. And there are thousands of people who pore over this supposed 'evidence' – one grainy little YouTube clip, arguably showing a rather goofy-looking girl turning lizardy and sprouting scales, has been watched nearly four million times.

26

CLAUDY BOMBING

THREE-WAY COVER-UP – THE COP,
THE CONSERVATIVE AND THE CARDINAL

When five Catholics and four Protestants were killed by IRA car bombs in the little village of Claudy in July 1972, the police, British government ministers and the Catholic Church were horrified.

It wasn't just that the atrocity had slaughtered nine innocent people, the youngest an eight-year-old girl. There was another complication that could have plunged community relations in this part of Northern Ireland into complete meltdown, six months after the 'unjustified and unjustifiable' killings of unarmed protesters in Derry's Bogside area, six miles away, on Bloody Sunday.

For all the plausible evidence detectives investigating the bombing had turned up pointed to one man as the ringleader of the bombing gang.

And that man was a local Catholic priest.

Father James Chesney, from the parish of Cullion, twelve miles away, was not arrested and not even questioned by police about the Claudy bombing.

The three bombs that shattered the life of Claudy on the morning of Monday, 31 July 1972, killed nine and injured more than thirty people. No warning was given, though macabre rumours spread later that the fleeing bombers had tried several times to phone in a coded signal but had been thwarted by out-of-order call boxes and a fault at the local telephone exchange.

As tensions rose after the bomb outrage, the police, the government and the Catholic Church conspired together to short-circuit the legal process and arrange for the priest to be sent quietly across the border to continue his career in a rural parish in County Donegal, in the Irish Republic.

WAS OBSTRUCTING THE LAW THE LESSER OF TWO EVILS?

There is no reason to doubt that church, state and constabulary colluded in a classic conspiracy to suppress evidence, prevent further investigation of a suspect and ensure that the truth about the Claudy bomb murders would never be uncovered.

Yet this was a far cry from the usual megalomaniac, self-seeking or hate-driven conspiracies we have seen elsewhere in this book. Though it was clearly wrong and involved the commission of a crime that would normally lead to jail sentences for each of the conspirators, the perpetrators were surely trying to choose the lesser of two evils. The motives may have been mixed, but it's quite possible that this is one bit of practical rule-bending that saved a lot of lives, Catholic and Protestant, during one of the worst periods of the Troubles in Northern Ireland.

JUSTICE DENIED FOR THE VICTIMS AND FAMILIES

What happened in the aftermath of the Claudy bombing was the result of a three-way conspiracy. The report of the Northern Ireland Police Ombudsman, Al Hutchinson, published in August 2010 after a detailed eight-year investigation, makes that explicit.

The questions are all about why, what it achieved and whether it was justified.

All the main people involved are dead, but it is clear the conspiracy took shape at a very high level. After the police passed the matter up the line, the discussions about what to do next directly involved the Conservative government's Northern Ireland Secretary, Willie Whitelaw (later Margaret Thatcher's deputy PM – 'Every prime minister needs a Willie', she once said), and the Primate of All Ireland, Cardinal William Conway.

They met and decided, with the agreement of Sir Gerald Shillington, Chief Constable of the Royal Ulster Constabulary, that Fr Chesney should be transferred to a parish across the border, in nearby Donegal. Shillington's acid comment that he would 'prefer a move to Tipperary' – 200 miles away – is recorded in the ombudsman's report.

This plan was presumably aimed at defusing the Ulster powder keg, at a time when there appeared to be a serious risk of an all-out sectarian civil war between Catholics and Protestants.

The intention may have been honourable. It may have saved lives, in a year which saw nearly 500 deaths from the Troubles in Northern Ireland. But in spiriting the suspect priest out of the country and protecting him from questioning and likely prosecution, the minister, the cardinal and the copper were committing a serious crime. Whichever way you look at it, this was a conspiracy to pervert the course of justice.

Fr Jim Chesney was a tall, dashing, charismatic man of thirty-eight, who liked to drive his Austin-Healey sports car far too fast along Ulster's winding lanes. He was a popular local figure, but the ombudsman's report said that detectives in 1972 concluded that Fr Chesney was also the Provisional IRA's quartermaster and director of operations in the area and that he was a prime suspect in relation to the Claudy bombing and a number of other terrorist incidents.

One suspect picked up in the week after the bombing provided an alibi in which he claimed to have been at Fr Chesney's home at the critical time. But the police claimed that a sniffer dog had found traces of explosives when Fr Chesney's car was stopped at a checkpoint. There was word, too – 'intelligence' it was called – from informers that strongly hinted at the priest's involvement.

'Police ombudsman investigators spoke to a former special branch detective who said he had wanted to arrest Fr Chesney in the months after the bombing,' the ombudsman's report stated, 'but that this had been refused by the Assistant Chief Constable, Special Branch, who had advised that "matters are in hand".'

If the officers involved were still alive, the report said, 'their actions would have demanded explanation, which would have been the subject of further investigation'.

Fr Chesney was ordered to take sick leave early in 1973 and was moved to the new parish in County Donegal later that year. He was interrogated several times by his superiors in the Church, but always denied any terrorist involvement. Living close to the border, he routinely crossed into Northern Ireland but was never once questioned by police about the Claudy bombs. He died of cancer in 1980.

In 2010, the head of the Catholic Church in Ireland, Cardinal Sean Brady, said that the actions of Cardinal Conway 'did not prevent the possibility of future arrest and questioning of Fr Chesney'. It has been suggested that part of Cardinal Conway's motivation may have been a dread that revelations of a Catholic priest's involvement in the bombings might have sparked Protestant paramilitary attacks on innocent congregations and Catholic churches.

Al Hutchinson, the Northern Ireland Police Ombudsman, accepted that some of the decisions that were taken should rightly be 'considered in the context of the time'. But the conspiracy had still meant that justice was frustrated.

'I accept that 1972 was one of the worst years of the Troubles and that the arrest of a priest might well have aggravated the security situation,' his report said. 'Equally I consider that the police failure to investigate someone they suspected of involvement in acts of terrorism could, in itself, have had serious consequences.'

The ombudsman concluded that the actions of the senior RUC officers who blocked the detective work and enlisted the help of the government and the Catholic Church had compromised the investigation. Whatever the motives that lay behind them, these decisions, he said, 'failed those who were murdered, injured or bereaved'.

27

JFK

WAS THE 35TH PRESIDENT MURDERED BY THE 36TH?

President John Fitzgerald Kennedy was promiscuous, ruthless, cynical, manipulative and charismatic. He double-crossed his friends and infuriated his enemies. He scraped into power ahead of Richard Nixon in the 1960 elections on the back of some barely disguised vote-rigging skulduggery cooked up by his father, Joseph Kennedy, and his mafia friends.

But he was young (forty-three), younger than any other elected president. He was handsome, in a Barbie-and-Ken sort of way. And he seemed, not just in America but around the world, to represent a new dawn and a new hope.

The American people as a whole – and not just the Democrats who had voted for him – took JFK to their hearts. But those who didn't buy the myth, the talk of 'the new Camelot', hated him with a passion.

Lyndon Johnson, Kennedy's own vice-presidential running mate, could hardly hide his contempt. The mafia associates who had helped JFK to power believed he owed them an easy ride and were furious when the president's brother, Bobby, was made Attorney General and set about trying to take them down.

The CIA and many senior military figures loathed Kennedy for leaving them high and dry when he abruptly withdrew his backing for the ill-fated CIA-organised invasion of Cuba by anti-Fidel Castro exiles that became known as the Bay of Pigs fiasco. White supremacists in the south thought his drive for black civil rights was ruining the country, while some right-wing Republicans appeared to believe he was a communist agent.

'Nobody likes him, except the public,' Kennedy's critics grumbled.

With so many powerful groups wishing him ill, JFK's security was always potentially under threat, quite apart from the risk posed to all public figures by lone obsessives with guns.

So it was shocking but not completely unpredictable when he was gunned down in Dallas on Friday, 22 November 1963, as his motorcade drove slowly through cheering crowds on a sunny Texas morning.

In the aftermath of the shooting, the police were quick to arrest Lee Harvey Oswald and put the word about that he had been acting alone, despite his claims that he had been set up as 'a patsy'. But, after the slapdash whitewash job compiled by the Warren Commission in 1963–64, the House Select Committee on Assassinations (1976–79) carried out the best of the official investigations so far and concluded that there was a strong chance there had been a conspiracy to kill the president.

The final HSCA report claimed Oswald fired three shots from his old-fashioned $12 Carcano rifle and that the president was killed by the second and third shots, which hit him from behind.

But the Select Committee then went on to say there was

'a high probability that two gunmen fired at President John F Kennedy' and that he was 'probably assassinated as a result of a conspiracy' – a conclusion opinion polls have shown 60 to 70 per cent of Americans have come to over the years.

After admitting it couldn't identify the other gunman 'or the extent of the conspiracy', the Select Committee's formal report then rolled out an extraordinary list of those it *didn't* think had been part of the plot.

It ruled out the governments of Fidel Castro's Cuba and Khrushchev's Soviet Union. It ruled out anti-Castro Cuban groups and organised-crime syndicates, while saying the evidence did not preclude the possibility that either individual Cubans or individual gangsters might have been involved. And it stated firmly that the US Secret Service, the FBI and the CIA were not involved in the shooting.

This confidence was surprising, when even members of the Warren Commission had been sceptical about some of the evidence they had been fed. The FBI's J Edgar Hoover, for example, seemed to have been far too quick to state, just hours after the shooting, that he was 'convinced' they'd got the right man.

Democratic Congressman Hale Boggs was one of the contributors to the Warren Report who was pretty sure the FBI hadn't told all it knew. 'Hoover lied his eyes out to the commission,' he said. 'On Oswald, on Ruby, on their friends, the bullets, the gun, you name it…'

Lee Harvey Oswald, the former CIA agent turned Marxist sympathiser who was arrested within two hours of the shooting and charged with killing the president, had been under close FBI surveillance for at least three years.

Jack Ruby, the sleazy small-time nightclub owner who stepped out of the crowd of pressmen and shot Oswald down as he was being moved from the Dallas police station to the county jail, died of cancer before 'coming clean', as he had promised. But it's probably safe to assume it wasn't a sense of moral outrage that motivated him to rub out the key witness, the one man who could have blown the conspiracy wide open.

'A NATIONAL FAIRY TALE'

Since 1963, there have been several major investigations, 4,000 books, countless films and television programmes and many academic studies focused on aspects of Jack Kennedy's assassination. But many people, including Oliver Stone, the Oscar-winning director of the movie *JFK*, believe Americans are simply unwilling to accept that there could have been a conspiracy.

Stone calls the official account of the killing 'a national fairy tale'. People cling on to it, he says, because, in the end, they'd rather be comfortable than right.

Those who believe there was a conspiracy point out that there are still many unresolved questions about what happened. Even those who don't are forced to agree with them about the shortage of answers. But, as always, what might be conspiracy might also be cock-up or coincidence.

For example, no one has come up with an explanation for the unusual decision, at the beginning of the Dallas motorcade, to withdraw the two Secret Service bodyguards who would normally have been standing on the platform at the back of the president's limo.

You can see a video clip of the bodyguards suddenly being told to back off on YouTube and their perplexed, shrugging reactions at being ordered to stand down. This is back at the beginning of the route, but there would normally have been agents on the rear bumper platforms or running alongside throughout the motorcade, as their job was specifically to throw their bodies in the way if JFK was attacked.

In the same way, whoever fired the shots, it is strange that the car did not accelerate away immediately. It even seemed to slow down for a second or two after the first impact, leaving the president horribly exposed to the final, fatal bullet to the head.

So many of these contributing factors could be put down to coincidence or cock-up. Over the years there have been several books, and a good BBC documentary film, that have swum against the tide by agreeing with the original Warren Commission conclusion that Oswald was acting alone.

The most telling argument in favour of this is probably that any well-organised group of conspirators, whoever they were, would have taken good care to kill off the mouthy and unstable Oswald as soon as possible. He would probably have been 'helped to escape' and disposed of immediately after the shooting, and certainly before he could be grilled for two days by police and FBI interrogators.

ONE FINGERPRINT POINTS TO LBJ'S 'ENFORCER'

The shooting of President John F Kennedy was the most closely scrutinised action of the entire twentieth century. The famous twenty-six-second snatch of blurry 8mm colour film shot by Abraham Zapruder has been examined, enlarged, enhanced and pored over by generations of puzzled policemen, historians, technical experts and conspiracy hunters.

Yet, if you showed this film to an intelligent Martian who knew nothing of the background to the shocking pictures, he would undoubtedly say that what he saw was a man, in a car, being shot, more than once. And he'd tell you, with absolute certainty, that the fatal shot to the head came from the front, from the general direction of the famous 'grassy knoll'.

But if the film does show JFK being shot from the front, then the person who fired that shot cannot have been Lee Harvey Oswald, the man on the sixth floor of the Texas School Book Depository, the man who was supposed to have pulled the trigger.

Though the car had turned the corner close to the depository, by the time the last shot was fired, Oswald's supposed vantage point was behind the car and off to the motorcade's right.

If you see the film that way, there is no doubt. It must point to a conspiracy, as the House Select Committee on Assassinations concluded. But who might have led that conspiracy?

Assuming the HSCA was right in crossing the Russians, the Cubans, the mafia, the CIA and the FBI off the list of conspiracy suspects, there is still one grim suspicion that needs to be examined.

With the assassination of JFK, his vice president, Lyndon Baines Johnson, was automatically sworn in as president. As soon as he succeeded to the White House, four separate sets of criminal allegations against him were dropped – serious accusations involving abuse of government contracts, money laundering, bribery and misappropriation of funds.

Johnson was a strange character, oddly liberal in his political commitment to civil rights, health and social welfare, but personally cruel and corrupt. He was nearly 6'4" tall, crude, bullying, scheming, insecure and foul-mouthed. The dead president's brother, Robert Kennedy, called him 'a mean, bitter, vicious animal', and LBJ, in return, referred to Bobby Kennedy as 'a grandstanding little runt'.

Johnson treated his wife badly and had two long-term mistresses over a period of thirty years. It was the second of these, Madeleine Brown, who claimed, after LBJ's death, that her lover had been at the heart of the conspiracy to murder Jack Kennedy.

Many years after the event, she gave a graphic account of Johnson's plotting with an unholy alliance of Texan oil barons, old-school Southern politicians, anti-Castro Cubans, CIA schemers and mafia hoods to get rid of the president. When you watch the interview in which she talked about the build-up to Jack Kennedy's visit to Dallas, it is hard not to be persuaded by her vivid description of LBJ's ferocious hatred.

Madeleine Brown described the meeting at which details were discussed of the welcome the conspirators had arranged for John Kennedy in Dallas. Johnson was angry and ruddy in the face.

'When he came out, he grabbed me by the arm and he had this deep voice and he said, "After tomorrow, those SOBs – the Irish mafia – will never embarrass me again. That's no threat. That's a promise." The Irish mafia. He referred to them as the Irish mafia.'

Madeleine Brown's tale seems damning. Yet she is a demonstrably unreliable witness. There is evidence that many of the people she lists as being at the conspirators' meeting in Dallas could not have been there. And Brown herself was convicted, in 1992, when she was sixty-seven years old, of the serious crime of forging a will.

Johnson had several strong motives for wanting to see the end of Kennedy. He had more power, connections and opportunity to make it happen than almost anyone else – and Madeleine Brown's flawed testimony is not the only finger that points his way.

Former CIA agent and Watergate burglar E Howard Hunt came out with a startling confession, immediately before his death in 2007.

Hunt claimed that he had conspired with Lyndon Johnson, a bunch of CIA operatives and a Corsican mafia sharpshooter called Lucien Sarti to execute the project they called 'the Big Event'. There have also been suggestions that the Kennedy-hating FBI chief J Edgar Hoover gave Johnson a helping hand or that LBJ planned the murder with the assistance of his long-time legal adviser Edward Clark, a former US ambassador to Australia, and his old friend Malcolm 'Mac' Wallace.

Those who believe Johnson was more than an innocent bystander generally have problems producing evidence that goes beyond hearsay. But there is a single fingerprint, found in the 'sniper's nest' in the Texas School Book Depository, that was finally identified in 1998 as probably belonging to Mac Wallace. One of America's most experienced fingerprint analysts, Nathan Darby, testified that he had found 'a fourteen-point match' between Wallace's fingerprint and the Dallas print.

Wallace was a convicted murderer, a former lover of LBJ's sister, Josefa, and a friend of Johnson's since the early 1950s. He was implicated in several savage killings over a number of years and often worked as an enforcer to sort out business or other complications for Johnson and his cronies.

If the tiny sliver of forensic evidence provided by that one fingerprint from Dallas can ever be confirmed, President Johnson will become a prime suspect in the murder of Jack Kennedy.

Failing that, we have only the unreliable evidence of what people said they heard, including the story of the White House photographer who claimed to have witnessed an extraordinary encounter between Johnson and Bobby Kennedy. He took a picture which seems to show the younger Kennedy punching a concrete pillar, while a shocked Johnson looks on. The explanation, the photographer said, was that Bobby Kennedy had just asked President Johnson the big question: 'Why did you have my brother killed?'

Why JFK was assassinated is the question that has troubled and frustrated millions for the last sixty years.

But LBJ himself knew exactly where he wanted people to place the blame for the shooting of President Jack Kennedy.

'He was trying to get Fidel Castro,' he said. 'But Castro got him first.'

28

MOON LANDINGS

LISTENING TO THE SILENCE FROM MOSCOW

'Ah, but did they really go there?'

The one superhuman, out-of-this-world technological achievement of the twentieth century that stands out above all others is the feat of putting a man on the moon.

At the same time, the most expensive, least productive, most utterly pointless effort of the same century is probably the same thing.

More than fifty years on from Neil Armstrong's 'One small step for a man, one giant leap for Mankind', there's no sign that we'll be going back any time soon.

Since Gene Cernan waddled slowly up the ladder and clambered back into the Apollo 17 lander on 19 December 1972, no one has set foot on the moon's surface. We're left with our pictures, our recordings, 382kg of the oldest rocks we've ever seen and our Teflon frying pans – a slender legacy from a project that cost nearly $30 billion (around $230 billion in today's money).

Six spaceships squatted on the dust of the moon. Twelve men walked on this other world.

In the decades that have passed since then, we retreated into the dull, sensible, still-dangerous routines of international space stations and intermittently deadly shuttles.

But the idea of human beings walking on the moon has never lost its hypnotic power. And there are many millions of people who do not trust that hypnotic power and simply don't believe the manned moonshots ever happened.

Polls seem to suggest the doubters represent an average of 20 per cent of people in most Western countries, though Cuba is the only country in the world where denying the moon landings is an official government policy and part of the school science curriculum.

The conspiracy theories come in many flavours. Some people simply believe we never went there – that the whole Apollo programme was faked, dummied up, scripted and filmed in some hidden studio in Houston, in the wilds of Nevada's secretive Area 51, in Disneyland or on Stanley Kubrick's original *2001: A Space Odyssey* sound stage at Borehamwood, in Hertfordshire. Some will quote you all the production credits for this imagined movie – sponsored by Disney, scripted by Arthur C Clarke, directed by Kubrick.

They believe the mountains of background data and documentation, voice recordings, telemetry records and tracking charts were all meticulously forged by an army of willing scientists and helpers, generously paid off and sworn to absolute secrecy.

Others are certain America reached for the stars but failed. They believe rockets and landers and moon buggies were built, astronauts were trained and launches happened. For them, it's all real until you get to earth orbit, but the giant leap outwards, away from earth's apron strings, could not be done and had to be counterfeited. Alternatively, people believe they went for the big one but fell fatally short, with cosmic rays or Van Allen Belt radiation killing off every one of the would-be space pioneers.

Images from the moon landings have become iconic, familiar, almost clichéd. The arguments used to challenge them are so familiar that they have almost become clichés, too.

The shadows aren't right, the doubters say. You can't see any stars in the photographs. The flag looks like it's fluttering, but there's no air so there can't be any breeze for it to flutter in. There should have been a blast crater under the lunar landing module. And anyway, if we got that far in 1969, how come we haven't been able to move on for the next fifty-something years?

MOSCOW WOULD HAVE GIVEN ANYTHING...

The one overwhelming, clinching reason to disbelieve the conspiracy theories and accept that the whole moon-landing story is true is the Soviet Union.

Those growing up after the end of the Cold War will never be able to believe the fear, intensity and aggression with which America and Russia squared up to each other for more than four decades after World War II.

Generations grew up completely convinced that their lives would end, sooner or later, in a nuclear holocaust. Gory military coups were organised, funded and armed by both sides in countries around the world. Spies were routinely killed, brainwashed or tortured. Ordinary people who tried to cross the Berlin Wall into West Germany were gunned down – men, women and children. The Cold War was not a theoretical concept. A lot of warm blood was spilled.

In this context, where prestige and global influence seemed to mean everything, there could not have been a more devastating propaganda success for world Communism than to show that America's space triumph was a fraud.

America had been shocked and humiliated in the late 1950s when the USSR took an instant lead in the space race with the launch of the first satellite, Sputnik 1, in October 1957.

A few years later, it got worse. I stood with hundreds of cheering schoolchildren at the side of the road in London in July 1961 to see Soviet cosmonaut Major Yuri Gagarin, the world's first real-life spaceman, drive past in his motorcade. Gagarin had orbited the earth on 12 April 1961 and six weeks later President John F Kennedy set his country the impossible target 'before this decade is out' of 'landing a man on the Moon and returning him safely to the earth'. No one believed then that it would really happen. And, if anyone was going to achieve a moon landing, everyone thought it would probably be the Reds.

But it didn't work out like that. As the USSR's own moon-landing programme slipped and slithered into a chaos of insoluble technical problems, anything Moscow could do to discredit the American achievements would have been given the highest possible priority. Scientists and spies, propagandists and politicians would all have worked non-stop to blow the credibility of the US space programme. Money and manpower would have been made available on a whatever-it-takes basis. The stakes could not have been higher. Yet they could not do it. America won the race to put a man on the moon – and repeat the feat again and again – and the Soviet Union was left looking weak, backward and inferior.

This would simply not have happened if the USSR had uncovered any way to expose the US and persuade the world the moon landings were faked. If the massed ranks of the Soviet and

Eastern European scientific and military establishment couldn't find the chinks in the armour, that's because they weren't there to be found.

And the clichéd challenges? Well, the shadows are complicated by sunlight reflected from the earth. The stars are invisible because the light is so bright, just as they're invisible, but still there, during a sunny summer's day on earth. The flag has a wire along the top edge and swings, pendulum-like, with no air resistance to slow it down, for a long time after being put in place. The blast crater exists, but the rock is compact below the fine surface dust and the crater is just a shallow depression, only about four inches deep at its lowest point, directly below the engine nozzle.

One other small but fascinating scrap of circumstantial evidence comes from the US National Archives. It's a memo, drafted while the Apollo 11 astronauts were already in flight, halfway to the moon, by a talented young spin doctor called William Safire, who was then working for President Richard Nixon.

The future *New York Times* columnist had looked reality in the face and planned ahead. He had crafted a strangely moving but obviously manipulative draft of the speech Nixon should make if and when it became clear that Armstrong and Buzz Aldrin were stranded and doomed to die on the moon.

'Fate has ordained that the men who went to the moon to explore in peace will stay on the moon to rest in peace,' the speech began.

In just eleven sentences, President Nixon would break this awful news to the waiting world. The phrasing is serious, sonorous, poetic, as befits a speech that would certainly have gone down in history. But its practical function is underlined by the somewhat brutal off-the-record note at the bottom of the memo that says: 'Prior to the President's statement, the President should phone each of the widows-to-be.'

This secret memo, addressed to Nixon's notorious Chief of Staff, HR Haldeman, was hidden away for decades before being released to the National Archives. It hardly seems likely that Safire would have had the foresight to draft it in 1969 so that it could be pulled out many years later in support of a moon-landing hoax master plan.

THEY'D HAVE NEEDED 400,000 CONSPIRATORS

One of the unspoken assumptions behind conspiracy theories is often the idea that new information is necessarily better. 'Ah, they believed that back then,' people are quick to say, 'but we know better now.'

That can be the case, but there's certainly no basis for believing, for example, that things we are fed today are automatically more likely to be true than yesterday's stories. There are more people in the world than there used to be and that probably means there are more liars, too. Thanks to the internet, there's definitely more opportunity for the liars and fakers to reach a wider public.

In the case of the moon landings, scepticism has grown and grown over time. New theories about how and why the conspiracy was perpetrated have arrived every few years. And, as the Apollo programme slips further into the past, the defenders of the official history haven't often been able to get their hands on fresh ammunition.

But that may be changing. New space programmes, clearly

beyond NASA's influence, are being put together by the Europeans, the Indians, the Chinese and the Japanese. As they start to find evidence of the manned moon landings, the doubters are likely to be thrown on to the defensive.

There were some 400,000 people directly or indirectly involved in the original Apollo programme, almost all of them in America. Pulling off the greatest con of all time, and keeping the lid on it, would have been incredibly difficult then. Now that distant countries with new space technologies are getting in on the act, the conspiracy would have to expand rapidly, with the grandchildren of the original spinmasters bribing or threatening their way around the world to keep up the pretence.

The cracks in the conspiracists' theories started to show a long time ago. In 2007, the Japanese SELENE lunar orbiter mission was able to see Apollo 15's blast footprint and captured excellent pictures of lunar landscape features which could be matched closely with images from the Apollo missions.

One of the best updates on what's been happening since we left came in July 2009, when NASA's Lunar Reconnaissance Orbiter (LRO) began sending back the first high-quality images of the lunar module descent stages left behind on the moon by all six Apollo landings.

But for those who insist on independent evidence with no NASA connections, these pictures are probably trumped by the newest images from the Indian Space Research Organisation's Chandrayaan-2 mission. In April 2021, the Chandrayaan-2 team captured clear, recognisable shots of Apollo 11's Eagle descent stage, using the highest-resolution camera yet fitted to a lunar orbiter. And the people who should know the truth – NASA and the astronauts themselves – have certainly continued to behave as if it were all real. Forty years on, NASA told lunar module pilot Edgar Mitchell, the sixth man on the moon, that he would have to give back the camera from Apollo 14 he had kept as a souvenir. The case quickly ended up in court, in November 2011, with Mitchell asserting his right to keep the moon camera – valued at $60,000 – or put it up for sale at auction.

For the true doubters, though, these scraps of circumstantial evidence are just further proof of an elaborate and sustained conspiracy.

In the end, some people will never be persuaded. Deep-dyed sceptics like Marcus Allen, a British writer and publisher of *Nexus* magazine, have long said that nothing will ever make them believe the Americans went to the moon.

Allen and his supporters are not impressed by any number of pictures of abandoned landers, as they have no problem with the idea that unmanned flights have been there and placed objects on the surface. They are unmoved by the fact that retroreflectors – effectively 'cat's eyes' – the Apollo crews left on the moon are still being used to measure its position to the nearest inch or so.

It's hard to think what might finally win them over. If we point to the traces of shuffling footprints in the lunar dust, we can be sure they will claim that NASA equipped the landers with shuffling-footprint machines. There won't be fingerprints on the rocks, as astronauts wear gloves. In the last analysis, those that won't be convinced will not budge. For them, it is an article of faith that the moon landings did not happen. And you can't shake faith with logic.

29

WATERGATE

WAS 'TRICKY DICKY' NIXON A VICTIM, TOO?

The iconic image of Richard Nixon never seems to fade. Sweating, scowling, tense and shifty, five-o'clock-shadowed, aggressive, haunted – here was a man sent direct from central casting to play the villain. He lost to Jack Kennedy in the 1960 presidential election, authorised the Watergate break-in and resigned in shame when on the brink of impeachment.

Yet this same Nixon was Ike Eisenhower's successful and popular vice-president for eight years. This Nixon would have beaten JFK to the White House if Daddy Joseph Kennedy hadn't, as has been said, organised some energetic vote-rigging and ballot-stuffing in Illinois and Texas, with the help of his mafia associates. This Nixon comfortably won the 1968 election and was re-elected with a landslide in 1972.

He ended the disastrous US involvement in Vietnam, opened a new era of contact with Communist China and speeded up desegregation in the American South. He raised social security benefits, chopped a third off defence spending and approved

NASA's space shuttle programme. Yet every good thing Nixon did made him enemies.

When the break-in at the Democratic National Committee offices in the Watergate hotel and apartment complex in Washington was traced back to the White House, Nixon was clearly seen to be implicated in both the planning and the cover-up. His fingerprints were all over the bungled operation to bug the Democrats' election planning, and his slippery and increasingly desperate efforts to deny the connection made everything far worse.

But the official version that history has accepted may not be the whole story.

Nixon's Watergate conspiracy was to do with covering up a relatively minor crime. Once he had given his enemies the ammunition, a new conspiracy took shape, with a much larger objective – to get rid of the president of the United States. This was something that had been done before. But this time there was the opportunity to do it using the law, instead of the bullet.

The five-man Watergate break-in team was led by James McCord, former Head of Security at the CIA's headquarters. He was a skilled and experienced officer and the others were also CIA-trained. At that time, CIA training and tradecraft were such that a 'black bag' squad like this would normally have ghosted in, done its work and vanished leaving scarcely a trace. But on 17 June 1972, the team that broke into the Democrats' offices behaved like rank amateurs.

The burglary that made the headlines was the third time the team had tried to raid the Democrats' Watergate offices. The first attempt, on 27 May, went wrong and was aborted. But the 'plumbers' had successfully planted three bugs and photographed thirty documents in a second raid the following night.

This third time round the break-in was discovered when a security guard noticed some sticky tape across the latches holding several doors unlocked in the stairwell of the Watergate building.

Tut-tutting to himself, he removed the tape and continued on his rounds. But when he came back an hour later and found the locks taped open again, his highly trained brain realised something was going on and he called the police, who arrested the five intruders.

Two days later, Bob Woodward and Carl Bernstein of the *Washington Post* broke the news that James McCord's day job was as Security Director of the Committee to Re-elect the President (otherwise known as the CRP, or as CREEP) and the burglary suddenly took on a much greater political significance.

THE TAPES THAT TIED A PRESIDENT IN KNOTS

Nixon was guilty. The infamous White House tape recordings, which only started to come into the public arena seventeen months later, made that perfectly clear. For more than a year after the break-in and arrests, no one knew that Nixon had secret recordings of every conversation that took place in his office. Once his refusal to release them, on grounds of executive privilege, had been overcome, it became steadily more obvious that he had been caught red-handed.

He had known about CREEP's dirty tricks campaign and he'd known from an early stage about the Republican slush fund's hush-money payments to the Watergate defendants and others as the White House team struggled desperately to keep the lid on the affair.

He had also had a deeply incriminating conversation with

Bob Haldeman, his Chief of Staff, just six days after the break-in, in which they discussed trying to bully the top men at the CIA into blocking the FBI's investigations on completely false national security grounds.

This particular conversation, laid bare on the so-called 'Smoking Gun' tape, which was released on 5 August 1974, sealed Nixon's fate. Three days later, he resigned.

WHY DID THE CIA DECIDE TO GET NIXON?

In this world of smoke and mirrors, though, nothing is what it appears to be.

The identity of Deep Throat, Woodward and Bernstein's secret source, was a mystery for more than thirty years, though many people asserted confidently that they knew it was Robert Bennett, boss of Mullen & Co, a thinly disguised CIA front company.

Bennett was undoubtedly a frequent source of leaked and confidential information for the *Washington Post* journalists. And he was the employer, at Mullen & Co, of one of the key conspirators, E Howard Hunt, even after Hunt joined the White House staff and planned the Watergate bugging.

Yet, in 2005, Bob Woodward revealed that the real Deep Throat had been Mark Felt, second in command at the FBI. Felt, who was then ninety-one years old, confirmed the truth of this revelation.

Nixon had discussed this possibility early on in the Watergate saga with Haldeman and they had even talked about making a 'move' on Felt in October 1972.

Oddly enough, a few years later, when Mark Felt was accused

and found guilty of ordering illegal burglaries aimed at disrupting a group of bomb-planting radicals called the Weathermen, Nixon contributed to his legal costs and appeared in court as an enthusiastic witness for the defence.

At the time of Watergate, the Nixon gang's first assumption was that the CIA was basically friendly and the FBI hostile. But with leaks coming to the journalists from both Bennett, from the CIA direction, and Mark Felt, from his lofty FBI vantage point, at least some elements in both organisations clearly had a considerable hand in bringing down the president.

Given their backgrounds and track records, neither Bennett nor Felt could credibly claim to be driven by motives of justice and purity.

It is obviously reasonable to ask the same question about both of them. If they were so concerned about the scandal of the Watergate cover-up, why did they both go talking to the *Washington Post*, rather than the Justice Department?

For the young reporters, this was all about uncovering the truth. For the spooks, it was about manipulating the situation, pursuing their own agendas and getting rid of Nixon.

Because wiretapping and bugging were involved, the Watergate break-in was automatically an FBI matter. That was bad news for the president, as the FBI was traditionally quite independent. But the CIA was generally seen as more or less the executive's private army. For the first few weeks after Watergate erupted, everyone seemed to be sticking to the script. The CIA, which had, after all, the closest of ties with the five burglars, seemed to be ready to help Nixon rein in the FBI and damp down the scandal.

But then, as the crisis rolled on, there was an abrupt change. Suddenly, the CIA was no longer interfering to assist Nixon and impede the investigation.

The untold conspiracy story of Watergate may well be that the CIA, which had its own dirty-tricks operations against the Democrats to worry about, decided that the best way to cover them up was to dump Nixon and make him and his henchmen take the rap for everything bad that was going on.

After this change of heart, Bennett's steady drip of information to the *Washington Post* made the newspaper the unwitting tool of a CIA operation to get rid of the president and cover up the agency's secrets. Given the CIA affiliations of the burglars, the planner (Howard Hunt) and many of the others involved in Watergate, it was remarkable how effectively Nixon's decline and fall distracted attention from the agency and its dirty deeds.

And maybe the stakes were even higher. If later suggestions and deathbed confessions from Howard Hunt and others are to be believed, it wasn't just a few break-ins and foreign adventures the CIA had to conceal, but, quite possibly, involvement in the shootings of one American president and one ex-Attorney General and Great White Hope.

30

THE PRINCE, THE NAZIS AND KLM

CASHING IN ON THE WAR CRIMINALS

Ever since the blockbuster Frederick Forsyth novel and film *The Odessa File,* there have been countless theories about the secret conspiracies and escape routes – known as 'ratlines' – that were set up to whisk Nazi war criminals and SS officers out of Europe to start new lives in South America.

Many of the stories sound like fiction. Many of them are. But we know that some are true because brutes like Adolf Eichmann and Klaus Barbie were eventually tracked down in South America and brought to trial for their crimes.

Eichmann, the architect of the Holocaust, and Barbie, the 'Butcher of Lyon', both went to Argentina, though Barbie was finally arrested in Bolivia. Other major Nazi war criminals, including Auschwitz 'Angel of Death' Josef Mengele and many lower-ranking SS officers, also made their escape via Argentina.

But one little-known aspect of the conspiracy to help SS war criminals escape from justice was the part played by KLM, the

Royal Dutch Airline, and Prince Bernhard of the Netherlands, the father of the much-loved Queen Beatrix, who came to the throne in 1980 and reigned until 2013.

During 1948 and over the next year or so, KLM staff in Switzerland allowed hundreds of suspected war criminals to board flights that would take them to freedom in Argentina.

The Odessa escape route networks are still shrouded in the secrecy and double-dealing of post-war Europe. Far too many known war criminals escaped justice and there were many ugly bargains struck between senior Nazis and the West German Secret Service or the US government and its newly formed Central Intelligence Agency. Odessa was a loose-knit tangle of contacts, routes, safe houses and international sympathisers dedicated to taking Hitler's murderers beyond the reach of the law.

KLM's role in helping senior Nazis escape to Buenos Aires remained a secret for more than half a century. But the cynicism of the airline's attitude towards the monsters responsible for millions of concentration camp deaths is still shocking.

After the war, KLM was close to bankruptcy and wanted the money from long-haul ticket sales. But there were few takers. A single ticket to Argentina, on a big airliner with just forty passengers and deluxe service including six-course meals, cost more than half a year's income for most Dutch people. When paying passengers turned up, it seems KLM did not want to know too much about where the money came from or who was really checking in. If there was a person with a passport and a roll of banknotes, that was good enough for KLM.

One of KLM's board members in the post-war years was Prince Bernhard, the German-born husband of Holland's Queen Juliana.

Bernhard was famously vain, inconsistent, controversial and corruptible. He was a Nazi Party member in the 1930s, though he ended up spending much of the war flying Spitfires with the RAF. In much later life, he was exposed for taking $1.1 million in bribes from the American aircraft manufacturer Lockheed. He was a founder and first president of the World Wildlife Fund, but was later accused of sullying the WWF's good name by using slush-fund money to recruit a private army of vicious mercenaries to fight game poachers in Africa.

KLM denies that the issue of Nazi war criminals taking flights out of Switzerland to Argentina was ever raised at board level. But if this traffic generated enough extra cash to be worth the political risk involved, its effects would obviously have been apparent to board members.

There is no absolute proof that Bernhard knew any details, but the airline's boss, Albert Plesman, and the pilot prince were good friends, as well as fellow board members. And Bernhard had strong personal connections in Argentina. He had got to know Eva (Evita) Peron in 1944, met her again in 1947 and even organised an arms deal for her in 1951.

Despite the denials that the men at the top knew about the traffic to Buenos Aires, Plesman and his boardroom colleagues were not the innocents they claimed to be. A BBC World Service programme in 2008 interviewed a witness who had overheard a furious row between Plesman and top KLM pilot Adriaan Viruly over the subject of flying 'the Black Monks' to Argentina. Viruly, a famous writer as well as an aviation pioneer, wanted to go public about what was going on and was threatened by Plesman, who said he would not let him ruin 'my KLM'.

MONEY TALKS

According to KLM, which is now owned by Air France, nothing in its archives indicates that the airline was involved in a conspiracy or broke any rules.

More than seventy years on, KLM acknowledges that some of its passengers may have been fleeing justice. But it denies that it tried to help them escape and claims it had no responsibility for carrying out background checks on passengers.

It says it was not the airline's job to check passengers against the list of those who were barred from leaving Germany without exit permits issued by the Allies, especially if they presented themselves in Switzerland, where the law did not require permits. For escaping SS officers, just slipping over the border and turning up at the airport with enough cash was the easy way to get to Argentina.

The Swiss themselves did not have a spotless record in dealing with Nazi fugitives. According to a US Army report from 1948, a payment of 200,000 francs (£35,000 at the time of writing) would buy Swiss residence papers, which would automatically allow the holder to come and go through Swiss airports with no questions asked.

KLM STILL IN DENIAL ABOUT 'RATLINE' FLIGHTS

KLM's denial of its part in a conspiracy to profit from helping the perpetrators of the Holocaust escape justice is questionable. No company would want to advertise its involvement in a dirty business like this, but traces of documentary evidence still survive.

A police memo uncovered by Dutch journalists in 2007 in Switzerland's federal archives proves KLM even approached the Swiss authorities and asked them to relax the rules about accepting passengers without full documentation.

The KLM request was not particularly subtle. The papers show a local KLM representative called Frick asking the Swiss border police chief to allow his airline's passengers from Germany to enter the country without the proper exit papers so they could fly to Argentina.

A memo from the Swiss police shows that Herr Frick's suggestion was formally refused, but there is plenty of evidence that many Germans were allowed to cross the border into German-speaking areas of Switzerland without authorisation. KLM admits its records are patchy, but claims it can find no trace of any employee named Frick. What motive would the Swiss border police have, however, for dreaming up the meeting?

The police memo about the direct approach from Frick is not the only new evidence that has come to light many decades after the fact.

Another more recent discovery is a letter dated February 1948 from the US ambassador in Amsterdam, who wrote to KLM saying, bluntly, that German citizens might be using KLM's planes to travel illegally to Argentina. The letter asked KLM to give US officials access to the passenger lists for all its flights out of Switzerland.

The airline stalled for some weeks and then agreed, apparently with some reluctance, 'to co-operate as far as was possible', though it had 'grave misgivings'. It pointed out, too, that it might take some time to release each passenger list.

This was an important factor, as the timing was crucial. Speed was one of the reasons escaping Nazis wanted to go by air. On a ship, the voyage from Europe to South America would take weeks and there might be nasty surprises waiting at intermediate ports. Once in the air, fugitives knew they could not be overtaken. By the time anyone knew they were gone, they would be safe in Argentina, where the autocratic President Juan Peron was happy to welcome them.

Peron was an admirer of the European Fascists – and he was not alone. In 1938, the Luna Park stadium in Buenos Aires hosted one of the largest-ever pro-Hitler rallies outside Germany, with nearly 20,000 people *Sieg Heil*-ing and singing Nazi anthems.

The US ambassador spent several weeks trying, and failing, to get a firm commitment from KLM that it would hand over passenger lists for the Americans to vet in real time. When it became clear that this was not going to happen, he concluded that simple greed was the motive behind the airline's attitude.

'It is the embassy's belief that KLM wants this business for purely commercial reasons, regardless of the type of persons being transported,' he wrote.

If the US diplomats in Amsterdam were angry about this, the Dutch embassy in Buenos Aires was also troubled about the well-worn path from the ashes of Nazi Germany to the bright lights of Argentina – and about KLM's role in the matter.

An internal embassy memo of the time expressed 'grave concern' and said it was 'undesirable' that there was such a 'strong German element' among staff members in KLM's Buenos Aires station office. These included, for example, Rolf Wilkening, once a leading SS officer, and a Dr Ehrle, grand-daughter of General Karl Litzmann, an elder statesman of the Nazi Party and close friend of Hitler's.

Though it has since been brushed under the carpet, the issue was highlighted at the time in a shrewd piece in a Swiss regional newspaper, the *Lucerne News*. This said, 'It is reasonable to ask the question whether there is a business connection between the mass import of known German National Socialists into Argentina and the interest that the Dutch airline has in the services of Nazis.'

It was a good question then and it still needs a bit more work now before it is finally untangled and laid to rest.

31

TWA FLIGHT 800

DEATH OFF LONG ISLAND

In 1996, 230 passengers and crew on board a TWA jumbo jet were killed when it exploded in mid-air, twelve minutes after taking off from New York's JFK airport on a flight to Paris.

The tragedy caused even more anguish and confusion than other air crashes because of what had come immediately before. Eyewitnesses – not just a few, but nearly forty – believed they had seen a missile streaking upwards towards the airliner.

More than two hundred other people said they had seen 'a streak', 'a flare', 'a firework' or 'something like a shooting star' somewhere near the plane before the explosion. So there was a huge amount of troubled speculation about what had happened to cause the death of so many men, women and children.

The US National Transportation Safety Board carried out a lengthy investigation, which cost more than $100 million and involved recovering more than 90 per cent of the wreckage from the bottom of the Atlantic Ocean. Its report concluded that the explosion had been caused by a short circuit near one of the main fuel tanks.

The loss of TWA Flight 800 was due to a mechanical failure, the NTSB declared, and those on board had lost their lives 'not as a result of a bomb or missile or other nefarious act, but as the result of a tragic accident'.

At just after 8.30 p.m., ten minutes before sunset on that clear July evening, three days before the opening of the Atlanta Olympics, there were unusual numbers of people out and about. Fishermen, tourists, a helicopter pilot and many others firmly believed they had seen one missile or even two heading towards the doomed 747 as it climbed away off the shore of Long Island.

What had they really seen? Had the jumbo been blown out of the sky by terrorists? Had there been some horrible mistake by a US Navy anti-aircraft missile unit? If there were two objects racing towards the airliner, was the second rocket a Navy interceptor sent up in a failed attempt to stop a terrorist-launched missile?

The problem for the NTSB, the Federal Aviation Administration, the FBI and everyone trying to establish what brought down TWA 800 was that there could be no such thing as a good answer. With 230 passengers and crew dead, it was vital to establish whether there was a mechanical or design fault in the Boeing 747, an airline workhorse that had been around since the 1970s and was still carrying millions of long-haul passengers every year.

But if the deaths were the result of a terrorist missile strike, that would raise all sorts of new and urgent questions, with big and disruptive implications for the security services, the travel industry, the government and the lifestyles of ordinary Americans.

And if the disaster was caused by a 'friendly' missile, that would imply that the US military had somehow managed to shoot down an American passenger jet in the skies off Long Island.

As official comments quickly moved from admitting three possible causes – mechanical failure, missile or bomb – to focusing wholly on the idea of a fault on the plane, suspicions grew that the authorities had launched some kind of subtle conspiracy to cover up the true story.

EYEWITNESSES NEVER BOUGHT THE 'ZOOM CLIMB' THEORY

The National Transportation Safety Board's account of the disaster was built around a scenario in which the plane climbed and gained over half a mile in height after an explosion had blown away the entire nose and cockpit section. This was known as the 'zoom climb' theory and it was illustrated and backed up by a CIA-prepared animation video.

According to this version of events, the witnesses on the ground had observed the stricken jumbo lurching upwards, trailing flames, and mistaken this, at a distance of several miles, for a missile.

Though 'zoom climb' became the official story of what happened to TWA 800, the CIA video did little to convince the witnesses that this was what they'd seen. It put forward a scenario many people found hard to believe, along with repeated assertions that 'the eyewitnesses did not see a missile', almost as if proving this point was the most important goal of the investigation.

One interesting piece of CIA evidence is buried deep in the paperwork of this case. The CIA experts considered the possibility of an attack by a shoulder-launched surface-to-air missile (SAM). But they said the small warheads on these missiles contained only two to three pounds of explosive and would not have been powerful enough to cause the catastrophic destruction of a Boeing 747. There had never been a total loss of an aircraft this big to a handheld SAM attack, they reported, in any war or any terrorist incident. When large aircraft had been targeted, they had always been hit in one engine and had been able to fly on safely.

NTSB SAFETY MEASURES 'TOO EXPENSIVE'

No one wanted the crash of TWA 800 to turn out to be anything but a terrible accident. The NTSB's verdict to this effect, given in August 2000, meant changes would be ordered that would stop similar accidents happening to 747s in the future. Altogether, there were fifteen main recommendations, mostly affecting fuel tank and wiring design and changes to maintenance procedures. There was also one key recommendation to do with introducing inert fuel systems to prevent fires and explosions.

These recommendations were seen as an appropriate and serious response to an accidental crash that had claimed so many lives. They seemed to back up the idea that the NTSB and the FAA were finally convinced about the cause of the disaster.

This impression was badly dented, though, in 2001, when the NTSB and the FAA dropped their recommendations on the grounds that they were 'too expensive'.

So the plane was at fault, it seemed – but whatever was wrong with it wasn't worth putting right for the sake of saving the lives of future passengers.

Many of the bereaved families and eyewitnesses felt there had been a determined effort to dismiss their testimony and exclude any explanation other than mechanical failure.

There was apparently no evidence to point to a bomb, with none of the telltale 'micropitting' of damaged surfaces that crash investigators have come to recognise. But no one in authority seemed ready to contemplate the idea that a terrorist with a handheld ground-to-air missile could so easily destroy an airliner leaving one of America's main transatlantic airports.

And if the fatal explosion was caused by a missile, but not a terrorist missile, the need for full disclosure was, if anything, even greater.

The US Navy was equipped with larger and more powerful ground-to-air missiles than the lightweight shoulder-launched SAMs the CIA documents discussed, and the navy had been conducting exercises in the area near Long Island, though these were supposed to have finished well before TWA 800 took off. It was eventually admitted that three unnamed US Navy ships were carrying out 'classified exercises' in the area at the time. But there was no official record of a missile launch and not a single whistleblower has ever come forward with details to back the idea that a navy missile was involved.

So for many – including most of the eyewitnesses, who stuck firmly to their accounts of seeing something rising towards the aircraft – a terrorist strike was always the most likely explanation of the crash.

This theory was also supported by a copy of a radar recording from the New York Terminal Radar Approach Control that was made public, under an affidavit, by an Air Transport Association official, James Holtsclaw. He claimed to have been given it by an NTSB investigator who believed it should not be suppressed. 'The tape shows a primary target at

1,200 knots converging with TWA 800 during the climb out phase,' said Holtsclaw's affidavit. If the tape was genuine, there could only be one type of target that would fit the description – a surface-to-air missile.

Few people ever found the 'zoom climb' story satisfactory, and the CIA video just seemed to make it all the more implausible. Pilots and aerodynamic experts insisted the plane would immediately tear itself apart, stall or dive under those conditions. With the nose and cockpit blown away, it would not have been climbing.

Boeing's immediate reaction to the video was interesting, too. The makers of the 747 said they hadn't been told what data the CIA's assumptions had been based on, but they did state: 'The video's explanation of the eyewitness observations can be best assessed by the eyewitnesses themselves.'

Since the reaction of the key eyewitnesses was one of disbelief and contempt, it is hard to accept that the CIA got it right.

The CIA video also includes one flat untruth, when it says that the first explosion (as distinct from the flare, streak or missile) was not seen by any known eyewitness.

At least three key witnesses did see what happened. Eastwind Airlines Captain David McClaine, en route from Boston to Trenton, saw TWA Flight 800 before, during and after the first explosion.

Captain McClaine first saw the 747 at a distance of about sixty miles. As the planes came closer and TWA 800 began to cross from left to right below him, about twenty miles away, he flicked on his inner landing light to signal that he was aware of its presence. With his co-pilot, First Officer Vincent Fuschetti, he watched in horror as the jumbo exploded, erupting into a ball of flame. The Eastwind crew's radio message to Boston Air

Traffic Control, ten seconds after the explosion, was the first report of the disaster.

And Major Fritz Meyer was even nearer, looking on from just ten miles away from the cockpit of his Blackhawk Air National Guard helicopter. The Vietnam search-and-rescue veteran had seen a lot of heavy fighting and a lot of explosions. On this fateful evening, he saw something 'red-orange in colour, moving very rapidly from my left centre away to my left', followed by 'a high-velocity explosion – unmistakably military ordnance', a second explosion, with a brilliant white light, and then, several seconds later, 'a huge, low-velocity fireball, four times the size of the setting sun'. As the fireball fell, hit the water and stayed there, blazing furiously, Meyer took the rescue helicopter down to fifty feet, dodging the falling debris, and began the vain search for survivors.

Another witness, US Navy trainer Dwight Brumley, was peering out to his right from the passenger cabin of US Air Flight 217, looking down from 21,000 feet on the TWA jumbo below him. He watched for seven to ten seconds as a 'flare-like object' climbed, pitched over and closed in on Flight 800, though he then lost his view of it and did not claim he'd seen the moment of impact.

These credible, qualified eyewitnesses were largely ignored as the FBI took control of the evidence-gathering, pushing the National Transportation Safety Board staff into the background, and the CIA took charge of the analysis.

Many of the eyewitnesses felt their evidence was undermined by the CIA's calculations about the time the sound of the airliner exploding took to reach observers several miles away. Witnesses who said they heard a bang and saw an explosion were more or less discounted, on the grounds that the wreckage of the plane would already have fallen thousands of feet during the time-lag of forty seconds or more before the sound reached them. That makes sense, in terms of the arithmetic. Anyone who claimed to have looked up in response to a bang was obviously confused about the timing. But which was more plausible – that people in the stress of a horrific moment should lose track of the exact order of events, or that so many normal, level-headed people should have dreamed up from nowhere the illusion that they had seen something streaking across the sky?

The eyewitnesses were so angry at the way their stories were dismissed that many chipped in towards the cost of angry full-page ads in several newspapers in the name of the TWA 800 Eyewitness Alliance.

These advertisements said: 'We are OUTRAGED that the FBI would not let a single one of us testify at the NTSB's public hearing… We are INCENSED that for four years the FBI refused to release its hundreds of reports of interviews with eyewitnesses who told them what we saw – the plane being hit by missiles that broke off its nose, blew up the fuel tank and sent the plane plummeting into the sea… And we are SHOCKED at the lengths to which the FBI, the CIA and the NTSB have all gone to discredit and ignore our testimony and hide the truth.'

For more than twenty years after the disaster, the ghost of TWA Flight 800 – a huge 3D jigsaw reassembled from 1,600 pieces of wreckage painstakingly collected by the navy and local fishermen – stood in a 30,000-square-foot hangar at the NTSB's accident investigation training centre in Ashburn, Virginia.

In 2021, just before a private twenty-five-year memorial service was held for the relatives of the victims, the NTSB announced that the reconstruction of the Boeing 747 would be minutely documented with modern scanning techniques and then destroyed.

NTSB managing director Sharon Bryson confirmed that the wreckage would be melted down, but admitted to CNN that even this might not be the end of the story. The TWA 800 affair 'may not be an investigation that you ever close the book on,' she said.

To this day, no-one can really be certain what happened to TWA Flight 800. Its fate remains one of the great mysteries of modern aviation. But almost nobody outside the American government agencies involved believes the official version was derived wholly from the facts of the case, rather than the political necessity to piece together a cover-up story.

32

KAREN SILKWOOD

THE WOMAN WHO BREATHED OUT PLUTONIUM

One Tuesday in November 1974, nuclear lab technician and trade union activist Karen Silkwood checked her radiation levels and found she was way over the legal contamination limit, with traces of plutonium on her hands and down her right side.

She went through the official decontamination process, but the next day she was found to be more highly contaminated, although she had been doing only paperwork all day and had not been near the potentially dangerous parts of the Kerr-McGee plant where she worked. Her car and locker were checked and found to be clean and she was decontaminated again and sent home.

On the third day, Thursday, 7 November, when she first arrived at work, she was found to be so dangerously contaminated that she was even breathing out particles of plutonium-239.

She was given the highest level of decontamination treatment and inspectors were sent to her home, where plutonium traces were found in the fridge and the bathroom. Urine samples taken at her home showed much higher radioactivity levels than those taken at the plant. Something very unusual was going on.

Karen Silkwood's involvement with the union at Kerr-McGee's Cimarron River plant in Oklahoma had begun several months before. Over the summer, she had complained about a series of spills, leaks and unsafe procedures for handling and storing the atomic power station fuel rods produced at Cimarron. She had reported these to the US Atomic Energy Commission and her own union's officials in Washington had asked her to collect evidence, including documents, to help them prepare a case against the company's illegal practices.

After the contamination treatment was over, the twenty-eight-year-old Silkwood went back to work and carried on with her union activities.

Less than a week later, she was driving from a local union meeting to an appointment with a *New York Times* journalist, David Burnham, and a senior union official in Washington, thirty miles away, when her car crashed off the road into a concrete ditch and she was killed.

The binder full of papers she had said she was going to hand to the reporter was not found in the car.

The fatal crash was classified by Oklahoma police as 'a classic one-car, sleeping driver accident', so there was no further police investigation into what happened. But private investigators hired by the union claimed that damage to the back of the car showed the little white Honda was shunted off the road by a second vehicle, raising the suspicion that Karen Silkwood was murdered.

This was the background to the 1983 movie *Silkwood*, starring

Meryl Streep, Kurt Russell and Cher and directed by Mike Nichols. The film attracted five Oscar nominations and clearly implied there had been a conspiracy to murder, prompted by the desire to cover up mistakes, falsified records or crimes within the nuclear industry.

Only a few months after Karen Silkwood's death, reports emerged that nearly 20kg of plutonium had gone missing from the Cimarron plant – enough to make three or four atomic bombs. This led to allegations that US and overseas intelligence agencies – including the CIA, Britain's MI5, Israel's Mossad and even some Iranian Secret Service agents – were co-conspirators with Kerr-McGee in a bizarre and politically sensitive plutonium-smuggling operation.

$1.4M DAMAGES, BUT NO ADMISSION OF LIABILITY

Though there was a high-profile civil court case, brought by Karen Silkwood's family against Kerr-McGee, it did not revolve around the question of whether she was run off the road and killed. It was simply about whether the company was responsible for her contamination with toxic and carcinogenic plutonium.

Damages totalling more than $10 million were awarded in the initial trial. This award was slashed to just $5,000 when Kerr-McGee appealed, but the original amount was reinstated in the US Supreme Court. The case was heading for a full retrial when Kerr-McGee settled out of court in 1986 for almost $1.4 million, though without admitting any liability at all.

The post-mortem on Karen Silkwood's body showed that the highest levels of radioactivity in her body were in the gastrointestinal tract, implying that she had somehow eaten some plutonium. There were plutonium particles in the lungs, too, meaning that she must have breathed in this material. The exceptional levels of contamination and strange distribution of radiation in her organs led to an expert investigation as part of America's specialist Los Alamos Tissue Analysis Program.

Silkwood had a double-dose level of methaqualone (Qaaludes) in her blood, with more of the drug not yet dissolved in her stomach at the time of death. Methaqualone is a barbiturate-like drug that was used in the 1970s as a sleeping pill, a sedative or a recreational 'love drug', though it would not usually be taken immediately before a thirty-mile drive. Police also found marijuana in the car.

DEADLY MATERIALS FROM THE LOCKED VAULTS

Karen Silkwood was not necessarily murdered. But she was always going to be a martyr for the union cause.

Lawyers for Kerr-McGee were keen to convince the court that she had deliberately taken radioactive materials and Kerr-McGee products home to her flat, intentionally contaminating herself to justify her accusations against the company. Not many people would have chosen that particular campaigning strategy, as every worker in the nuclear industry knows plutonium is highly toxic and causes cancer.

But if the lawyers failed to make that unlikely point of theirs stick, there would obviously be awkward questions about how the plutonium got there, especially as the materials involved were kept under tight security.

There are still many unresolved issues around Karen Silkwood's death, from the details of the crash itself to the mysterious contamination of her body in the week or so before she died.

Silkwood's Honda car, shown in the Hollywood movie as a battered second-hand wreck, was actually only a few months old. It had not been in any previous accidents, so the dents and traces of rubber and paint on the damaged rear end could have provided valuable clues to support the theory that she had been forced off the road. Two union crash investigators concluded the car had been hit from behind, though later Justice Department and FBI reviews said there was nothing suspicious and two Congressional subcommittees dropped their investigations.

If the car was deliberately bumped off Highway 74, of course, it may not have been done by amateurs. It would take some skill to nudge a car off the road at the right point to ensure a fatal accident and for the attacker to do it without leaving evidence or risking crashing his own vehicle. This may point to the involvement of outside agencies, rather than non-specialists.

Soluble plutonium in Karen Silkwood's body was traced back to pellets which were kept locked in the Cimarron plant's vaults, which she could not visit.

And there was never any explanation of the fact that other Kerr-McGee products found in Silkwood's home came from closed areas of the plant that she had not had access to for many months. Nor could anyone say why her flatmate, Sherri Ellis, and her live-in boyfriend, Drew Stephens, both had only minute traces of plutonium contamination.

After Silkwood's death, there was a federal investigation into safety and security at the plutonium plant. Kerr-McGee pulled out of the nuclear energy business the next year and decided to concentrate on oil and gas.

But the issues wouldn't go away. Over the next twelve years, a number of witnesses and people connected with the case died or disappeared in odd circumstances, while lawyers for the Silkwood family claimed to have been attacked and received death threats.

On one level, the Karen Silkwood story is all about a whistleblower who had uncovered embarrassing truths about the way her employers went about their business – and paid an awful price for her discoveries. On another, it looks to many people like the tip of an iceberg of international nuclear skulduggery. And, when the stakes get that high, it seems that individuals are simply crushed underfoot.

33

CHEMTRAILS

ARE WE IN OVER OUR HEADS?

Look up in the sky on a clear blue day and you'll see crisp white lines etching themselves across the heavens as thousands of airliners carry millions of people to and fro.

These vapour trails, otherwise known as contrails, have been part of the scenery of people's lives since the early years of aviation. But look in an increasing number of books and websites dedicated to the subject and you'll see hair-raising accounts of a massive international conspiracy.

The conspirators are supposedly using doctored contrails to dose innocent civilian communities with mind-control potions, infertility agents, chemical poisons or drugs to suppress and undermine human immune systems. Or they are secretly vaccinating us all against biological warfare agents that might be used by an enemy power – or even by our own governments.

Either that or they are attempting to control climatic and weather conditions, littering the upper atmosphere with metallic particles to reflect sunlight and reduce global warming or seeding clouds to make it rain.

Contrails – condensation trails – have been with us since the Great War of 1914–18, when soldiers in the trenches reported strange and beautiful patterns traced across the sky by the slow, low-flying biplanes of the day. As planes flew higher and faster and jet airliners came into service in the 1950s, ushering in the era of cheap foreign travel, more and more white contrails crisscrossed the sky.

But chemtrails are said to be different. The people who investigate them believe that, because they are made up of more than just frozen water vapour, they behave differently from ordinary contrails. They point to the strange, spreading patterns that can stretch across the sky for hours after a single plane has passed and claim that a normal vapour trail would not hang around for so long. They talk about the 'typical X formations' that they associate with these sinister chemtrails, though the US, for example, has a formal grid of north/south and east/west flight lanes that will always lend itself to the creation of noughts and crosses in the sky.

According to those who believe in the chemtrails conspiracy, the plot began to be implemented in the mid- to late 1990s.

The original accusations centred on the US Air Force, which was said to be using contrails as a means of spreading 'mysterious substances' and secretly delivering doses of poisons or pathogens to an unsuspecting population. But military flights are few and far between, compared with airline traffic (about 45,000 flights a day in US airspace and 20,000 a day in Western Europe). So the suspicion soon arose that commercial airliners were being used as well to lay the chemical trails across the sky.

But who would want to do these dastardly things? The answer depends on who you ask. The extreme conspiracy theorists say it is all part of the megalomaniac Illuminati conspiracy to create a New World Order, which apparently requires the global population to be trimmed by at least a couple of billion in the next two generations. As a mechanism for world population control, of course, repeated spraying centred on the United States and Europe is obviously inefficient, but the assumption is that other methods are being used in other continents, where population growth is much faster. China is supposedly excluded from all this, because it is destined to be the superpower focal point of the new order. The contrails you see there are real vapour trails, so China's 1.4 billion people are safe for now. Elsewhere, chemtrails are supposedly intended to help reduce the population steadily but imperceptibly, by causing infertility and by reducing immunity and resistance to respiratory diseases and flu viruses.

Some chemtrails conspiracists believe the chemicals in the clouds are to do with mind control and producing a docile, lethargic public that will do what it's told, while others think we are being immunised against the evil bugs that would be used in germ warfare. All of them, however, are convinced that there is a massive and malign conspiracy to affect our health and wellbeing without our permission.

THE PRACTICALITIES MIGHT BE DIFFICULT

Conspiracy theorists who point to the sky and cry foul have a hard time convincing the sceptics, who always like to pick and niggle away at questions about how the chemicals or pathogens are supposed to be carried and delivered by civilian airliners.

Jet engines run very hot, at 1,000 to 1,500 degrees Celsius. These temperatures are higher than the melting points of metals like aluminium and silver, meaning that it would not be possible to eject small particles of these metals through engine exhaust in solid form.

High-altitude aerosol spraying of viruses or bacteria would face the same temperature problem, so there is no chance that biological agents could survive if they were mixed into the fuel. The payload could not pass through the engine, so there would have to be a dispenser on the outside of the engine cowl. Too near and the bugs would fry. Too far away and people would notice that the contrail was coming from the wrong place. Apart from these snags, it would be hard to keep this extra hardware hidden from the prying eyes of the world's reporters and plane-spotters, and to ensure that all pilots and maintenance crews maintained total secrecy for years on end.

While many who are worried about chemtrails see them everywhere they look, some of those who have taken the issue more seriously believe they are only produced by adapted military tankers or specially equipped aircraft hired from civilian contractors. One source describes chemtrail materials as being 'expelled from multiple ports along the entire wing'. This kind of delivery system would create the appearance of a wide band trailing back from the aircraft, totally distinctive and quite unlike any normal vapour trail. The same source says that planes laying chemtrails 'always fly back and forth over a set area, creating circular or zig-zag patterns'. Applying these two criteria and ruling out agricultural crop-spraying activities would certainly drastically reduce the number of alleged sightings of chemtrails.

CHAFF AND CLOUD-SEEDING – BUT IS THERE MORE?

The dismissive refusal of governments and aviation authorities everywhere to admit that chemtrails exist is a red rag to a bull as far as conspiracy hunters are concerned.

When the US Environmental Protection Agency, the Federal Aviation Administration, NASA and the National Oceanic and Atmospheric Administration got together to put out a factsheet to try to clear the air, back in 2000, this was immediately seen as proof that the American government had something to hide. But just because the authorities say something isn't true, that doesn't mean it is. Nor does it mean it isn't.

In California, Utah and Ohio, and across the border in Ontario, Canada, communities claim to have suffered the health effects of chemtrails – including 'severe headaches, chronic joint pain, dizziness, sudden extreme fatigue, acute asthma attacks and feverless "flu-like" symptoms' – after extensive spraying by air force tankers. In some places, it has even been linked with an increasing incidence of Alzheimer's, though local health authorities say the evidence for that is far from conclusive.

But few samples have been studied of the stuff that comes down from the chemtrail clouds. In California, there were reports that 'skeins of white, waxy material' had been collected at ground level. But this was never identified and the US Environmental Protection Agency now refuses to test samples brought in by the public. Independent testing seems to have established that there is aluminium oxide in some field samples gathered up after apparent chemtrail activity. But even the conspiracy hunters tend to admit their case needs the support now of clean, uncontaminated samples, collected in mid-air under controlled conditions and analysed by independent chemical and pathology laboratories.

It is now officially admitted that British planes carried out aerial spraying of toxic and potentially carcinogenic chemicals and 'simulated' biological warfare agents over large areas of Dorset, Devon and Wiltshire, Bedfordshire and Norfolk during the 1960s and 1970s, as part of a programme run by Ministry of Defence scientists at Porton Down. There are now declassified MoD documents that confirm that two major cities, Salisbury and Norwich, were targeted.

Both British and American air forces routinely drop large quantities of metallic chaff to confuse missile guidance systems and radar in training and defence exercises, and both countries have carried out plenty of weather-control experiments with cloud seeding over the years. So there is a lot of strange material up there. If these are the operations we know about, it is highly likely that there will also have been other, more secretive, tests and development programmes involving spraying or seeding, though these would probably be on a smaller scale. The challenge for the chemtrail conspiracists is to prove their theory that something very much bigger, darker and more frightening has been going on over our heads for the last twenty years or so.

34

THE PHILADELPHIA EXPERIMENT

WAS THE US NAVY TRYING TO MAKE ITS WARSHIPS INVISIBLE?

For more than sixty years, there have been strange rumours of a dramatic wartime experiment in which the US Navy tried to develop a high-tech 'cloak of invisibility' to hide its warships.

JK Rowling fans will remember the scene in the first Harry Potter movie, *Harry Potter and the Sorcerer's Stone*, where he unwraps an unexpected Christmas present that turns out to be the wondrous gift of an Invisibility Cloak. But hiding a boy is one thing; invisiblising a 300ft-long warship with 216 men on board is a much bigger project.

At the centre of this mystery were the port of Philadelphia, the newly built convoy-escort destroyer *USS Eldridge* and the greatest scientist of the twentieth century, Albert Einstein.

The Philadelphia Experiment was said to be based on Einstein's promising but uncompleted work on his 'unified field theory' linking magnetism, electricity and gravity. The aim would be to use powerful electrical equipment to bend or refract light around a large object so as to make it invisible.

During World War Two, the wild-haired genius with the blackboard covered in formulae was actually employed as a part-time technical consultant to the US Navy. Einstein had signed the fateful letter, drawn up with his friend Leo Szilard, that told President Roosevelt an atomic bomb might be possible and led to the first $6,000 budget for experimental work. But he didn't take part in the atom bomb project. Nor did he work with the navy on any experiments based on unified field theory. His consultancy contribution involved theoretical research on conventional explosives and the physics of explosions.

There are many versions of what happened in Philadelphia, but most of them agree that the first experiment on *USS Eldridge* took place in late July 1943.

It is claimed that the 1,200-ton destroyer briefly vanished from sight, to be replaced, some said, by wisps of greenish fog. When it reappeared, it was clear that the crew had suffered, with many feeling extremely sick and one sailor trapped with his hand embedded deep in a steel bulkhead.

After adjustments, the experiment was supposedly repeated in October 1943. This time, the vessel vanished again, but suddenly appeared in the harbour at Norfolk, Virginia, 200 miles away, where it was said to have been seen by the crew of a cargo ship, the *SS Andrew Furuseth*. It then reappeared in Philadelphia, leaving many of the crew nauseous and suffering from shock and a range of mental disorders. The theory is that the authorities dropped any further experiments after seeing the harm that had been done to crew members and implemented a complicated cover-up to ensure no information about the programme leaked out.

CREWMEN DENIED THEY WERE 'DISAPPEARED'

When major military technologies are invented, they don't usually get uninvented again.

If the Americans had once managed even a partly successful experiment along these lines, it is hard to believe they would have simply given up on an idea with such obvious wartime applications.

At a crew reunion more than fifty years later, sailors and officers who had served on *USS Eldridge* laughed off the idea that they and their ship had vanished or been teleported to Norfolk, Virginia, and back.

Official US Navy records show the ship did not leave New York until mid-September and that it was nowhere near Philadelphia in late 1943. Needless to say, though, it has been suggested that these records could have been falsified as part of a cover-up and that crew members involved in such an extraordinary project might well have been brainwashed afterwards in the interests of national security.

TALL TALES MAY HAVE BEEN A RED HERRING

Oddly enough, something mysterious really was going on in Philadelphia's navy base at that time. And it was something that was being kept firmly under wraps.

Sailors from another destroyer moored there, the *USS Engstrom*, noticed that there was a lot of large-scale experimental equipment around the base, which they were told, confidentially, was to do with degaussing the ships. Degaussing meant using powerful electrical currents to scramble the electromagnetic signatures of these escort destroyers and make them 'invisible' to magnetic mines and the magnetic torpedoes used by Hitler's U-boat packs as they preyed on the Atlantic convoys.

There may be a parallel here between invisibility cloaking and carrots. During the war, the story was spread far and wide that the success of the RAF's night fighter squadrons in locating enemy bomber streams was because the pilots ate a lot of carrots, which supposedly gave them lots of vitamin A and remarkably acute night vision. In fact, the ability to find bombers in the dark had a lot more to do with top-secret British developments in the field of airborne radar, but the carrots story helped to confuse the issue and mislead the enemy. In the same way, tales of invisibility experiments may have been deliberately circulated to muddy the waters and distract attention from new work on these advanced degaussing technologies.

Degaussing worked, and it eventually became a widely used technique, saving many lives. But it doesn't quite have the magical appeal of a light-bending Invisibility Cloak that would have enabled the *USS Eldridge* to ghost past enemy defences and give the US Navy total control of the sea lanes.

35

JOHN LENNON

THE DREAM IS OVER

Kennedy was American. Lord Mountbatten was from another era. For at least two generations of British kids, the one violent death that will be etched on the memory like no other is the murder of John Lennon.

As Britain woke up that Tuesday morning, the radio bulletins were there to break the news that the most famous man in the world, the man who had said, tactlessly but justifiably, 'We're more popular than Jesus now,' had been shot.

The numbness came and stayed. For some of us, it has never gone away.

Lennon was not just a musician, a singer, a songwriter, the heart and soul of the greatest rock and pop group of all time. He was the curious, arrogant, vulnerable, mouthy, funny, intuitive, energetic, naive and radical spokesman for a band and a generation. He was responsible for a vast amount of social change. With his fellow Beatles, he put Liverpool on the map, sparked the jaunty, overblown Swinging London phenomenon, helped knock down the barriers to careers in music, art, writing, photography and fashion, fought prejudices, changed attitudes and outraged adults and politicians everywhere.

John Lennon was shot dead outside his New York home in the Dakota Building by Mark Chapman on the evening of 8 December 1980 (making the date of his death 9 December in UK terms).

They had met briefly a few hours earlier, when Lennon had autographed an album sleeve for Chapman among a cluster of fans waiting on the sidewalk. As the star arrived home with his wife from mixing a Yoko Ono track called 'Walking on Thin Ice', Chapman lurked in the shadows and waited while he walked past. Then he pulled out a five-shot Charter Arms Undercover .38 Special revolver and unhurriedly fired four hollow-nosed dum-dum bullets into John Lennon's back.

As Lennon staggered up the five steps to the Dakota's security booth, Chapman made no attempt to run from the scene. He walked around a bit, took off his coat and hat and sat down on the sidewalk to wait for the police, holding his copy of J D Salinger's *Catcher in the Rye*.

When the Dakota's doorman shouted, 'Do you know what you've done?' Chapman merely said, 'Yes. I just shot John Lennon.'

On top of the shocked outpourings of grief, the world quickly became aware that there were odd aspects to this murder. Chapman didn't seem to be motivated by hatred, envy or even the lone loser's typical desire for fifteen minutes of fame. If anything, he seemed keen to avoid publicity. He had made no attempt to avoid capture and punishment. After several ingenious lawyers had spent six months preparing his defence, with psychiatrists diagnosing paranoid schizophrenia, he wrong-footed them all and pleaded guilty.

Chapman was clearly mentally ill, yet he was tried as an ordinary criminal and sent to an ordinary jail. His life sentence meant he was potentially eligible for parole after twenty years. By 2020, he had applied for and been refused parole eleven times. His twelfth application was scheduled for late 2022.

Chapman has claimed that he heard a voice in his head when Lennon walked past that said, 'Do it, do it, do it,' over and over again. He said he didn't remember aiming and that he felt 'no emotion, no anger'.

The sheer random brutality of John Lennon's death, coupled with Chapman's weird mental state, soon gave rise to rumours that there was more to the murder than met the eye. Detectives had commented that he seemed blank or robotic and it was claimed that he might have been hypnotically programmed and sent to shoot the millionaire working-class hero on the orders of a right-wing group or even the arch-conspirators of the CIA.

CHAPMAN WAS ON HIS SECOND MURDER MISSION

Mark David Chapman was unquestionably mad, crazy enough to do anything, including collecting an autograph from a pop hero at 5 p.m., like any other fan, and then gunning him down in cold blood less than six hours later. There was no need to invoke a conspiracy to explain his murderous behaviour.

Over a period of ten years, he had been through drugs, from LSD to heroin, and aggressively evangelical born-again Christianity. He had started studies at three colleges and dropped out of each course. He had tried to commit suicide twice and been saved by other people both times. 'I was such a failure, I even failed at killing myself,' he said.

He had come from Hawaii to New York to stalk and kill Lennon, a trip he had also made a few weeks earlier. That time, though, he had overcome the 'master inside himself' and flown back elated, the snub-nosed revolver safe in his suitcase. 'I've won a great victory,' he told his wife, on the phone. 'I'm coming home.'

The victory didn't last long. He made an appointment to see a psychiatrist, but didn't turn up. On 6 December, he was back on the plane to New York. On 8 December, he was outside the Dakota.

'Mr Lennon,' he said, as the ex-Beatle walked by. Then five shots, the first missing, the rest finding the target, and the eerie calm as he waited for several minutes to be arrested.

'IF ANYTHING HAPPENS ... IT WASN'T AN ACCIDENT'

After the angst, drugs and compulsive hellraising of the post-Beatles 1970s, John Lennon had settled back into happy domesticity with his wife and child in New York. Several quietly unproductive years had ended with the release of *Double Fantasy*, which contained at least half an album's worth of excellent, well crafted and highly individual Lennon songs, including 'Watching the Wheels' and the single 'Starting Over'. Because of his history, Lennon could get the world's attention at the drop of a hat, but in truth he was no longer a threat to anyone.

The full-on conspiracy theory about John Lennon's death says that he was killed on the orders of right-wing obsessives in the US government, who had always hated everything he stood for.

In this account of events, Mark Chapman had come into contact with CIA agents while working as a children's counsellor in refugee camps in the Lebanon. They had recruited him, at some level, and he had eventually been drugged, brainwashed and hypnotised to carry out the mission of stalking and shooting his target, under the notorious and well-documented MKULTRA mind-control programme run by the CIA and the US Army Chemical and Biological Weapons Division.

According to this hypothesis, he was the classic, zombified Manchurian Candidate-style assassin, attacking without fear, malice or conscience and with no memory of why he had done it. He may even, unconsciously, have offered a clue himself, when he said, 'It was almost as if I was on some kind of special mission that I could not avoid.'

There was no mystery about why right-wing Americans might hate Lennon. His music and attitudes had triggered a seismic shift in American youth culture in the 1960s, drawing the kids on from harmless pop to hippy idealism, drugs, anti-war demonstrations, feminism and radical politics. President Nixon and J Edgar Hoover, the evil spider of the FBI, both loathed him, and Lennon's long struggle to get the Green Card that would let him live in the US was legendary.

The FBI file on the ex-Beatle ran to over three hundred pages and the star was well aware of the potential threats to his life and liberty. 'Listen, if anything happens to Yoko and me, it wasn't an accident,' he told comedian Paul Krassner in 1972.

Lennon had been quiet and the bulging FBI file had not gained a single new page while the Democrats were in power in America, from 1976 to 1980. But *Double Fantasy* was bringing him back into the spotlight just as the Reagan administration was taking control, with a much more socially divisive and internationally combative agenda.

John Lennon was never famous for staying out of

controversial issues and would almost certainly have found ways to make himself a nuisance for the new regime. But it's a big jump from that to assuming the existence of a Republican-linked assassination plot. If he was killed for political reasons, however, there is no doubt that the plotters had the perfect cover in the addled, suggestible psyche of Mark Chapman.

36

PONT-SAINT-ESPRIT

**THE TOWN THAT DIDN'T KNOW
WHAT HIT IT**

**One summer's day in 1951, the little medieval French town of
Pont-Saint-Esprit, a few miles from Avignon, suddenly went mad.**

Pont-Saint-Esprit was hit by an outbreak of poisoning that
caused wild hallucinations and deadly delusions. More than 300
people were poisoned. Five died, two committed suicide and fifty
had to be locked up in lunatic asylums.

An eleven-year-old boy tried to strangle his mother. Men and
women tore off their clothes and ran naked and sobbing through
the town. A man shouted, 'I'm a plane,' and jumped out of a
second-floor window, breaking both legs, before getting up and
hobbling fifty metres down the road before he could be helped.
Another saw his heart escaping through his feet and begged a
doctor to put it back.

Time magazine reported horrific scenes. 'Among the stricken,
delirium rose. Patients thrashed wildly in their beds, screaming
that red flowers were blossoming from their bodies, that their
heads had turned to molten lead…'

Townspeople fled through the streets, convinced that they were being chased by 'bandits with donkey ears'.

Léon Armunier, the local postman, was on his rounds when he was suddenly overwhelmed by wild hallucinations and nausea. 'It was terrible,' he said. 'I had the feeling I was shrinking. I saw snakes and I saw fires. I saw serpents around my arms and they gnawed at my body.'

Like so many others, the postman was put in a straitjacket and taken straight to hospital in Avignon, where he shared a room with three teenagers who had to be chained to their beds to keep them under control.

'Some of my friends tried to get out of the window,' said Armunier. 'They were thrashing wildly, screaming. The sound of the metal beds and the jumping up and down… the noise was terrible. I'd rather die than live through that again.'

Investigations immediately after the incident seemed to point to the town's bread as the source of the problem. The Spiripontains, as they call themselves, closed all eight bakeries and stopped eating bread at all.

Local doctors were convinced it was an outbreak of ergotism, a disease caused by fungal contamination of flour that hit many communities in the Middle Ages. In medieval times, it was known as St Anthony's Fire, but there'd been no cases anywhere in France since the year after Napoleon's defeat at Waterloo. The black ergot fungus grows on damp grain and produces a hallucinogenic alkaloid, ergotamine, which is used in making lysergic acid diethylamide, or LSD.

The grain used in the suspect bakery, Roch Briand, was traced back to a mill 300 miles away, in Poitiers, and the miller was charged with involuntary homicide.

Later investigations again blamed the bread supply, but

focused on the possibility that it was an accidental case of mercury poisoning, due to ingestion of a mercury-based fungicide used to treat seed grains before planting. There have been hundreds of deaths around the world from this kind of poisoning, in Pakistan, in Central America and in repeated incidents in Iraq. In each case, mercury-treated grain had been sold on and used to bake bread, instead of being planted.

In 1982, French researchers made out a case against *Aspergillus fumigatus*, a fungal toxin that can be produced in grain silos. But *A. fumigatus* is also present in soil, in rubbish heaps and generally in the air. In normal life, it turns out, most people will breathe in several hundred spores every day. Only those with damaged immune systems are unable to shrug it off and many of the Pont-Saint-Esprit victims were young and fit. One of the dead was a previously healthy twenty-five-year-old man.

Until 2009, the latest and most advanced theory about the Pont-Saint-Esprit disaster had come from French-born Cornell University history professor Steven Kaplan. His 2008 book, *Le Pain Maudit* (The Accursed Bread), argued that large amounts of nitrogen trichloride – a nasty chemical that can explode and also produce tear gas-like symptoms – might have been used to bleach the flour in the bread, causing the mass poisoning. The flour bleach was sold in the mid-twentieth century under the name Agene, but was later banned after it was found that poisons formed by its reaction with amino acids in flour could cause convulsions and fits.

Not one of these theories has ever been proved, but everyone has always been sure it was the bread that caused the tragedy. So it was a huge shock when an American author, Hank P Albarelli Jr, claimed, in 2009, that the poisoning of Pont-Saint-Esprit wasn't an accident at all.

It was deliberate, he said. An experiment that got out of hand but yielded useful data. Not an Act of God, but a flagrant act of infamy by the CIA. Not an accident, but a conspiracy involving a handful of Frenchmen and US Secret Service agents who preferred to risk the lives of French provincials than American citizens.

The CIA, Albarelli claimed, had sent the whole town on a wild and terrifying LSD trip.

FOR SOME, THE NIGHTMARE SYMPTOMS CAME ON SLOWLY

There is a general rule when dealing with mysteries, cover-ups and conspiracy theories – especially those dating from the 1950s through to the early 1970s. If there's no obvious explanation, blame the CIA.

The US Central Intelligence Agency's reach, its funding, its obsessions and its arrogance, during the Cold War period, were so great that CIA people thought they could do anything and justify it on the grounds of protecting America.

In many ways, Albarelli's theory fits with what we know about the CIA's attitudes and activities. But it doesn't necessarily fit so well with events on the ground.

The write-up of the Pont-Saint-Esprit nightmare in the *British Medical Journal* at the time describes in detail what the doctors on the spot observed. They saw, among other things, that some of the worst symptoms seemed to take six days to occur. They couldn't help noticing that most of the patients stank (or, as they put it, 'had a disagreeable odour') and they noted that one of the women who died had developed gangrene, which fits with ergotism's symptom of narrowed blood vessels.

Most tellingly, they were surprised to see that some cases

showed delirium as the first serious symptom after a very long delay, 'ten to twelve days after the first onset of the poisoning'.

This is not usually the experience of people who have been poisoned with LSD. Indeed, LSD would probably never have had its brief popularity as a recreational drug in the late 1960s if 'trippers' had had to wait a week and a half to experience its effects.

DID THE CIA REALLY SEND A WHOLE TOWN ON AN ACID TRIP?

CIA strategists and agents were always being urged to get one step ahead of their Cold War enemies and think the unthinkable.

In this case, Albarelli's book suggested, administering LSD to hundreds of unsuspecting civilians deep in rural France, to see what effect it would have, was by no means unthinkable. In the course of his research, he had turned up a declassified 1949 document in which a director of the Edgewood Arsenal, where many US government LSD studies were carried out, urged the army to begin 'field experiments' with the new drug.

There was also a CIA document from 1953, disclosed after a Freedom of Information request, in which a representative of Sandoz Chemicals, the world's only producer of lysergic acid diethylamide, was quoted as specifically mentioning Pont-Saint-Esprit.

'The Pont-Saint-Esprit "secret" is that it was not the bread at all,' said the Sandoz man. 'It was not grain ergot. It was a diethylamide-like compound.'

Albarelli's book, *A Terrible Mistake*, claimed the scientists who volunteered two of the most widely accepted explanations for the poisoning were both Sandoz employees deliberately engaged in misleading the world.

He quoted a letter from a Federal Bureau of Narcotics agent, George Hunter White, who was also working for the CIA. His letter, dated October 1954, specifically talked about the Pont-Saint-Esprit experiment and called it 'that little French village's Stormy epidemic'. In White's coded CIA jargon, 'Stormy' meant LSD.

But Albarelli believed he had found what he called 'the real smoking gun' in an official White House document submitted to the Rockefeller Commission, set up in 1975 to investigate CIA abuses. It linked the names of two French nationals secretly employed by the CIA, a senior US Special Operations Division officer and a CIA biological warfare expert, and it referred directly to 'the Pont-Saint-Esprit incident'.

The latest book on the affair, *Les Raisons Cachées* (*The Hidden Reasons*) by Tony Jagu, came out in 2018. Jagu, who agrees the CIA were behind the events in Pont-Saint-Esprit, offers proof that the French government deliberately sabotaged the inquiry afterwards and was also deliberately secretive about the claims submitted by the victims and their descendants, in an effort to conceal the true story.

The civilians of the little town of Pont-Saint-Esprit suffered a terrible ordeal in 1951. But whatever the new theories or evidence that may emerge, many of the survivors and their children are not keen to see the subject reopened.

'That story is taboo here,' said deputy mayor Jean-Pierre Colombet in 2009, shaking his head at the idea of the new 'crackpot theory' of a CIA conspiracy to send his little town on a communal acid trip. 'We were all taken for fools, but there were deaths, botched investigations and ruined families, starting with that of the baker.'

37

ALEXANDER LITVINENKO

LIES, SPIES AND A FATAL SURPRISE

On the evening of 1 November 2006, London-based Alexander Litvinenko, a former officer in the Russian security services and a passionately outspoken critic of Vladimir Putin, began to feel ill.

Over the next three weeks, as Litvinenko's condition got rapidly worse, it eventually became known that he was dying of radiation poisoning. He seemed to age by the day. His weight fell away, his hair fell out and his overall health quickly declined as his immune system collapsed. By 23 November, he was dead.

As the outline of what had happened became clear, the world's media focused in on Litvinenko's hospital bed. This was murder. But it was murder with global political implications.

Rare radioactive isotopes are not available to every common or garden killer. And why would whoever murdered Litvinenko choose such a slow, public, expensive and sensational way to get rid of him?

Conspiracy theories abounded. The radioactive material involved turned out to be polonium-210, a substance that is formed inside nuclear reactors. Therefore, Litvinenko's death must presumably have been a state-sponsored assassination, using polonium brought in from somewhere else, probably Russia. And, indeed, the detectives who ended up following a trail of polonium traces around London, soon found themselves at Heathrow Airport, where they identified three BA planes on the London–Moscow route that had been mildly contaminated.

On the other hand, the Russian security services have vast experience of black ops and many tried, tested and discreet methods of eliminating enemies.

Litvinenko had been an officer in the KGB and then its successor, the FSB, holding the elevated rank of lieutenant colonel. His last job in Russia had been as head of the FSB's anti-corruption department. If his former colleagues had been told to get rid of him, they could easily have arranged an accident, a heart attack or some other death that would not point directly to Moscow and would not be played out in a three-week glare of media publicity.

If this was an FSB killing, it was clearly planned to send out some unmissable messages to other dissidents in exile or perhaps to make a broader international statement to the effect that Russia really doesn't care too much what the rest of the world thinks.

But perhaps that's what we're meant to believe. The fact that Moscow's fingerprints appeared to be all over the murder weapon could actually mean that the assassination was staged by anti-Putin elements, anxious to frame the Kremlin and draw attention to the Russian leader's ruthless methods.

Litvinenko had two informal meetings arranged for the day he was poisoned. He met three other Russians – Andrei Lugovoy, Dmitry Kovtun and Vyacheslav Sokolenko – at the

Millennium Hotel in Mayfair, first in a fourth-floor room and then downstairs, where they drank tea in the hotel's Pine Bar.

His next appointment was to have lunch in the Itsu sushi bar in Piccadilly with an Italian security consultant called Mario Scaramella. They had something urgent to talk about, as Scaramella wanted to show him a hit list he said he had been emailed by a contact in Moscow. The list of targets, apparently drawn up by Russian intelligence agents, had five names on it. Two of the names were very familiar – Litvinenko and Scaramella.

But they had hardly started talking about the list when Litvinenko said he felt extremely ill.

That evening, at home, he felt dreadful. His wife, Marina, assumed he had food poisoning and cleared up when he was sick, every twenty minutes, never guessing she might be handling radioactive materials. After three days, as he got steadily worse, he was taken into hospital, never to come out again. It soon became clear that he'd been poisoned. But it was three weeks later – and just three hours before his death – that scientists at the Atomic Weapons Research Establishment at Aldermaston finally identified the fatal substance as polonium-210.

Polonium is rare. Global yearly production totals about three ounces and 97 per cent of it is produced in Russia.

Officially, there is only one source of polonium-210 for commercial purposes in the world – a nuclear plant in the sealed 'atom city' of Sarov (twinned with Los Alamos, New Mexico). But polonium could equally well be made by the Indians or Pakistanis, Israel or China, or even the maverick North Koreans. The amount thought to have been involved in the poisoning of Litvinenko would have been worth up to a million dollars, because of polonium's key role in making detonators for nuclear bombs.

This material, which emits alpha radiation, rather than the more familiar gamma rays, is unbelievably toxic – 250,000 times more poisonous than cyanide. Alpha radiation cannot penetrate human skin, but once inside the body it causes terrible damage to tissues and organs. The minute amount Litvinenko ingested, apparently slipped into his teapot, could have been enough to kill him 200 times over.

THE PRIME SUSPECT ACCUSES EVERYONE ELSE

It may be hard to say whose finger was on the trigger, but there is surely no reason to doubt that Alexander Litvinenko was murdered as the result of an international conspiracy.

The only alternative theory anyone has put forward is that Litvinenko himself had somehow got his hands on the polonium and was planning to use it for his own purposes.

He could, perhaps, have decided to inflict this horrific and agonising death on himself in order to become a high-profile martyr and shine a powerful light on Vladimir Putin's evil ways.

But most of us would find that notion a little too hard to swallow. Litvinenko was young and fit, only forty-three, with a loving wife and a young son in London, and he could definitely have found other ways to make his point.

The heretic's version of the story is that the polonium itself was not a weapon but merchandise. In this scenario, either Litvinenko himself or one of the men he met on the day he was poisoned had brought the polonium into London as part of an international nuclear smuggling operation.

The main man in the trio seemed to be Andrei Lugovoy, another former FSB officer, though Dmitry Kovtun had the same background and had actually known Lugovoy since infant school. The arrogant, aggressive Lugovoy was the man the British Crown Prosecution Service saw as the prime suspect in Litvinenko's murder. It believed it had quite enough evidence to charge him.

An attempt to extradite Lugovoy from Russia for questioning was turned down shortly after Litvinenko's death and he was then elected, in December 2007, as a 'Liberal Democrat' member of the duma, the Russian parliament. As duma members are immune from prosecution, that effectively blocked that line of enquiry. Lugovoy is viewed as a hero by many people in Russia, though one sceptical Russian who saw him in Moscow remarked that his skin was a strange yellow colour and commented that he 'probably glows in the dark'.

By his own account, the former KGB bodyguard was cruelly misjudged. He was the innocent victim of circumstance, conspired against by the conniving British.

'They think that they found a Russian James Bond that penetrates the nuclear facilities and, in cold blood, poisoning his friend, and at the same time poisoning himself, his friends, his wife and children,' he said.

Lugovoy didn't know for certain who killed Litvinenko; he just knew it wasn't him – or, of course, Putin's people.

He wasn't short of accusations, though, claiming it was the UK's MI6 intelligence agency or the Russian mafia, or maybe exiled oligarch and Putin opponent Boris Berezovsky, who carried out the assassination. Berezovsky, a close friend of Litvinenko, was found dead in 2013, having apparently hanged himself, in the locked bathroom of his home near Ascot, a few months after losing a high-stakes court battle with the then owner of Chelsea Football Club, Roman Abramovich.

THE RUSSIANS DID IT, BUT WHAT IS BRITAIN HOLDING BACK?

Alexander Litvinenko's poisoning happened just three weeks after the murder of campaigning journalist and Putin critic Anna Politkovskaya. She was shot dead in the lift of her Moscow apartment block, but the three accused were eventually acquitted and the case remains unsolved.

Litvinenko had written about similar themes to Politkovskaya. His book, *Blowing Up Russia*, for example, accused Putin and the FSB of conspiring to place bombs in Moscow apartment blocks and blaming Chechen separatists, as an excuse for sending the tanks into Chechnya.

When Litvinenko died, many people, even inside Russia, thought they saw a connection between the two murders.

In the American embassy in Moscow, Ambassador William J Burns wrote a blunt and confidential cable to Washington, running through the list of assumptions and conspiracy theories about Litvinenko's death that were circulating in the Russian capital. Thanks to a WikiLeaks release in December 2010, we can hear his frustration with the situation.

'The media have variously traced Litvinenko's demise to suicide, Putin's Kremlin, Putin himself, those determined to undermine Putin, FSB agents unhappy with Litvinenko's alleged betrayal of their organisation, those unhappy with Litvinenko's co-operation with Israel-based businessman Leonid Nevzlin on the Yukos affair, and the United States or "other" countries,' he wrote, adding that much of this speculation was 'self-serving'.

Despite the shortage of facts to go on, most people took a pretty cynical view, especially as Moscow had its own battle for power going on behind the scenes.

'All of the above putative versions of events are handicapped by a lack of evidence and by the existence of other motives for the killings and other potential perpetrators,' said Burns.

'Whatever the truth may ultimately be – and it may never be known – the tendency here to automatically assume that someone in or close to Putin's inner circle is the author of these deaths speaks volumes about expectations of Kremlin behaviour as the high-stakes succession struggle intensifies.'

WikiLeaks material has also shone new light into other corners of the mystery. For example, a couple of weeks after Litvinenko's death, US Ambassador-at-Large, ex-spook and terrorism expert Henry Crumpton had a long and friendly talk in Paris with his Russian opposite number, Anatoly Safonov. In the middle of this amiable chat, in the context of the Litvinenko case, Safonov suddenly referred to both Russia and Britain apparently knowing in advance that illegal polonium was being brought into London.

According to the account in the diplomatic cable, written by Karl Hofmann, the highly experienced Deputy Chief of Mission at the US embassy in Paris, Safonov said Russian officials in London had 'known about and followed individuals moving radioactive substances into the city, but were told by the British that they were under control, before the poisoning took place'.

This is potentially hot stuff. It would point to an Anglo-Russian conspiracy that's very different from the generally accepted scenarios, though there's nothing else in the conversation that amplifies this throwaway line.

The main evidence supporting the more conventional conspiracy theories about Litvinenko's murder is largely forensic.

Lugovoy, for all his denials, left a radioactive trail in his wake wherever he went. Polonium traces were eventually found at the Parkes Hotel, in Knightsbridge, where he stayed in mid-October, at the Sheraton Park Lane, where he stayed on 25 October and on the three BA 767s on which he went backwards and forwards to Moscow. The radiation was also found at the Millennium Hotel, where he stayed with Dmitry Kovtun over the time of the poisoning and at the Emirates Stadium, where Arsenal played CSKA Moscow on the night of the fatal meeting.

Kovtun was also pushed into the spotlight by further WikiLeaks revelations. These concern the number of hits found by German police looking for polonium-210 traces in Hamburg, dating from the three days he spent there after arriving from Moscow and before his flight to join Lugovoy in London.

The US Consulate General in Hamburg cabled Washington that Kovtun had left polonium traces on everything he touched, including 'vehicles, objects, clothes and furniture'. The Germans wanted to check the Aeroflot jet that brought him in from Moscow and were preparing to ground it for tests, but somebody leaked. 'Russian authorities must have found out about German plans, because at the last minute Aeroflot swapped planes,' the cable said, noting that the Germans 'did not expect Aeroflot to fly the other plane to Germany any time soon'.

In October 2011, London coroner Dr Andrew Reid announced the opening of the inquest into Litvinenko's death. He also said, against the urgings of the UK government's lawyer, that it should look at the wider issues involved. This was a reward for sustained lobbying by Marina Litvinenko and was prompted by the discovery of new documentary evidence, which also led Crown Prosecution Service lawyers to name Dmitry Kovtun as a second suspect.

The inquest process actually got under way in 2013, with a High Court judge, Sir Robert Owen, acting as the coroner. There were early complications, though, including the British government's submission of a PII – a public interest immunity certificate – which insisted that government information about Russian state involvement and about whether British intelligence could have done anything to prevent Litvinenko's death should be excluded. Another new factor was introduced by Marina Litvinenko's surprise admission that her husband had worked for MI5 and MI6, a fact she had denied for several years.

In June 2013, Owen asked for the inquest to be replaced with a public inquiry, which would be able to take statements under oath and hear secret evidence. He was turned down flat. But after a political U-turn, the then Home Secretary, Theresa May, agreed that there would be a public inquiry, with Sir Robert Owen in the chair, starting in January 2015.

A year later, the inquiry report was published. It found that Alexander Litvinenko had been killed by two Russian agents, Lugovoy and Kovtun, and that there was 'a strong probability' that they were acting on behalf of the FSB. One key section, paragraph 10.6, said: 'The FSB operation to kill Mr Litvinenko was probably approved by Mr Patrushev [FSB director Nikolai Patrushev] and also by President Putin.' It was, Prime Minister David Cameron told the world, 'state-sponsored murder'.

Whatever the tangled webs and loyalties that might lie behind Litvinenko's death, it may be the most banal pieces of forensic evidence that give the strongest clues as to what happened.

The Russian authorities, the suspects and Moscow's media always hinted that their poor, misunderstood people were set up or contaminated by Alexander Litvinenko himself, who, they claim, had the original polonium.

Sure, Lugovoy and Kovtun said, the hotels we stayed in, the restaurants we ate in, the lapdance club we visited, the taxis we used and the planes we went home on all showed traces of polonium, because we had been around Litvinenko. Naturally, everything we touched after that would be contaminated.

But there's one tiny exhibit that's hard to square with all that.

Litvinenko, who had to watch the pennies, came into town from Muswell Hill that fateful morning on a big red double-decker bus. Police confirmed that the bus was free of any contamination. And the £1.50 bus ticket in his pocket – touched then, but not since – bore no trace at all of the radioactive poison.

38

GLENN MILLER

MISSING WITHOUT TRACE

Everyone knows what happened to Glenn Miller.

1) The great bandleader's plane iced up or suffered engine failure and crashed into the sea off the French coast.

2) Or it was picked off by a German interception squad that had been tipped off about the flight and set out to shoot down the slow, unarmed aircraft.

3) Or Miller arrived in France, got himself into a highly compromising situation in a Parisian brothel and died of a heart attack under awkward circumstances that the authorities were determined to hush up.

4) Or he was captured, tortured and eventually killed as he carried a secret message from General Dwight D Eisenhower to dissident German generals plotting to overthrow Hitler and make peace with the Allies.

5) Or he died of gunshot wounds in a hospital in Ohio, weeks after the papers had announced his disappearance over the Channel.

6) Or, as his younger brother, Herb Miller, also a bandleader,

insisted, the chain-smoking trombonist died of lung cancer in an American forces hospital.

7) Or, as many people have tried to prove in recent years, the plane was hit from above by unused bombs jettisoned over the sea by a group of 138 RAF Lancaster bombers returning from an aborted raid on Germany.

The fact is, nobody can be sure of anything about Miller's death. Except that it was odd, unexpected, hard to explain and potentially embarrassing.

Alton Glenn Miller was the biggest star of his day. In 1939, something like a quarter of all the records on America's 300,000 jukeboxes were by the Glenn Miller Orchestra. He was awarded the first-ever gold record for 'Chattanooga Choo Choo'. After talking his way into the US forces, despite being too old, he formed his fifty-piece Army Air Force Band and played eight hundred concerts to entertain Allied troops in Europe in just six months.

Yet, in December 1944, on a cold, foggy day, he climbed into a cramped single-engine aircraft, with a pilot and a single military colleague and took off for France, never to be seen again.

Miller was effectively hitching a ride to Paris with a senior officer, Lt Col Norman Baessell, whose plane was already scheduled to fly from RAF Twinwood Farm, near Bedford, on 15 December 1944. He had only met Baessell the day before, and the soldier had offered him the spare seat in the Canadian-built Noorduyn Norseman. There was no room for Miller's manager, Don Haynes, so it had been agreed that he would follow on as soon as he could.

The official line is that Major Glenn Miller's plane crashed and was never found, leaving him formally classified 'missing in action'.

But Miller was more than an ambitious, energetic and

patriotic bandleader. He and his band were seen as one of America's secret weapons, in terms of forces morale and anti-Nazi propaganda.

One top US military flyer, war hero General Jimmie Doolittle, told him, 'Next to a letter from home, your organisation is the greatest morale builder in the European theatre of operations.'

When the band went into London's Abbey Road Studios, it was to record propaganda programmes in which the music was mixed with anti-Hitler messages aimed at the Nazi forces, including Glenn Miller himself talking in painfully coached German.

So Miller had military and even political significance. And his death in an unconfirmed flying accident was bound to spark suspicion and rumour, though few people would have expected that to go on unresolved for nearly eighty years.

NO FLIGHT PLAN, NO WITNESSES

Planes crash, especially in winter, especially in wartime. The tiny fabric-covered UC-64A Norseman had a reputation as a rugged little workhorse, originally designed for use by bush flyers in Canada and Alaska. It was often flown in cold conditions, but that does not rule out the possibility that icing-up could have led to a fatal accident. UC-64As had a history of carburettor and wing icing problems.

Single-engined aircraft are always vulnerable if something goes wrong, and flying over water increases the risk. With or without any intervention by the enemy, a crash in the Channel has always been the most likely explanation for Glenn Miller's death.

The fact that the star bandleader's disappearance was not reported in the press until ten days later is not necessarily suspicious, either. In the fog of war, odd things happen, communications are unreliable and nobody will have been exactly rushing to announce a high-profile death like Miller's, especially when there was no body and no wreckage to confirm it.

After Miller was declared missing in action, it was generally assumed that the true story of what happened would emerge over time. Even without direct evidence of a crash, documentation such as flight plans and witness statements would normally clear up any mysterious loose ends. But the Norseman's pilot, Flight Officer John Morgan, had failed to register any flight plan at all and there were no witnesses to anything that happened after the plane crossed the English coast.

A book published in 2006 included the rather belated claim, by an American former anti-aircraft gunner, that his ack-ack battery on the coast at Folkestone had accidentally shot down Miller's plane. This theory was generally dismissed on the grounds that the alleged date of the incident was three months before Miller's death and that the bandleader had played dozens of gigs in front of tens of thousands of witnesses during the intervening period.

THE ALTERNATIVE SCENARIOS WOULD BE EVEN WORSE

Everything about Glenn Miller's death lends itself to the suspicions of conspiracy theorists. Even the brief summary of seven explanations that starts this chapter doesn't exhaust the tales that have grown up around it. Some people believe, for example, that Miller did get to Paris, but was then rubbed out by black market operators, shot because of alleged spying activities or accidentally killed by a US military policeman.

Whatever actually happened to Glenn Miller, his disappearance caused consternation among America's top brass in Europe. This was something they didn't want to have to announce. But they had other things on their minds, too. They were largely caught on the hop by the surprise German counter-offensive in the Ardennes, which began the next day and developed into the intense and bloody Battle of the Bulge.

It was not until 23 December, more than a week after Miller vanished, that his wife, Helen, was telephoned and told that he was missing.

Supreme Headquarters Allied Expeditionary Force (SHAEF) and Washington did not want to say anything until the plane's loss was confirmed, but there was a Glenn Miller special scheduled for Christmas Day and a press statement was urgently needed. The newspapers and BBC radio carried the news of his death the following day, on Christmas Eve.

Though he was never in the front line – and certainly was not involved in spying or secret trips to meet German generals – Glenn Miller was undoubtedly seen as important to the war effort.

To lose a key figure like this in a straightforward flying accident was bound to look bad, but it would not be nearly as damaging as any of the other explanations.

If the Norseman was intercepted by Luftwaffe pilots who knew what they were looking for, that would immediately imply that there were serious security leaks to worry about. If it was knocked out of the sky by carelessly discarded bombs from RAF Lancasters on their way back from a cancelled raid, that would raise a lot of questions, too.

And, of course, if Miller had died in the arms of a French

prostitute or at the hands of Gestapo spyhunters, some kind of cover-up operation would have been essential to avoid a major propaganda setback.

Whatever the true story, it is unlikely that more than a handful of people would ever have known what was real and what was smoke and mirrors. The decision to announce that the plane had apparently been lost without trace over the sea was almost inevitable, as the only practical way to handle the situation. But whether that was what really happened to Glenn Miller, no one will ever be completely sure.

39

9/11

100 MINUTES THAT CHANGED THE WORLD

More than twenty years on from America's great human tragedy of September 2001, a recent opinion poll, conducted by Statista, claims that 23 per cent of Americans – 75 million people – agree with the proposition that '9/11 was an inside job'. Some 11 per cent say they 'strongly believe', while 12 per cent say they 'somewhat believe' that the US government staged the apocalyptic events of that day or knew in advance and failed to stop them.

Overall levels of scepticism about the validity of the official account are high, both in the US and in Britain. Repeated polls have shown that at least 40 per cent of Americans still believe their government has either hidden important evidence or left crucial questions unanswered. Ask people under thirty years old and it is taken as read, by a large majority, that the truth has been suppressed.

The two main conspiracy theories – both quite horrifying, if you truly believe them – are that the George W Bush administration allowed the attacks to happen or that it, or its agents, actually carried them out.

Nearly 3,000 people died as a direct result of the September 11th attacks. The world was stunned and disbelieving as the first hijacked plane smashed into the North Tower of the World Trade Center in New York. Horror turned to near-panic fifteen minutes later, at 9.02 a.m., as a second Boeing 767 streaked in over Manhattan and drove into the side of the South Tower.

At this point, of course, people had no way of knowing whether more planes would dive in to target landmarks like the Empire State Building, the Chrysler Building and Brooklyn Bridge. When news came that two more aircraft had been hijacked, New York feared the worst. But it had suffered enough shocks for one dreadful morning.

Attention switched first to Washington, DC, where the third airliner spiralled down out of the sky and rammed the side of the Pentagon at 9.35 a.m., and then to the drama being played out on the fourth plane, which eventually crashed into fields near Shanksville, Pennsylvania, after the passengers stormed the cockpit.

Just before ten o'clock, the 110-storey South Tower, once the world's tallest building, collapsed in a few seconds, leaving a gaping hole in the New York skyline. Onlookers couldn't believe their eyes. 'Oh, God,' a nurse said. 'So many people.'

After burning fiercely for another twenty minutes, the North Tower shook, rumbled and folded down into a mountain of rubble, kicking up a writhing, acrid plume of smoke, grit and dust.

The Twin Towers, and the people inside them, had gone.

Could this really be a conspiracy? Could Americans really have done this to their fellow countrymen? What motivation could ever make that worthwhile?

In less than 100 minutes, the face of New York had changed, 3,000 people had died and the politics of the world had changed, too.

Suddenly, the War on Terror had begun. The Bush administration was quick to blame the hijackings on terrorists from the al-Qaeda network of Islamic extremists, masterminded – or at least, inspired – by the dissident son of a rich Saudi family, Osama bin Laden. The bin Laden and Bush families go back a long way. In the 1970s, George Bush Sr received funding for his Arbusto oil company from Salem bin Laden, Osama's half-brother. And indeed, on the very morning of 9/11, Bush Sr was at the Carlyle Group's investment conference, also attended by Shafiq bin Laden, another of Osama's dozens of half-brothers, at the Ritz-Carlton Hotel in Washington.

After the attacks, homeland security was abruptly tightened and al-Qaeda was identified as public enemy number one. Afghanistan was invaded, eventually followed by Iraq, and the offshore Guantanamo Bay detention centre was opened. Nearly ten years after 9/11, on 2 May 2011, US special forces shot bin Laden dead, in a raid on his secret compound in Pakistan. But that wasn't the end of the story. Two decades on from the assault on the Twin Towers, the consequences of September 11th are everywhere and relations between America and much of the Islamic world are still at a historic low.

The 9/11 tragedy was the worst terrorist incident in American history. The White House accused Osama bin Laden, and al-Qaeda was proud to claim it as a victory. First there was a grainy video of Osama bin Laden, followed by an interview with al-Jazeera television in which Khalid Sheikh Mohammed said he was head of al-Qaeda's military committee and that 9/11 was his operation.

But it did not take long for the rumours to start. After the shock and the immediate recriminations about lack of preparedness for this kind of attack, people started to ask more questions.

Would the impacts and the burning fuel really have been enough to bring down the Twin Towers? No large steel-framed skyscraper had ever collapsed before, anywhere in the world, even when major fires had blazed for hours.

Didn't the way the towers fell down in seconds look more like one of those controlled demolition jobs, where charges are detonated at many points around a building? Didn't survivors say they heard several explosions? Didn't videos show puffs of smoke that looked like explosions far away from the impact points?

Then there were all the questions about the hijackers. There had been nineteen of them altogether, but only four had filled in proper visa forms. How had they been so successful at dodging the CCTV cameras when boarding the flights? If they hadn't been under observation beforehand, how was the FBI so quick to identify them, even tracing some back within a day to the flying schools they'd trained at? How had ringleader Mohammed Atta's passport survived and been found so quickly amid the chaos and mangled confusion of 1.6 million tons of debris?

At the site of the Pentagon crash, people doubted whether the narrow-looking hole punched in the building's strengthened outer wall could really have been the impact point for a 100-ton Boeing 757 with a 12-foot-wide fuselage, a wingspan of 124 feet and big three-ton engines slung under each wing.

And when it came to the fourth plane, it was argued that the anguished mobile phone calls between passengers and their friends on the ground simply couldn't have happened. Cell phones would not have worked under those conditions, the conspiracy theorists insisted. It followed, of course, that the bereaved relatives and friends who had received these calls were supposedly lying as part of this huge conspiracy – an accusation many of them found hurtful and despicable.

To add to the confusion, nearly ten years after 9/11, in February 2011, one of the multitude of US diplomatic cables released by WikiLeaks revealed sensational new evidence and raised a whole batch of new questions.

Apart from the four groups that hijacked the planes, this US embassy cable shows there may have been a fifth terrorist gang, either targeting the White House or intending to spread the terror by hijacking an airliner in California.

According to the WikiLeaks cable, three Qataris – Meshal Alhajri, Fahad Abdulla and Ali Alfehaid – had been on a reconnaissance mission to New York and Washington that was linked to the 9/11 attacks, conducting surveillance at the World Trade Center, the Statue of Liberty and the White House. They had allegedly then gone on to California, where they linked up with another suspect. The Qataris then apparently waited for two weeks, holed up in a three-bed room in an airport hotel in Los Angeles, equipped with pilots' uniforms, pin-feed printouts with aircrew names and flight details, several laptops and American Airlines tickets to fly to Washington on 10 September.

Something seems to have changed their plans, though, as they failed to board this flight and flew home to Qatar via London. The plane they had been scheduled to fly on was the one that was hijacked on leaving Washington the next day and crashed into the Pentagon, killing 184 people.

It has even been suggested, since the embassy cable was leaked, that the Qataris may have been planning to hijack their overnight BA flight to London, timing their action for the very last leg of the journey so that it would be synchronised with the New York attacks.

The three Qataris were among 300 people on an FBI 'wanted for questioning' list that was leaked in 2002, though it was said that those named were not necessarily suspects. The FBI now claims it has proof that the flight tickets for the three men were 'paid for by a convicted terrorist'.

The existence of this fifth hijack team was only revealed for the first time when WikiLeaks published the secret cable, dating from early 2010, which had been sent to Washington from the American embassy in Doha, Qatar.

RUSSIA WARNED SUICIDE PILOTS WERE TRAINING

Ranged against the conspiracy theories are some impressive investigative efforts since 2001. The initial 9/11 Commission was unsatisfactory, but it was not the straightforward whitewash job some people expected.

It did expose quite a number of warnings and tip-offs that should have alerted the government, the FBI and the CIA to the risk of terrorist activity on US soil. Intelligence reports had specifically talked of Osama bin Laden gearing up for action. In July, Russia had told the CIA that suicide pilots were training to attack US targets, while Mossad had helpfully handed over a list of terrorists who had sneaked into America. Four of the names on the Mossad list were 9/11 hijackers.

The 9/11 commissioners also made it public that they had found the government less helpful than it should have been. President George W Bush had dragged his feet over the commission in the first place, funding was inadequate and both the chairman and vice chairman yelped that they'd been 'set up to fail'. The *Washington Post* reported that the Pentagon's obstructive answers to questions about what happened on 9/11 frustrated the ten commission members so much that they thought of asking the Justice Department to bring criminal charges.

But much of the careful unpicking of the tangled factual and technical evidence about aircraft impacts and structural damage to buildings was left to the National Institute of Standards and Technology (NIST). NIST produced its main report in September 2005, with a follow-up report on the third World Trade Center tower, WTC 7, in 2008, and is widely thought to have done a good job.

The main set of NIST reports totals 10,000 pages and settles a lot of the standard questions about what happened and how. It confirms that the North and South Towers were hit by the two Boeing 767s and that it was a Boeing 757 that rammed the Pentagon, and not a cruise missile, as some people have suggested.

It explains that the Twin Towers collapsed, not because the steel structures melted, but because they weakened and deformed at much lower temperatures. It also says, incidentally, that the steel might well have retained enough strength to support the building if the crash impact had not wrenched the spray-on fireproofing off the metal surfaces.

The damage far below the impact points was caused by blazing jet fuel gushing down utility risers and lift shafts, while the puffs of dust and smoke expelled from the sides of the building were not explosions but the result of floors collapsing. As each floor pancaked onto the one below, there would be ever more weight bearing down and it was this that eventually caused the chain reaction that pulled the towers down.

There is much, much more besides and probably enough to convince most people what happened. The focus of the conspiracy thinking then shifts to why it happened as it did.

AMERICA'S PAIN – AND DOUBTS – WON'T GO AWAY

The combination of a great national disaster and the new internet video technologies created the first blockbuster of the Conspiracy Age. An angry, raw, impassioned documentary film called *Loose Change 9/11: An American Coup* hurled together every possible conspiracy theory, survivor soundbite, video clip, expert interview and paranoid fantasy it could find into a fascinating mishmash that has been viewed on YouTube, in its various forms, some twenty million times.

Written and directed by twenty-seven-year-old Dylan Avery, *Loose Change* is rivetingly watchable. But hard-line '9/11 Truthers' see it as lightweight and criticise it for focusing too much on WTC 7, the third tower, the Salomon building.

This was the forgotten aspect of 9/11. It was a forty-seven-storey tower, linked to the World Trade Center plaza by an elevated walkway, that was damaged by flying debris in the original attacks, burned virtually untended all day and finally collapsed just after 5.20 p.m. Its fate encouraged speculation, partly because it wasn't directly hit by either aircraft but also because of its tenants. Besides investment bankers Salomon Smith Barney, these included the Securities & Exchange Commission, the stock market regulator, and the US Secret Service, the Department of Defense and the CIA.

Ever since the slaughter of 9/11, there has been a steady and very intense exchange of accusations and counter-accusations between those who believe the broad outline of the official version of events and those who don't. The objectors are, naturally, cast as wild-eyed fanatics with paranoid delusions.

How, their mainstream critics ask, can they possibly believe that anyone within the US system of government, with all its checks and balances, would even dream of killing off 3,000 of its own people to provide a pretext for attacking Islam, invading Afghanistan or securing oil supplies by marching into Iraq?

How can you be so naive? asks the other side. What about Pearl Harbor, where Roosevelt certainly did less than he could to protect the American sailors? What about Operation Northwoods, the plot cooked up by the army and vetoed by JFK in 1962? That depended on staging terrorist outrages in American cities and faking attacks on US bases and blaming it on Fidel Castro as an excuse to invade Cuba.

For those who believe that politicians are often corrupt or self-seeking and unduly warlike, but unlikely to be monsters of Nazi-like depravity, there is no comfortable middle ground. Either 3,000 died by accident or 3,000 died by design.

The questions persist about how the al-Qaeda team was allowed to execute its plan. For example, why were fighters not scrambled? Unbelievably, there was no direct link between air traffic control and the North American Air Defense Command (NORAD). Air traffic controllers literally had to pick up the telephone and dial NORAD – and it didn't do much good. Their information was wildly inaccurate, too, as, once the hijackers had turned the planes' ID transponders off, the controllers were left trying to keep track of the right targets in a sea of 4,500 similar blips. Two F-15 fighters and three F-16s were eventually scrambled, but it was all over before they got anywhere near. NORAD's sophisticated radar systems all pointed outwards, as nobody was expecting to face threats from planes starting in US airspace.

There are currently nearly 7000 books about 9/11. But the flow is not dying down. Publisher's lists for the following year show dozens more on their way. Many, inevitably, will be full of crackpot conspiracy theories explaining how Bush, Vice President Dick Cheney, Big Oil, the Illuminati, the rabid right, the still-red left, the anti-Muslims, the pro-Muslims, the Israeli government, the United Nations and a dozen other candidates all stood to benefit from the events of America's cruellest morning. That doesn't mean that, in among the elements of cock-up and grim farce, there were not conspiratorial elements, too.

But, in the end, all we can be sure of is that al-Qaeda attacked the US and killed nearly 3,000 people by hijacking four aircraft and crashing them into targets that included the Twin Towers. Most of the rest, at this distance, has become a matter of belief, rather than fact.

40

HAROLD WILSON

THE KREMLIN'S PUPPET IN
NUMBER TEN?

When Harold Wilson's great rival for the Labour leadership, Hugh Gaitskell, died abruptly in 1963, it was a major shock. A tired Conservative government was already running out of steam and Labour had its best shot at power for twelve years.

Gaitskell, who had been fit enough to travel to Moscow on 1 January for talks with Soviet leader Nikita Khrushchev, fell ill as soon as he got back on 4 January. He was suffering from an almost unknown autoimmune disease, lupus disseminata, and within two weeks he was dead.

Wilson became the prime minister-in-waiting. But the disease that had killed Gaitskell was so unusual, so fast-acting and so rare in the UK that his doctor even got in touch with MI5. He was suspicious that Gaitskell might somehow have been infected as a form of bio-assassination, during his brief trip to Russia.

No evidence was uncovered to support this theory, though a Soviet defector, Anatoliy Golitsyn, later claimed that the KGB's

'Department of Wet Affairs', Assassinations Department 13, had been plotting to kill a leading Western politician in order to insert one of its own stooges or 'agents of influence'. If Gaitskell was the victim of Department 13, that implied Wilson was the agent.

The security services had taken an interest in Wilson since the late 1940s. They knew he had shown some Communist sympathies as a student at Oxford before the war, and MI5 had noticed the number of trips he made to the Soviet Union when he was President of the Board of Trade, from 1947 onwards.

Harold Wilson was definitely a high flyer. At thirty-one, he was the youngest cabinet member in living memory. He obviously enjoyed his trips to Moscow and became friends with Communist leaders like Molotov and Mikoyan. Some MI5 agents believed he was recruited as a KGB informer by means of a traditional 'honey trap' operation, in which he was seduced by a female KGB staffer and filmed or photographed in compromising situations to provide ammunition for blackmail.

Nothing was ever found in the KGB files to back up this idea, but security service suspicions were kept simmering when Wilson seemed less than hawkish about the Korean War. He was kept under observation during the 1950s, while Labour was in opposition, but it was Gaitskell's death that marked a change of gear.

Wilson took over the party leadership and enjoyed the immediate good fortune of the Conservatives' embarrassment over the Christine Keeler/John Profumo sex scandal, in which the Secretary of State for War turned out to have shared a bed-mate with a Russian spy and a West Indian drug dealer and then blustered and lied about it to Parliament before eventually resigning.

Harold Macmillan stood down and was replaced as prime

minister by the lofty Sir Alec Douglas-Home, who had to give up a peerage to sit in the Commons and was never likely to win the hearts of ordinary people.

With the general election of October 1964, Harold Wilson became prime minister. For the next twelve years, in office and out of it, Wilson was watched and sometimes plotted against by a group of security service spooks who could never bring themselves to drop the idea that he was being run from Moscow.

Wilson was thought of as a dull, uninspiring leader, though he did have moments of real wit ('I'll offer them a deal. If they stop telling lies about us, we'll stop telling the truth about them'). He never quite claimed personal responsibility for Swinging London, building the supersonic Concorde airliner, the introduction of colour television or England winning the World Cup in 1966, but he was happy to take credit for all the good things that happened on his watch.

The Americans disliked him for keeping the UK out of the war in Vietnam and the CIA's head of counterintelligence, James Jesus Angleton, repeated to British Secret Service officers that his sources told him the prime minister was a Soviet spy. For MI5 staff like Peter Wright, who later wrote the banned book *Spycatcher*, the idea would not go away. Throughout Wilson's first term of office, which lasted until May 1970, this group within the security services watched his every move.

They may have listened to it, too, as Harold Macmillan had told MI5 to plant bugs in the cabinet room, the waiting room and the prime minister's study. They were removed when Macmillan went, but replaced within months on the orders of Sir Alec Douglas-Home.

Neither Wilson nor the next PM, Edward Heath, knew

anything about these bugs. Wilson was back in 10 Downing Street after two election victories in 1974, still knowing nothing about the hidden microphones, which were finally removed in 1977, a few months after Jim Callaghan took over as PM. There was an interesting coda to this, as the next prime minister, Margaret Thatcher, carefully and deliberately lied about this surveillance in a formal statement a couple of years later. 'Lord Wilson has never been the subject of a Security Service investigation or of any form of electronic or other surveillance by the Security Service,' she said.

Meanwhile, there were genuine plots being hatched.

But they were anti-Wilson conspiracies, rather than plans for a Communist takeover.

WILSON WAS PARANOID – BUT THEY WERE OUT TO GET HIM

Wilson himself always said he was against Communism. The official MI5 line, after repeated investigations of him over many years, was that he had no relationship with the KGB. So it is unlikely, from that point of view as well as from the point of view of common sense, that the British prime minister was part of some conspiracy to bring Britain under Soviet domination.

On the face of it, it seems just as unlikely that the UK's secret security services would plot to undermine a serving prime minister or to swing a general election against one particular party. There never was an officially sanctioned anti-Wilson conspiracy, though up to thirty MI5 agents appear to have thought it was their patriotic duty to look for opportunities to remove him from office.

Wilson was often portrayed as the most paranoid of British

prime ministers. He certainly believed there were people in the security services who were keen to see the back of him.

Later on, during his second spell in power, he was shocked when the army mounted a sudden exercise that involved surrounding and taking over Heathrow Airport, with roadblocks at key points and tanks on the runways. His close friend Marcia Williams, a key member of Wilson's 'kitchen cabinet', claimed the PM hadn't been told about this and that it was being used as a dry run for a possible military coup. No evidence of this was uncovered at the time and no declassified documents seem to support the idea.

PLOTTING AND PLANNING FOR A VERY BRITISH COUP

The most extraordinary conspiracy in modern British politics apparently lasted just a few minutes. And we only have the word of one person that this dramatic meeting did occur. But, if it did, it must be one of the few clear attempts to launch a treasonous plot to take over the country that didn't end in a beheading.

Hugh Cudlipp, the long-time editorial director of the *Daily Mirror*, claimed he was told to set up a meeting in early May 1968 between his boss, the head of the International Publishing Corporation (IPC), Cecil King, and Lord Louis Mountbatten, a great British war hero, last Viceroy of India and uncle of the Duke of Edinburgh.

Once the doors were closed, Cecil King apparently told Mountbatten that Wilson's ineptitude meant the country was heading for a crisis, in which the government would collapse and law and order would disintegrate. There would be blood on the streets and the army would have to take control. There would then be a desperate need for a great leader who could work in the national interest to steer the country off the rocks. The key question, he said, was whether Mountbatten would allow himself to be put forward as the head of the new administration.

Mountbatten said it sounded like treason and he would not get involved. The revolution was over, for the time being. Three weeks later, Cecil King, who was also an MI5 agent, was relieved of his post at the top of IPC.

But if this short-lived conspiracy sounds outrageous, it wasn't the last time the name of Mountbatten, who was murdered by an IRA bomb on his boat in 1979, was involved in something similar.

Thirty years on, a ninety-minute BBC documentary named several right-wing military and security figures who, it said, had plotted against Wilson again in 1975 and had even started forming private armies to save the country from the threat posed by the Soviet Union and British trade unionists. The BBC claimed this was a royalist coup and that it was backed, and even partly planned, by Mountbatten and other close relatives of the Queen. Again, the conspirators saw Mountbatten as the right figurehead for a government of national salvation. Their plans even went as far as asking the chairman of Cunard, John Mitchell, if he would lend them the QE2 as a floating prison for Harold Wilson's cabinet.

This potential Establishment revolution was never acknowledged, but even the official history of MI5 finally conceded in 2009 that there was a group ('a few, very few, malcontents') inside the service that had serious grudges and 'gave vent to these and spread damaging and malicious stories about the Labour government'.

In other words, Prime Minister Harold Wilson was quite right to think that members of his own security services spent years conspiring to smear him and bring about his downfall. It was an outrageous situation. But, because this happened in Britain, no one was shot, no one was jailed and, at least as far as the public record is concerned, no one was even fired from a job.

41

MARTIN LUTHER KING

THIS SHOOTING WAS NO LONE GUNMAN

The Reverend Dr Martin Luther King was shot from a distance, once, through the neck, on his motel balcony in Memphis.

It was the quickest, cleanest, most clinical shooting of all the high-profile assassinations that jarred and reshaped the course of American history in the 1960s. On that basis alone, you'd expect to see the murderer exposed as a professional, a contract killer or a military marksman gone bad.

You would not expect the lone gunman convicted of this shooting to be a petty jailbird, an unsuccessful crook with a background of minor thefts and burglaries and no history of gun crime.

James Earl Ray, who pleaded guilty after being told he'd get the electric chair if he put up a defence, was sentenced to ninety-nine years and almost immediately began trying to withdraw his confession.

He was framed, he claimed, by a gun smuggler called 'Raoul' or 'Raul', who had used the room Ray had checked into in a boarding house opposite King's motel, made sure Ray's fingerprints were on the rifle and fired the deadly shot while Ray waited in the car. Raoul had then run down the street, dropping the rifle and a holdall containing several items that would identify and incriminate Ray, jumped into the car and made sure they were far away before the police could react and set up roadblocks.

It was a dramatic tale and most people didn't believe a word of it.

Attempts to substantiate Ray's story led nowhere. But there were plenty of reasons to believe that James Earl Ray had been set up as a patsy by someone or some organisation that was a lot more formidable than he was.

The shooting of Dr Martin Luther King took place on 4 April 1968. He was in Memphis, with other leaders of his Southern Christian Leadership Conference, to mediate in a sanitation workers' strike. The day before, he had been held up by a bomb scare as his plane was about to take off. That evening, in his speech, he mentioned threats that had been made against him. 'And then I got to Memphis. And some began to say the threats... to talk about the threats that were out. What would happen to me from some of our sick white brothers?' There had been more than fifty death threats, but he was determined not to show fear.

He ended his last speech on a note of prophetic optimism: 'And I've seen the Promised Land. I may not get there with you. But I want you to know tonight, that we, as a people, will get to the Promised Land. And I'm happy, tonight. I'm not worried about anything. I'm not fearing any man. Mine eyes have seen the glory of the coming of the Lord.'

Less than twenty-four hours later, he was dead. A wave of

horror shook the country and there were serious riots in sixty American cities.

Despite a huge manhunt, it was two months before the fugitive suspect was picked up. Ray was actually caught in London, at Heathrow Airport, travelling on a false Canadian passport in the name of Ramon George Sneyd. He was trying to board a plane to Belgium on his way to start a new life as a mercenary in white-ruled Southern Rhodesia.

This seemed strange, in itself. This failed criminal and chip-on-the-shoulder racist had somehow got the $10,000 and the false papers he needed to slip out of the United States and travel first to Canada and then on to Britain, to Portugal and back to London again on a complicated flight from justice.

When stopped, he was carrying several fake identity documents, including more papers in the name of another Canadian called Eric S Galt. This was an alias Ray had used before, but it was not made up. The real Galt did exist, was Canadian, looked a lot like Ray and was known as a skilled rifleman. Ray, however, had never been to Canada until he arrived there after the shooting, met up with someone referred to as 'The Fat Man' and was apparently given a wad of money to pay for his flights.

IF RAY WAS THE KILLER, DID HE DO IT FOR MONEY?

Either there was no conspiracy to kill Martin Luther King or this was the most effective 1960s cover-up of them all.

Everything about the assassination is suspicious, circumstantial and hard to take at face value. Yet there has been an enormous amount of time and effort spent trying to test the various theories and nobody has come close to proving that Dr King's death was not the work of one ugly, ineffectual, small-time bigot who wanted to make a name for himself.

The apparent incompetence of the Memphis police, the plain-clothes agents who were never far from Dr King, the FBI detective teams and the later investigators from the 1977 House Select Committee on Assassinations and the 1999 Justice Department case review may be the real thing. Or it may just be that there is no conclusive evidence to find.

James Earl Ray was not bright. He was not even good at being a crook. He was greedy and vain, but he'd shown no previous signs of being motivated by anything other than money.

If he did shoot the great civil rights activist of his own accord, it must have been one of the few actions he ever took that was prompted by a principle – however wildly misguided – rather than the desire for an easy buck. And if he did it for money, then we are immediately back on the conspiracy trail.

THE HOUSE COMMITTEE CALLED IT 'A CONSPIRACY'

According to the official account, the single shot that killed the youngest-ever Nobel Peace Prize winner was fired from a 'sniper's nest' set up in the bathroom of the boarding house opposite the motel. One handprint and a few other smudged fingerprints supposedly placed James Earl Ray in the bathroom, while the bundle of belongings dropped in the street outside included the gun, Ray's binoculars and radio and even some personal papers.

The gun was a problem. Two inconclusive sets of ballistics tests failed to match the bullet from Dr King's body closely enough to prove that the Remington Gamemaster recovered by police was necessarily the murder weapon.

The position of the gunman was also problematical. There is a famous picture taken just a few seconds after the shooting, with Dr King lying on the balcony and several of his friends pointing at bushes near the top of a steep bank opposite the motel. The arms are almost exactly parallel, but the direction they all point in is not towards the boarding house. (You can see this graphic black and white photo online. Just search for 'MLK assassination' and click 'images').

Because of James Earl Ray's guilty plea, there was not an extensive trial at the time. Subsequent investigations have been patchy and unsatisfactory and have done little to clear the air and remove suspicions of conspiracy and cover-up.

The House Select Committee on Assassinations, in 1977, looked at evidence that Ray's false identity documents might have been supplied by CIA agents and concluded that it did not stack up. Its judgment asserted that Ray was guilty, though, extraordinarily, it also ruled that it was likely he hadn't acted alone.

'The committee believes, on the basis of the circumstantial evidence available to it, that there is a likelihood that James Earl Ray assassinated Dr Martin Luther King as a result of a conspiracy,' it said. 'No federal, state or local government agency was involved in the assassination of Dr King.'

With the CIA apparently out of the frame – and despite the blanket reassurances of the committee – attention switched to the FBI, which had shown a consistent and rabid hatred of Martin Luther King. FBI statements had attempted to smear Dr King's reputation with lurid references to his adulterous lifestyle and a letter had even been sent to him urging him to take his own life. One FBI agent said he'd seen notes in Ray's white Mustang with Raoul's name and FBI contact numbers.

When Attorney General Janet Reno ordered new investigations and a review of the evidence by the Department of Justice, the investigators dismissed the FBI connection and the Raoul story. The judgment, in 2000, also found 'no reliable evidence' to support another conspiracy theory, which had convinced Dr King's widow and family, that revolved round a Memphis café owner, Loyd Jowers, who claimed to have been at meetings where local police, government agents and mafia gangsters got together to arrange the killing.

For all the investigations over the years, it is hard to believe that James Earl Ray operated entirely alone. He may well have acted in league with other Tennessee racists or been motivated by the $50,000 'blood bounty' offered for King's death by John Sutherland, a racist St Louis lawyer.

But the thought inevitably occurs that the poisonous, insane ferocity of the FBI's loathing for Dr King, and the crisp efficiency of the murder, must make the bureau the prime suspect. FBI chief J Edgar Hoover had called King 'the most notorious liar in the country', 'an evil beast' and 'the number one threat to American security'.

Although the most secret FBI documents and tapes from its surveillance of Martin Luther King will not be released until 2027, it is unlikely that anything will ever be proved for certain. Whether or not Ray actually pulled the trigger or was set up and then set running, some degree of FBI complicity seems the most likely explanation.

The Reverend Jesse Jackson, who was on the balcony with his friend when he was murdered, had no doubt. In 2004, he said, 'There was this ringing shot that hit him in the neck. He never knew he was hit. But I will never believe that James Earl Ray had the motive, the money and the mobility to have done it himself. Our government was very involved in setting the stage for, and, I think, the escape route for, James Earl Ray.'

42

BOB MARLEY

A SUSPICION OF FOUL PLAY

Bob Marley died in hospital in Miami on the morning of 11 May 1981. The cause of death was recorded as being tumours of the lungs and brain as the result of an unusual type of skin cancer, known as acral lentiginous melanoma, that had originated in the big toe of his right foot.

Many music fans were sceptical of the idea that this lean, active man in his mid-thirties – Marley was a vegetarian and a dedicated amateur footballer – had just died abruptly of natural causes. They looked for darker forces at work and suspected foul play and CIA involvement. Others pointed out that his sporting lifestyle may have contributed to the fatal illness. In July 1977, he broke his big toe and lost the nail when he was injured during a football match. Later, the malignant tumour was found in the area of the wound. It metastasised to the brain and lungs and eventually killed him.

Bob Marley's Rastafarian beliefs may also have contributed indirectly to his death. The toe could have been amputated to stop the spread of the disease, but the singer refused to have the operation. Rastafarians like Marley believe that the body must remain whole and the singer was also concerned that amputation of his big toe would affect his dancing and balance on stage.

The possibility of CIA involvement in Bob Marley's illness and death has not been given much consideration by mainstream observers, though many Rastafarians and admirers of Marley's music have heard the rumours.

The story goes that he was targeted by the US Secret Services, not just as a subversive influence on American youth but, more specifically, because of his enormous authority among the ordinary people in Jamaica, where a bitter and violent political power struggle was taking place.

As usual in the smaller countries that were seen as America's backyard, the US had effectively taken sides and was backing the more right-wing opposition, the Jamaica Labour Party (JLP), while covertly trying to destabilise the socialist government. The new CIA head of station, Norman Descoteaux, was keen to make his mark and was bringing guns, drugs and money into Jamaica to encourage JLP supporters, who included the gang boss and drug runner Lester Coke, also known as Jim Brown, founder of Jamaica's brutal Shower Posse.

Following a failed assassination attempt by gunmen using more conventional automatic weapons, Marley was said to have been made ill by a pair of boots prepared by CIA scientists. Those who smell a conspiracy claim the CIA labs had developed the ability to give injections that would induce cancer and that the world's first reggae superstar was a victim of this top-secret technology.

Marley was supposedly given a handsome new pair of boots by an unknown admirer. But when he tried them on he jabbed his toe on what seemed to be a protruding spike of copper wire inside the right boot. From this tiny pinprick wound, it is said, the health problems developed that led to his death.

The initial treatment for his illness, in America, was clearly not working. When his doctor in Jamaica, the dreadlocked Pee Wee Fraser, saw he was going downhill, he suggested seeking treatment from an unconventional German cancer therapist, Dr Josef Issels.

Dr Issels's clinic, in the German Alps, south of Munich, had often been in the headlines. His unorthodox techniques were based on a belief that tumours could not grow in a healthy body. His regime was based on a strictly controlled diet, surgery to remove 'reservoirs of infection' like tonsils and root canal tooth fillings and an exercise programme that included the advice to 'Go climb a mountain'. He called this approach 'integrative immunotherapy'.

In 1961, Issels had successfully defended himself against charges of fraud and manslaughter, after being accused of offering cancer treatments that actually killed his patients faster. A report from Britain's Medical Research Council called the Issels treatment 'worthless' and pointed to very low survival rates among his patients. But others, including Bob Marley's doctors, believed Issels might offer a chance when all other treatments had failed.

A VOICE THAT RANG OUT AROUND THE WORLD

Ever since Marley's group, The Wailers, first attracted overseas attention with their fifth album, *Catch A Fire*, recorded in Kingston but reworked for Chris Blackwell's Island Records in the

UK, it had been clear that Bob Marley could speak to audiences far beyond his native Jamaica. As his fame grew, his words seemed just as relevant to black audiences in Africa. In the countries of Southern Africa, songs like 'Africa Unite' and 'Zimbabwe' became much-loved anthems of the liberation movements.

Marley's lyrics might change attitudes, but he was not a direct threat in a way the CIA would normally recognise. It is unlikely that the top people at the agency's Langley headquarters would have identified him as a significant target, though the local CIA agents, within Jamaica, might well have seen him as rather more threatening.

But, even if its bosses had decided Marley must die, is it really likely that the CIA would use a carcinogenic boot as its weapon of choice?

CIA director William Colby had revealed to a US Congressional committee in 1975 that his people had already developed the perfect device for quick and discreet assassinations. Colby showed off a silent electric gun that could fire a minute poison dart, the width of a human hair and a quarter-inch long. The poison was deadly and quick-acting, but left no detectable traces in the body. In most cases, the victim would die within minutes, without even knowing he had been attacked. Compared with inducing an illness that would take nearly four years to kill the target, this James Bond-style gadget might have been a better bet.

Was the eccentric and unconventional German doctor somehow in on the plot? It seems unlikely. Josef Issels had undoubtedly been a Nazi, but he was always out of step with authority and he did provoke the party's wrath by quitting when he was ordered not to treat Jewish patients. As a punishment, he was sent to an army unit on the front line, where he was captured by the Russians and spent years in a Soviet prisoner of war camp. Issels's methods were always controversial and sometimes dismissed as unscientific, but he had often represented a last hope for other high-profile cancer patients, including Britain's Olympic 400m silver medallist Lillian Board.

MARLEY HAD SURVIVED ONE ASSASSINATION ATTEMPT

Musicians are trouble – and rock, rap and reggae musicians are the worst, not least because they can articulate messages about politics, drugs and revolution to large and enthusiastic international audiences of impressionable young people.

Bob Marley was generally seen as a benign and peace-loving Rastafarian, wreathed in smoke and hair, and motivated by real compassion for those suffering injustice and oppression. You might wonder why the CIA would find him particularly threatening. But documents released under the US Freedom of Information Act have shown that the CIA and other US government agencies did have files on the singer and took more than a passing interest in his career.

Marley was no fan of the CIA and its covert activities. As Jamaica slid into economic chaos in the mid-1970s, undercover CIA operatives were at work in Kingston, bent on destabilising the left-leaning government of Michael Manley's People's National Party (PNP). The PNP had infuriated America by taxing the profits of the US corporations that exploited Jamaica's aluminium ore deposits and by cosying up to President Fidel Castro's Cuba.

So the song 'Rat Race', on Marley's 1976 album *Rastaman Vibration* (his only US Top Ten album), was both heartfelt and topical when it said: 'Don't involve Rasta in your say-say, Rasta don't work for no CIA.'

Lyrics like this convinced PNP opponents in Jamaica that Marley was a Manley supporter. As both political parties were in the habit, at that time, of using goon squads armed with guns and machetes to settle their ideological differences, there were definite risks involved in voicing clear political loyalties.

Later in 1976, during rehearsals two days before a free 'Smile Jamaica' concert organised by Michael Manley, gunmen broke into Marley's home and shot him, his wife, Rita, and his manager, Don Taylor. Rita and Taylor were badly hurt before the raiders were driven off, but Bob escaped with minor wounds to his chest and arm. Some of The Wailers, probably wisely, disappeared from view, but Marley went on to play a defiant set at the concert, making up the numbers with the help of musicians from another local band.

The assassination attempt was undoubtedly carried out by enforcers from the CIA-backed Jamaica Labour Party. The seven-man hit squad was said to have been led by Lester Coke/Jim Brown, the father of present-day Jamaican gang boss Christopher 'Dudus' Coke, currently serving a twenty-three-year sentence in New York, and Carl 'Byah' Mitchell.

While there are arguments about the timing of the 'Boots of Death' story, many people claim that it was just a couple of days later, at the Smile Jamaica event, that Bob Marley was handed the poisoned gift.

The boots were apparently presented to him by a young cameraman/director who was filming the performance. But this cameraman actually turned out to be Carl Colby, son of the CIA's director, William Colby. The younger Colby had a perfectly good reason to be there, as he was making his film on behalf of Island Records, but the family ties with the CIA have always seemed too much of a coincidence to ignore.

Several of Marley's friends, including film-maker and former Black Panther activist Lee Lew-Lee, claim to have seen him try on the boots and jab his toe. But it was hardly a major incident at the time and it was only later that suspicions began to gather around the boots, the CIA and Colby.

No one has ever been clear whether the CIA really did produce injectable cancer-causing materials as assassination weapons, as part of its ultra-secret MKNAOMI bio-warfare programme. Trials were certainly conducted with chemicals such as beryllium compounds in the 1950s and there were also persistent reports over twenty years of experiments with potentially cancer-causing monkey viruses. There is now plenty of declassified documentary evidence about various other bizarre MKNAOMI activities, though records were always kept to a minimum and some key documents have still been held back. This part of the bio-weapons programme, if it did exist, is likely to be among the last of America's Cold War secrets to be revealed.

43

NEW COKE

WAS IT REALLY THE REAL THING?

It's not a matter of life or death, but the story of what happens when a big international corporation wants to make a possibly unpopular change is interesting. And Coca-Cola certainly didn't want to take any unnecessary risks with its product's global popularity. So simply announcing that it was changing Coke once and for all, like it or lump it, was never going to be the best business solution.

The debate, ever since the New Coke fiasco in 1985, has always been whether the Coca-Cola Company pulled off a massive worldwide con or made one of the most glaring mistakes in American corporate history. It's the usual question – conspiracy or cock-up? Nobody died, but there were billions of dollars at stake.

In the early 1980s, Pepsi was catching up fast on Coke. There were a number of reasons, but the main one was that people liked it better. Coke's market share was slipping, while Pepsi's was on the up, year after year.

Coke had a fast-growing success of its own in Diet Coke,

which had been introduced in 1982 and quickly built a huge following. It used artificial sweeteners instead of sugar. But it was a double-edged sword. As more and more drinkers were drawn away from the classic sugar sodas, the preference for Pepsi among the shrinking pool of traditionalists was all the more marked.

Coke bosses had a brainwave. Take the popular taste of the artificially sweetened Diet Coke and work on that. Take out the slimline stuff and replace it with full-flavour sugars, tweak the flavour balance a bit, taste-testing at every stage, and then unleash the new, unstoppable monster that is to be… New Coke.

Every tasting told Coca-Cola they had got it right. The new mix was smooth, sweet and preferred at every blind test session to either Coke or Pepsi. But Coca-Cola's marketers couldn't risk having three products fighting it out and dividing the market between them. Leaving the Diet Coke segment aside, it just wouldn't work to have two sugary Cokes splitting the vote when they were up against a single powerful brand in Pepsi.

The company stopped, took a deep breath, and in April 1985, pulled the world's most popular cold drink off the market and replaced it with New Coke.

It was a sensation. For the next month or so, Coke was all over the media. It was in every conversation, in homes and bars and workplaces across the country. It was the talk of the town. And the talk was overwhelmingly bad.

People felt robbed. Something was being taken away from them and it clearly wasn't just about flavour. Coke had dented a shiny little part of America's history and self-image, and America didn't like it. New Coke didn't stand a chance.

In the South, the abandonment of the original recipe was widely felt as a betrayal of the Dixie heritage. Coke's headquarters in Atlanta, Georgia, received more than 400,000 calls and letters from irate customers. Even less patriotic voices were raised in protest.

In Cuba, Fidel Castro, a lifelong Coke drinker, dismissed the switch to New Coke as yet another symptom of the decline of capitalism.

It took ten weeks for Coca-Cola to take the hint, realise things weren't suddenly going to change for the better and decide to do one of the most public U-turns in US business history.

On 11 July 1985, Coca-Cola's top two executives announced that the original formula was coming back.

With a barrage of suitably syrupy schmaltz, the company's president declared that the company had been caught by surprise and trumpeted the rebirth of 'a wonderful American mystery, a lovely American enigma'. The return of the original, now relabelled Classic Coke, was framed as a dramatic sign of Coca-Cola's responsiveness to its customers' wishes. 'We have heard you,' said Coke's chairman, Roberto Goizueta, who had earlier been quoted as saying it was 'New Coke or no Coke'.

WAS IT ABOUT UNDERMINING PERU'S COCAINE INDUSTRY?

Was the whole New Coke saga a put-up job? The reborn Classic Coke came roaring back with a vengeance over the next few months, regaining the market share it had lost over the summer and going on to overtake Pepsi again by the next spring. By reminding people sharply of the part the hundred-year-old brand played in their lives, the episode actually put new life into the product.

But who would have bet a career on that? No marketer or

chief exec who valued his skin would have proposed such a high-risk strategy. And the costs of retooling, rebranding, even just redistributing one product and then the other must have been enormous. Coca-Cola could have bought a lot of billboards or TV ad time with the money that went on that. On the other hand, observers pointed out that no one, not a soul, was given his or her marching orders after this apparent shambles.

Despite the furore, Coca-Cola's 'original' formula had actually been tweaked and trimmed many times over the years, most notably in 1929, when the last traces of active cocaine were finally removed from the recipe. Despite that, derivatives of the coca plant (described as 'spent coca leaves') were still part of the secret formula in early 1985.

Conspiracy theorists have claimed this was the secret behind the New Coke operation. Since the US Drug Enforcement Administration was trying to wipe out coca as a crop, the Peruvian government-owned coca farms that supplied Coca-Cola were becoming a political hot potato, they allege. After the double-shuffle around New Coke, the 'reinstated' Classic Coke formula no longer called for any coca plant materials, they say, to the relief of the executives involved.

This attractive theory has one flaw. Even now, Coca-Cola still uses coca leaf extracts (as does Red Bull Cola, launched in 2008). The coca is still supplied by America's only authorised importer, the Stepan Company of Northfield, Illinois, which buys one hundred tons of the leaves each year from Peru's state-owned National Coca Company, sells the processed cocaine-free leaves to Coca-Cola and passes on the cocaine itself to licensed pharmaceutical manufacturers.

'WE ARE NOT THAT DUMB – AND WE ARE NOT THAT SMART'

People who claimed they could taste a change in flavour when old Coke made its return quickly focused their suspicions on the sweetness of the drink. Rumours sprang up that claimed the whole thing was an elaborate commercial conspiracy, a charade that was deliberately set up as cover for a switch away from cane sugar to a much cheaper sweetener, high-fructose corn syrup.

In fact, Coca-Cola had already slipped the first major change past its customers in 1980, when it swapped half the cane sugar in Coke for high-fructose corn syrup. Some bottlers had gone over completely to corn syrup by 1985, but some were stubbornly holding out against the switch, which they felt changed the flavour of the product. Coca-Cola took the opportunity to put pressure on them to get into line in the weeks while 'old' Coke was supposedly dead and buried.

This has since been denied many times. But, when Classic Coke was reintroduced in July 1985, America's Sugar Association, the industry's trade body, published a furious full-page ad criticising Coke for using only corn syrup for all bottling of the old formula. As they were the companies on the receiving end of this blow, the Sugar Association members' yelps of pain – and willingness to pay for the advertising – are fairly convincing evidence of genuine concern.

Even today, there are Coca-Cola customers in America who go out of their way to hunt down Coke that tastes the way it did in their childhood. Imported sugar-sweetened Mexican-made Coke is available in some parts of the country, sold at up to twice the normal price alongside 'regular' Coke in stores like Costco. When the special yellow-capped kosher Passover Coke appears on sale each year, it is eagerly snapped up by many non-Jewish drinkers. There were just one or two old-fashioned bottlers, in areas like Cleveland, Ohio, and in Pennsylvania, who doggedly refused to change over to high-fructose corn syrup, but they have finally made the switch in the last few years.

Whether the New Coke episode was really the result of an accidental misjudgement or a calculating conspiracy is never likely to be established now. After all, the art of a good conspiracy is to leave everyone guessing. But Coke's president in 1985, Donald Keough, certainly came up with the best quote to emerge from the whole saga: 'Some critics will say Coca-Cola made a marketing mistake. Some cynics will say we planned the whole thing,' he said. 'The truth is we are not that dumb – and we are not that smart.'

44

PEARL HARBOR

WHY DIDN'T THEY SEE IT COMING?

On Sunday, 7 December 1941 – shortly before Japan declared war on America – 2,400 people died when Japanese warplanes attacked the US Pacific Fleet in Pearl Harbor, Hawaii.

It was 'a date that will live in infamy', to use US President Franklin D Roosevelt's unforgettable phrase. It was a terrible slaughter, the 9/11 of its day.

America was not at war with Japan. America was not at war with anyone.

America was neutral and opinion polls showed that 90 per cent of Americans wanted to stay neutral – to stand well clear while the old nation states of Europe sorted out their differences in the war that had started in September 1939.

But the president believed allowing Hitler to finish the job of taking over Europe by defeating Great Britain would leave the US in a situation where war with the Nazis would end up being inevitable. So Roosevelt wanted his country to join in on the Allied side. And he was ready to do almost anything to make that happen.

At the time, patriotic American fury against Japan's murderous sneak attack meant there was no longer any question of the US staying aloof from the conflict.

The country rallied behind its president as he declared war on the aggressor. Hitler's Germany responded, as it was bound to under its defence treaty with Japan, by declaring war on the United States. Suddenly Britain, America and the Soviet Union, which had switched sides in June 1941, were allies. Europe's war had become a true world war.

Roosevelt led his country forward and the only people blamed for the massacre, apart from the Japanese, were the two officers in charge of the naval and army forces at Pearl Harbor that had been caught so badly unawares.

Admiral Husband Kimmel and Lieutenant General Walter Short were heavily criticised by the Navy Secretary, Frank Knox, who carried out a brief investigation a few days later, and by the first inquiry into the disaster, in early 1942.

They were blamed for dereliction of duty and relieved of their posts. But they were never court-martialled, perhaps because a court martial would drag other more powerful people into the spotlight. A lot of the evidence and many of the key documents could not be revealed at the time, in the middle of a war.

There were several further investigations in the next few years, but it was not until the Clausen Inquiry in 1946, with Roosevelt dead and the war over, that fuller evidence could be examined. Responsibility for leaving Pearl Harbor unaware and largely unprotected shifted up the military and political ladder as it became clear that there had been many clues that an attack was imminent, including a large number of Japanese messages that had been intercepted and read by US codebreakers.

The 1946 inquiry placed much of the blame for the Pearl Harbor tragedy on the Army Chief of Staff, General

George Marshall, and Admiral Harold Stark, Chief of Naval Operations. It also, for the first time, implied some criticism of President Roosevelt's handling of the information that was coming in to him.

These days, with the help of long-secret documents that are now declassified and first-hand accounts from people who could not talk at the time, historians and others have been able to piece together a much fuller view of what really happened. And many are quite appalled at what they think they see.

It is now generally recognised that Franklin Roosevelt (FDR) had a great deal of information about the build-up to the Japanese attack on the battleships, cruisers, destroyers and aircraft of the US Pacific Fleet. By the time it happened, he may have known the date and even the timing of the onslaught.

Roosevelt knew he could not rely on winning the backing of the American public to join in the war. So it was essential to his plans that Japan should strike the first blow – and that the Japanese blow should be seen as a cowardly, underhanded, illegal and barbaric outrage.

But was it also essential that the defenders of Pearl Harbor should be left so ill-informed and unprepared that more than 2,000 of them would be killed?

EVERYONE KNEW WAR WAS IMMINENT

Exactly one week before the Pearl Harbor assault, the local newspaper, the *Honolulu Sunday Advertiser*, carried the front page headline: 'JAPANESE MAY ATTACK OVER WEEKEND!'

Although the Japanese carrier fleet had already set sail four days earlier, nobody has seriously suggested the journalists of

Honolulu had secret inside information about what was about to happen. Everyone was aware that the diplomatic dance was coming to an end and the Pacific was on the brink of war.

If the president, or anyone else, had known quite how unready Pearl Harbor was for a massive air strike, something would surely have been done about it. General Short had been sent several messages warning that war with Japan was getting very near, but he had responded quickly and explained that he had already raised his alert level and taken extra security measures.

These included carefully parking all the Army Air Corps planes bunched up, wingtip to wingtip, in the middle of each airfield and making sure all the ammunition lockers were securely locked. The aircraft thus became sitting ducks for bombing and strafing and could not be scrambled in a hurry, while anti-aircraft gunners could not hit back because they had no ammunition.

But these apparently suicidal measures made perfect sense at the time. Short had been told to expect a wave of attempted sabotage by Japanese exiles living in Honolulu and elsewhere on the island of Oahu in the run-up to a declaration of war. Planes and ammunition stores would be key targets, so he had taken sensible, practical measures to safeguard these assets.

As Washington watched the tension mount and saw war was looming, it failed to emphasise to General Short that he might have more than just local saboteurs to deal with, while he failed to explain just how limited his extra precautions were.

It is also easy to underestimate how carefully the Japanese set up their sneak attack. For example, one reason the carriers came in from the north was because Japan's radio direction-finding trackers had spotted that reconnaissance flights out of the Hawaiian islands always concentrated on the areas to the south and west.

Similarly, while the attack fleet sailed under strict radio silence, with valves removed from wireless equipment and bits of card stuffed between the contacts of transmitters to stop any mistakes, the ships' radio operators had been left behind and ordered to keep up a 'normal' chatter of signals. This was picked up, of course, and fooled US intelligence officers into assuming the carriers were still at home in Japanese waters.

There are a few people who believe President Roosevelt was one of the greatest conspirators and double agents of all time. They claim that he was, all along, an undercover Communist agent, working for Joseph Stalin and the USSR while ruling the United States of America. Similar accusations have been levelled at John F Kennedy as well, but they are hard to take too seriously in either case.

Even those who think Roosevelt was desperate for Japan to strike first and give America some martyrs to avenge don't usually suggest that he deliberately kept Hawaii in the dark in the hope that there would be mass slaughter on this scale.

LOSSES COULD HAVE BEEN FAR WORSE

The assault on Pearl Harbor lasted less than two hours, but the Japanese had been planning and training for it for nearly a year. Special Thunderfish aerial torpedoes had been made, with extra wooden fins attached to make them stay near the surface in the shallow water of Pearl Harbor. All six of Japan's aircraft carriers took part and 353 aircraft attacked, in two waves, starting at 7.49 am.

Just five minutes later, the Japanese operation commander was able to radio that total surprise had been achieved, using the infamous code signal 'Tora! Tora! Tora!' ('Tiger! Tiger! Tiger!').

By 9.45 a.m., 21 American ships had been hit, including eight battleships, and 263 aircraft had been destroyed or severely damaged. As well as 2,345 service deaths, 1,238 sailors, airmen and marines were wounded.

Frank Knox, Secretary of the Navy, told a colleague later that he'd seen Roosevelt just after he'd heard the scale of the Pearl Harbor losses. 'FDR was as white as a sheet,' he said. 'He expected to get hit, but not hurt.'

Roughly eighty minutes before the air attack began, the destroyer *USS Ward*, patrolling outside the entrance to Pearl Harbor, spotted a periscope, opened fire and sank a two-man midget submarine. This, technically, was the first attack of the war in the Pacific. The incident was over in minutes and should have rung alarm bells throughout the region. Yet the messages from *USS Ward* were not seen as important enough to pass on to Admiral Kimmel and General Short. As a result, a crucial hour was lost during which they could at least have made sure the anti-aircraft guns were manned and had ammunition to hand.

Later, as the 183 Japanese aircraft in the first wave headed in towards the island, they were clearly picked up on the radar screens of Oahu's new early-warning system. The two inexperienced operators on duty had never seen a group of targets that large and passed the alarming news up the line, but it was dismissed as nothing significant by a junior officer at the intercept centre. He had been told to expect a flight of US bombers that was due to arrive at about that time, so he was not worried by the shoal of blips on the radar screens.

Several American planes that were unlucky enough to meet up with the first wave of Japanese aircraft were shot down. At least one managed to radio a garbled warning message, but this was unclear and again was ignored.

As a result of all this sleepy Sunday-morning slackness, the fleet and the army were wide open to attack. Men woke up to the sounds of sirens, gunfire and exploding bombs. The navy's big 5"/38-calibre guns didn't fire a single anti-aircraft shell and only a quarter of its machine guns ever got going, as the fighters swooped and turned and came in on repeated strafing runs. The army had over thirty anti-aircraft batteries, but only four were able to put up a fight.

Admiral Kimmel's evidence to the Congressional investigation in 1946 damned Washington for leaving him, and Pearl Harbor, high and dry.

'We needed one thing, which our own resources could not make available to us,' he said. 'That vital need was the information available in Washington from the intercepted dispatches which told when and where Japan would probably strike.

'I did not get this information. It is my conviction that action by the Navy Department… in furnishing me the information from the intercepted messages would have altered the events of 7 December 1941.'

Argument still rages about whether FDR and his staff had specific time and place details gleaned from decoded naval messages. But codebreakers on both sides had been reading secret diplomatic messages, unknown to each other, for at least a year before Pearl Harbor. The Americans had also intercepted messages from a spy in the Japanese consulate in Hawaii which included a 'bomb plot' diagram that told Tokyo exactly which ships were berthed where in the harbour.

When the Americans saw the decoded transcripts of Japan's 'one o'clock message' – a thinly veiled declaration of hostilities due to be delivered by diplomats at 1 p.m. Washington time, or 8 a.m. in Hawaii – Roosevelt muttered 'This means war.'

It was obvious Pearl Harbor needed to be warned.

But Army Chief of Staff George Marshall did not pick up the scrambler phone to General Short. Instead, he sent a cable. And that cable was held up by delays in encryption and transmission. It lost its 'urgent' marker before it eventually arrived in Hawaii and was delivered to General Short several hours after the deadly attack had ended.

There are still American (and British) documents relating to naval code intercepts and other key details from 1941 that have not been declassified. Without them, we will never be certain exactly what was going on in the build-up to Pearl Harbor. Cock-up clearly had a massive hand in the disaster, but it is also clear that President Roosevelt and his top brass did conspire to hold back information that could have saved lives when the Japanese attacked.

Chester Nimitz, America's greatest admiral and the man who took over from Kimmel as C-in-C US Pacific Fleet, probably had the best perspective of all on the tragedy. His view was startling, but realistic.

Nimitz was sure Admiral Kimmel would have sailed bravely out to take on the Japanese force, if he had known it was there. This would have been suicidal. Without air cover, the battleships would have been no match for the aircraft carriers and would have been sunk with all hands, far out in deep water, with 20,000 casualties, rather than 2,400. In the shallow waters of Pearl Harbor, men could mostly be rescued or swim ashore and six of the battleships were eventually refloated and repaired. In fact, he said, if the Japanese had not decided to go for a sneak attack, the disaster would have been far worse.

Only a great war hero like Nimitz – the kind of man you name your aircraft carriers after – would have had the track record and credibility to be able to get away with saying what he did in a speech in 1962 without being howled down.

'It was God's mercy that our fleet was in Pearl Harbor on 7 December 1941.'

45

PRINCESS DIANA

HOW ACCIDENTAL WAS THE ACCIDENT?

At the final inquest into the death of Princess Diana, in early 2008, a letter was produced in evidence. It was written in Diana's large, untidy handwriting and it claimed that Prince Charles was plotting to have her killed.

'This particular phase in my life is the most dangerous,' the note said. 'My husband is planning "an accident" in my car – brake failure and serious head injury in order to make the path clear for him to marry Tiggy. Camilla is nothing but a decoy, so we are all being used by the man in every sense of the word.'

Diana's note was written to her butler, Paul Burrell, in 1995, two years after Diana and Prince Charles had separated. Diana claimed Charles wanted to marry Alexandra 'Tiggy' Legge-Bourke, once the nanny to Princes William and Harry, and that Camilla Parker-Bowles, now the Duchess of Cornwall, was 'nothing but a decoy'.

Legge-Bourke, incidentally, married in 1999, while Charles and Camilla went on to marry in 2005.

The actual crash that killed 'the people's princess' and her new lover, Dodi Al Fayed, in the Pont de l'Alma tunnel in Paris, happened on 31 August 1997.

Diana's death unleashed a huge public outpouring of grief, followed by troubled speculation about the causes and circumstances of the accident – and even questions about whether it was accidental.

In particular, Dodi's father, former Harrods boss and Fulham football club owner Mohamed Al Fayed, insisted that it was not an accident, but murder. Year after year, he repeatedly accused the royal family, led by the Duke of Edinburgh, of conspiring with the Secret Intelligence Service (MI6) and others to arrange the deaths of Diana and Dodi.

Al Fayed's conspiracy theory pivoted on the assumption that the royal family could not bear the idea of Diana marrying Dodi and having a Muslim baby.

He claimed that the couple had become engaged and that Diana was pregnant at the time of her death, though this was contradicted by several witnesses. One of her closest friends, Rosa Monckton, told the inquest that Diana had had a period ten days before, while they were on holiday together on a small boat in the Greek islands. The autopsy doctor was also clear about this: 'She was not pregnant,' he said. 'I have seen inside the womb and there was no pregnancy.'

But Mohamed Al Fayed's accusations seem understated compared with those of some of the ultra-conspiracy theorists to be found on the internet. They believe in a bigger, worldwide conspiracy that involves the security services of Britain, France, the US and Israel.

They say the black Mercedes had been stolen and damaged some weeks before and that when it was returned it was secretly rebuilt with a hidden radio-control mechanism that would allow a remote controller to override the driver's actions.

They say the driver, Henri Paul, was not drunk but deliberately poisoned.

These extreme conspiracists talk of Princess Diana being relatively uninjured, walking around and stepping into the ambulance after the crash.

They point to the fact that one hour and forty-three minutes elapsed between the time of the crash and Diana's arrival at the Pitié-Salpêtrière hospital, less than four miles away. And they offer a gruesome explanation for this. They believe that Diana was indeed pregnant and was subjected to a forced termination procedure in the ambulance, parked at the roadside, before being delivered to the hospital on the verge of death.

In this cloak-and-dagger smoke-and-mirrors world, the British want the couple dead for all the reasons Mohamed Al Fayed put forward. American and British governments and arms manufacturers want to silence Diana's anti-landmines campaigning. The Israelis want Diana and Dodi eliminated for fear that he will influence her to become a high-profile spokesperson for the Palestinian cause.

And the actual killers? They are, according to these all-seeing truth-seekers, 'an international conglomerate' of spooks known as Defence Intelligence Services, or Group 26, based, naturally enough, in Bristol.

Libya's Colonel Muammar Gaddafi, always keen to accuse the European nations of conspiracy, was quick to blame the British and French security services. Many more respectable Arab commentators also took it as read that it was a murder motivated by naked racism.

'The British intelligence service killed them,' veteran Egyptian author and journalist Anis Mansour wrote. 'They could not let the mother of the future king marry a Muslim Arab.'

LAST-MINUTE CHANGES RULE OUT THE AMBUSH THEORY

The idea that Diana was not seriously hurt in the catastrophic collision with the thirteenth pillar and the side wall of the Alma tunnel contrasts strongly with the painful descriptions given by the medical experts at the scene.

Like the others in the car, she had not been wearing a seatbelt and she was twisted into the footwell behind the front seat, broken, bleeding and battered. It took twenty minutes just to get her out of the remains of the vehicle and she then went into cardiac arrest and had to be brought back to life with ventilation and heart massage.

French emergency medicine for traffic accidents works differently from the UK model, focusing on using well-qualified doctors and well-equipped ambulances to try to stabilise patients on the spot, rather than transporting them as quickly as possible to hospital. So there was nothing strange about the fact that it was another hour before the ambulance could set off on its journey.

Even then, progress was deliberately cautious, as the doctor on board knew that acceleration and jolting could greatly increase the chance of Diana's heart stopping again. A few minutes short of the hospital, near the Gare d'Austerlitz, the doctor saw her blood pressure fall sharply and halted the vehicle while he administered more dopamine, successfully preventing another cardiac arrest. The whole journey of 3.8 miles took twenty-five minutes.

Diana arrived at the hospital barely alive, unconscious and in deep shock. It was the best place in Paris for dealing with multiple injuries and had an exceptional range of surgeons and specialists on duty that night. They opened her chest and tried to find the source of the internal bleeding, but she was slipping away fast. When the end came, they tried everything – massage, adrenaline and repeated defibrillation – to restart her heart, but it was no good. After over an hour, at 4 o'clock in the morning, Diana, Princess of Wales, was declared dead.

The two eminent specialists appointed by the French examining magistrate to review the handling of Diana's case were highly impressed by the performance of all those involved. They had done all they could. 'The type of injury found is commonly fatal, regardless of the treatment given,' their report said. 'It is exceptional for patients with this type of injury to reach hospital alive.'

Suggestions that the accident could have been the result of a plot to ambush the car tend to be undermined by the unpredictability of Diana and Dodi's movements that evening. As the Operation Paget Report, prepared for the inquest by Sir John Stevens, former Metropolitan Police Commissioner, pointed out, almost all the details had been changed, virtually at the last minute.

At about 12.20 a.m., Diana, Dodi and the bodyguard, Trevor Rees-Jones, set off on the final journey from the back entrance of the Ritz Hotel, in a black Mercedes S280 driven by the deputy chief of security at the Ritz, Henri Paul. They were heading for Dodi's flat in rue Arsène Houssaye.

In the last hour or so before their departure, the car, the driver and the point of departure had all been unexpectedly changed. Paul, who had gone off duty at 7 p.m. and had had several drinks, was called back in to do the driving. The Mercedes S600 the couple had been using that afternoon was used as a decoy car, leaving from the front of the hotel, while the VIPs left from the rear in the S280.

The route Henri Paul chose, slipping along the Seine to avoid the busy Champs-Élysées, was the usual route professional drivers in Paris would use. But the fatal last-second decision to go past the usual turning and take the Pont de l'Alma tunnel was not something anyone would have anticipated.

To contrive a pre-planned accident as part of an assassination plot would have taken a great deal of organisation under any circumstances. It would be virtually impossible to have enough people and resources in place to put such a plot into operation when the time, the place, the equipment and the personnel were all impossible to predict.

The Operation Paget Inquiry Report, which took three years, fourteen police officers and nearly £4m to produce, provided 832 pages of evidence, witness statements and conclusions. It was originally intended to be an internal police report into allegations of a criminal conspiracy to murder, but was eventually published, during the inquest, in response to the intense public interest in the death of Princess Diana.

WAS HENRI PAUL A 'SUICIDE MERCENARY'?

The whirlwind romance between Diana and Dodi Al Fayed had started only a few weeks earlier, in mid-July 1997, when Diana had accepted an invitation to take a short holiday on Mohamed Al Fayed's yacht in St Tropez.

Diana had been involved in a two-year relationship with a

gentle, unassuming Pakistani heart surgeon in London called Hasnat Khan. She had only been in St Tropez for a couple of days when Al Fayed's son, Dodi, flew in. The two hit it off immediately. Two days later, another guest arrived. This was Dodi's fiancée, Kelly Fisher, a beautiful American model he had been living with, on and off, for a year and a half.

Fisher has always claimed that she and Dodi were due to get married a few weeks later and she was certainly not at all pleased with the developing situation involving Dodi and Diana. When the long-delayed inquest into the crash deaths was held in London, starting in late 2007, she gave evidence to the jury at the High Court that included a transcript of a taped twenty-minute phone call with Dodi. In the call, dating from mid-August, two weeks before the fatal crash, Kelly Fisher's sense of bewildered betrayal was only too clear.

'You even flew me down to St Tropez to sit on a boat while you seduced Diana all day and fucked me all night,' she said, while Dodi hurled back accusations that she was 'crazy' and 'hysterical'.

There was no doubt that the relationship between Diana and Dodi had gone ahead very fast. They were both enjoying themselves and Dodi had bought a ring and was apparently about to propose to her. The ring, still in its box, was found in his apartment after the accident.

Whether Diana would have given him the answer he wanted is not so clear. Within the previous three days, she had made pointed comments to at least two friends, saying, 'I've just got out of one marriage and I'm not going to get involved in another one,' and 'I'm being spoiled and I'm having a wonderful time. I need marriage like I need a rash on my face.'

The conspiracy theorists who believe Diana's relationship

with Dodi was enough reason for dark forces to want her killed usually accuse them of being motivated by a desire not to have the future king of England closely linked to a Muslim family of Egyptian ancestry (Mohamed Al Fayed said they didn't want to be related to 'the son of a Bedouin camel trader'). This does not make sense, though, in view of Diana's deep and passionate two-year relationship with Dr Hasnat Khan, himself a Pakistani-born Muslim, which had only just ended and had certainly not been kept secret.

More understandable, if less flattering for the Al Fayed family, was the possibility that Dodi's dubious personal reputation made him a potential embarrassment. Everyone knew he could be bright and charming, but there were also persistent accusations that he couldn't handle money and was permanently in debt. And there were even louder rumours about his personal habits.

During the inquest, the Al Fayed legal team alleged Prince Philip had once referred to Dodi as 'an oily bedhopper', though this phrasing was ridiculed by Paul Burrell, Diana's friend and former butler.

What did crop up, time and again, outside the courtroom, were claims that Dodi had used cocaine for many years and in spectacular quantities. It was said he spent $15,000 a week on the white stuff at one stage, buying it by the kilo for his own use and to entertain friends.

If the Establishment had decided to get rid of Dodi, and perhaps Diana as well, some aspects of the Alma tunnel conspiracy scenario might have made sense.

A tunnel is a good place for an assassination, as there can be few witnesses and it is a controlled environment. A murder in a foreign country always makes it easier to muddy the waters, because of different legal, cultural and medical rules and conventions. It can also make it easier to share out parts of the operation between different agencies – in this case, it is suggested, MI6, the French Direction Générale de la Sécurité Extérieure and the CIA.

Mohamed Al Fayed's people claimed Henri Paul, who had fifteen different bank accounts containing $350,000 and died with $2,500 in his pocket, was working for both the British and French Secret Services, though the Operation Paget report has him acting only as a low-level, unpaid informer for the French internal security service, the DST.

If there was a conspiracy, Henri Paul has to have been the key man. Without the co-operation of a driver willing and able to deliver the victims to the appointed spot at a prearranged time, no plan for a staged accident could be made to work. Yet few people – even paid informers – would willingly put their own lives on the line.

We are used to the idea of suicide bombers. We all know there are mercenaries who will kill for money. But unless Henri Paul wanted to be the pioneer in a completely new category, the world's first 'suicide mercenary', it is simply not plausible that he drove the car into a deadly ambush for a fistful of dollars.

Henri Paul was supposedly way over the drink-drive limit, though there are genuine questions about the blood samples that were tested. He was also driving too fast, at least twice as fast as the tunnel's speed limit. And he definitely lost control of the two-ton car on the slope down into the tunnel, hitting the right-hand wall and cannoning off into the fatal collision with the thirteenth pillar.

Beyond that, nothing is certain. After all these years of sleuthing, guesswork and speculation, the death of the people's princess is still anything but an open-and-shut case.

46

WINDSCALE FIRE

WHEN BRITAIN WAS MINUTES
FROM MELTDOWN

'Stopp Sellafield' said the posters on the sides of the council dustcarts in Tromsø, capital of Norway's Arctic region. You didn't have to be much of a linguist to get the message. It was 2010 and even here, 1,250 miles northeast of the closed-down British nuclear reactor and 210 miles inside the Arctic Circle, people were worried about Sellafield's long and sinister legacy.

Sellafield used to be known as Windscale. It is on the Cumbrian coast and it's the site of a 1940s weapons-grade plutonium-239 production plant and nuclear power station that ceased operations in the 1990s. The decommissioning process that started then still has some way to go. A date of 2037 is sometimes mentioned, but it could all take a good deal longer.

Windscale/Sellafield boasts the remains of Calder Hall, the world's first atomic power station. Among the relics on the site is Building B30, 'the most hazardous industrial building in western Europe', according to George Beveridge, Sellafield's deputy MD. Nearby is Building B38, officially ranked second.

In more recent years, apart from the decommissioning work, Sellafield was busy reprocessing spent nuclear fuel and manufacturing new MOX (mixed oxide, plutonium and uranium) fuel assemblies. The MOX plant was built at a cost of £470m and was supposed to produce 560 tons of fuel in its first decade of operation. In those ten years, it managed a total of fifteen tons, while costing the taxpayer £90m a year. A highly confidential cable from the US embassy in London, released to the world by WikiLeaks, said Sellafield's MOX plant was 'a white elephant' and called it one of the 'most embarrassing failures in British industrial history'.

Up in Norway's Arctic fishing ports, they have been watching anxiously, knowing that the prevailing currents sweep any pollutants leaked or dumped into the Irish Sea off Cumbria right up the entire length of Norway to the northernmost tip of Europe. One particular, virtually harmless, man-made radioactive substance, technetium, provides a marker for radio-active pollution, as it is only created in nuclear processing. Technetium has been found in shellfish in Tromsø – and the locals know who they blame. They want all discharges into the Irish Sea stopped, now and for always.

But if the future of the complex is controversial, it is Windscale's murky past that makes Brits as well as Norwegians distrustful.

Back in October 1957, a white-hot three-day fire in Windscale's Pile Number 1 reactor led to the risk of a catastrophic nuclear meltdown.

This could so easily have been Britain's Chernobyl.

The fire burned for two days before anyone realised. Nobody knew what to do, as the temperature in the 2,000-ton graphite core of the reactor rose higher and higher, beyond all known limits. After several failed efforts to control the fire, managers at the plant risked everything by cutting off the air supply and drenching the reactor with water, which could potentially have led to a huge explosion with widespread and 'dirty' nuclear fallout. The gamble came off, though the reactor could never be used again and large amounts of radioactive material were released up the 400-foot chimney and into the atmosphere.

This was the world's first big atomic disaster and it remained the most serious nuclear accident in Europe until the Chernobyl explosion in Ukraine, nearly thirty years later. Chernobyl was a Level 7 event on the International Nuclear Event Scale, like the 2011 Fukushima catastrophe in Japan, and is expected to have been responsible for 4,000 deaths. Windscale (rated Level 5, an 'accident with wider consequences') was nothing like as bad as Chernobyl, but is still officially believed to have caused more than 200 additional cancer deaths.

The political fallout from the Windscale fire was potentially huge.

Britain was desperately trying to prove its nuclear virility – it had tested its first hydrogen bomb four months earlier – in order to be seen as a superpower and hold on to a permanent seat among the Big Five on the United Nations Security Council. The prime minister, Harold 'You've Never Had It So Good' Macmillan, could not afford any slip-ups, so he ordered a comprehensive security blackout, arranging for most of the details to be classified and kept under wraps for at least thirty years.

This blackout eventually succeeded in hiding weaknesses in Britain's nuclear design expertise and covering up the health effects of the Windscale disaster for half a century.

A COVER-UP BASED LARGELY ON IGNORANCE

The cover-up over Windscale was on nothing like the scale that would have happened in many other countries. Reporters were given relatively free access to the site and the personnel involved, but the accident was so unprecedented that most of the journalists just didn't know the right questions to ask.

Though the health and safety implications of the fire and the radioactive releases were clearly played down, ignorance was probably as much to blame as the desire to avoid public panic and official embarrassment. No one knew exactly what or how much had escaped into the air or what the likely levels of radioactive contamination might mean for people's long-term health.

Immediate safety precautions consisted mainly of instructions to local residents to stay indoors as much as possible and the destruction of all milk produced on farms within a 250-square-mile zone around Sellafield for the next four months. Surprisingly generous compensation was arranged for those farmers whose milk had to be poured away unused, and statisticians noticed later that dairy production during the period appeared to be rather higher than the previous year.

BUT THE ACCIDENTS AND LIES WENT ON FOR DECADES

Windscale's safety record did not support the reassuring stories sold to the British public in 1957 and it continued to be shockingly bad throughout the active life of the early reactors.

Between 1950 and 1977, there were nearly 200 accidents at

the site. Eleven involved fires and forty-five caused radioactive plutonium to be released. Apart from the 1957 fire, there have been five Level 4 ('accident with local consequences') and fifteen Level 3 events at the Windscale/Sellafield site.

The near-meltdown at Windscale spewed a catalogue of radioactive materials out into the environment. These included caesium, strontium-90, the highly toxic polonium-210 and iodine-131, which readily enters the food chain, is concentrated in the human thyroid gland and causes cancer.

The initial political cover-up was based on suppressing the report on the fire produced by the UK's chief scientist for nuclear research, Sir William Penney.

Penney reported that design faults caused the accident.

Macmillan buried his report.

When a toned-down, edited and distorted version of the report was eventually put out, some weeks later, it even had a carefully spun introduction from Prime Minister Harold Macmillan himself. Penney was ordered to go on the radio and tell the world the near-disaster had been caused by operator error. Brave, determined staff who had risked their health and their lives to grapple with the problem and bring it under control were blamed and stigmatised as the cause of the fire, just so that questions would not be asked about the flawed British technology.

When Penney's original report was finally released, in 1987, after being locked away under the thirty-year rule, it became clear that the cover-up had been highly political. *New Scientist* magazine wrote a polite but damning article, burning with indignation at the way Penney's views had been twisted to mislead the public and suit the prime minister's nuclear agenda.

And half a century after the Windscale fire, major

reassessments had to be made of the amount of radioactive material released and the potential health damage, which had clearly been underestimated.

'We have had to double our estimates of amounts that were released,' said one former UK Atomic Energy Authority research scientist in 2007.

The original calculations in 1957 showed, reassuringly, that emissions after the fire would only have caused a small handful of cancer cases.

That was convenient and the figures went unchallenged for many years. But in 1990, radiation health experts worked out that 200 cases of thyroid and breast cancers and leukaemia could have been triggered.

No one can point to individual cases, many years later, and say that they were caused by the Windscale leak. But the grim reality that has emerged is that many more cancers have occurred than doctors would have expected.

By 2007, the latest research showed that that figure of 200 needed to be revised upwards again. Nobody could say by how much the problem had been underestimated, but the scale of the 1957 disaster was becoming even more evident.

'Several dozen more cancer cases may have to be added to our total,' said epidemiologist Professor Richard Wakeford, from Manchester University.

Over the decades, the safety record of Windscale/Sellafield has been poor and official attitudes to concern over public health issues have been consistently secretive, high-handed and conspiratorial.

In the early days, as Britain raced to build its own atom bombs with plutonium made at Windscale, radioactive waste was diluted with water and discharged from the site into the sea.

A total of 200kg of plutonium was deposited, making the Irish Sea one of the most contaminated seas in the world and leading to calls from the governments of Ireland, Denmark and Norway for the plant to be shut down.

During the fifties and sixties, clouds of plutonium and irradiated uranium oxide particles were regularly and deliberately discharged into the air.

In 1983, a nearby beach was closed and Sellafield's operators were fined after it was discovered that highly radioactive discharges containing ruthenium and rhodium had been pumped into the sea.

In the 1990s, staff at the MOX fuel plant systematically falsified quality data over several years. The Nuclear Installations Inspectorate (NII) found that four of the five shifts had faked results, though only one worker admitted doing it. 'The level of control and supervision... had been virtually non-existent,' the NII reported.

In 2005, the Thorp fuel reprocessing plant had to be closed down for two years, when it was found that 18,000 gallons of radioactive nitric acid solution had been leaking, unnoticed, into a steel and concrete safety tank over a period of nine months. The leak of fluid involved 20 tons of uranium and 160kg of plutonium and was classified internationally as Level 3, a 'serious incident'.

Slowly, slowly, the news they didn't want people to hear has filtered out. In November 2010, another shameful cover-up was unmasked. An inquiry headed by Michael Redfern QC reported to parliament about claims that organs had been removed, usually without permission, from sixty-four nuclear industry workers from Sellafield who died between 1960 and 1991.

Redfern's 650-page report confirmed that brains, hearts,

livers, lungs and testicles had been stripped from the bodies for radiation testing.

Bones had been taken, too, including ribs and thigh bones, which were crudely replaced with bits of broomstick so mourners would not become suspicious at funerals. Relatives of the dead said the report had uncovered an 'old boys' club' among pathologists, coroners and Sellafield scientists that 'mutilated' the bodies and conspired to put the aims of the nuclear industry above the rights of the dead workers and their families.

The original Windscale fire cover-up in 1957 was justified afterwards on the grounds that it was necessary in Britain's national interest. Unfortunately, it was not a one-off. Instead it set the tone for decades of arrogant mishandling of vital political, environmental and health issues that should have been the concern of every individual and family in Britain.

47

LECH WAŁĘSA

FIGHTING DIRTY FOR FREEDOM

Life's odd. In five years, Lech Wałęsa went from unemployed shipyard electrician, to trade union leader, to political prisoner, to 1983 Nobel Peace Prize winner. Seven years later, he was president of Poland.

As the man who pulled the first brick out of the wall of Communist oppression, he started the process that led to freedom for the countries of Eastern Europe and the crumbling of the Soviet Union and its empire.

Yet there are well-supported claims that the chunky, blunt-spoken guy with the droopy walrus moustache, the people's hero and founder of the Solidarity trade union, may also have been Agent Bolek, a spy for the SB (Służba Bezpieczeństwa, the State Security Service, the Polish equivalent of the KGB).

Papers have been unearthed that indicate Wałęsa may have been a paid SB informer from 1970 to 1976. But the same applies to hundreds of thousands of his fellow Poles. In a nation of thirty-eight million, half a million names were found listed in the secret police archives. Who was approached, who became involved, who was paid and who actually spied for the Communists became the key questions.

Some of the records from the SB files are deeply incriminating. Some are clearly forgeries or represent wishful thinking by spymasters whose approaches had been turned down.

Wałęsa himself always admitted that the SB tried to recruit him, but said they had failed. His old enemy, Poland's Communist hard man General Wojciech Jaruzelski, who had him imprisoned under martial law in 1981, thought the accusations that Wałęsa was a grass were laughable: 'I regard them as something not to be taken seriously,' he said in 1993. 'They are part of some game.'

And anyway, if there was a dark conspiracy between the hero of Solidarity and the government security apparatus, how did that fit with the fact that Lech Wałęsa led the movement that loosened the iron fist and tipped the Communists out of power?

THE MAN WHO WALKED THE TIGHTROPE

In a case like this, common sense says that actions speak louder than files. Documents can be faked or altered. Revolutionary changes in the society and politics of a whole country are more likely to give a true impression.

Those on his own side who didn't buy into the Wałęsa myth often criticised him for what they saw as a lack of principle. They said he was ruthless and cynical, inconsistent and compromising, equally happy to deceive friends or enemies, and far too concerned with being all things to all men.

But, for Solidarity to achieve freedom for Poland, Lech Wałęsa had to maintain his political relevance. He had to stay in the game. He had to make himself valuable to the Communists, so they kept talking to him and believing he was less dangerous than the other Solidarity leaders. At the same time, he had to avoid losing credibility and support within the trade union and the wider movement. For at least twelve years, Wałęsa was walking a tightrope, and only the ends could justify the means.

NO FLAWLESS HERO, BUT HE HELPED SET EUROPE FREE

The secret files from the SB archives are now under the control of the Institute of National Remembrance – Commission for the Prosecution of Crimes against the Polish Nation (the IPN). In 2008, two senior employees of the IPN published a massive, scholarly book that analysed Wałęsa's secret police records and reproduced 300 pages of declassified documents.

The book was a bombshell.

If the documents were real, it showed that Lech Wałęsa was a registered 'secret collaborator' for the SB from 1970 to 1976, under the name 'Agent Bolek'. It showed he had been especially active during 1970 to 1972, when strikes and rioting in the Lenin shipyard in Gdansk, where he was on the strike committee, led to the deaths of thirty workers. And it showed he had been paid for his work as an SB spy.

Many of the IPN documents referred to in the book were faded or photocopied. But the authors said other papers, in better condition, had been unearthed in different archives.

'These files still had their original seals and it could be proved that they hadn't been opened since the 1970s,' they claimed. 'Manipulation was out of the question.'

Altogether, the papers showed there were about twenty

colleagues of Lech Wałęsa who had suffered harassment or persecution by the authorities as a result of his connection with the SB.

The conspiracy seemed real. The future president had, it appeared, spied on his fellow workers for the secret police.

But, like everything in Poland, it was more complicated than that. Wałęsa grew unhappy with the Communists and decided to stop informing, so the SB deregistered him. When he became active in the Free Trade Unions movement in 1977, the SB tried to recruit him again. He said no, and cleared the air by confessing his previous sins to his union colleagues.

But he stayed in touch with his SB contacts from time to time and was able to make it pay when he took over the leadership of the crucial strike in the Gdansk shipyard in August 1980 that led to the founding of Solidarity, the first non-Communist trade union in Eastern Europe.

During the strike and his imprisonment the next year, under martial law, he convinced the regime that he was effectively a double agent. He'd got rid of the extremists in Solidarity, he said, and he was the man to talk to. So it went on, right through until 1989, with the Communist government still seeing him as an enemy, but the least worst of all the options.

And in the end, in 1989, Wałęsa was able to make a power-sharing election deal with the Communists that made them think they'd won, until they suddenly found themselves in the dustbin of history, with Wałęsa installed as the first president of post-Communist Poland.

All this plotting and double-dealing has only recently been revealed and documented in detail, not least because many of the key pages from Lech Wałęsa's SB files were illegally removed and destroyed during the years of his presidency.

Lech Wałęsa has denied the recently published evidence and insisted the documents were falsified by the Communist authorities to blacken his name. In 2009, he began a libel case against Poland's president, Lech Kaczyński, for repeating the allegations that he had been involved with the SB. The trial ended abruptly in April 2010 when Kaczyński and 95 other Polish leaders and VIPs were killed in the Smolensk air disaster.

Kaczyński was once a comrade in the struggle against Communism and Wałęsa has since refused to be drawn into criticising him, though he continued to insist that the documentary evidence was faked by the secret police many years ago.

Then, in February 2011, he decided to come clean. In a Polish television interview that has never been picked up and reported by the British or US media, Lech Wałęsa admitted, for the first time, that he had co-operated with the SB.

'It was the only way to outplay them,' he said. 'I wasn't going over to the other side, or betraying people. But I could do more, and save more people, if I did it this way.'

The controversy about Wałęsa's actions and motives resurfaces every few years. In 2016, after incriminating SB documents were seized from the home of the recently deceased General Czesław Kiszczak, a Communist-era minister of the interior, Wałęsa went on the offensive again, denouncing the 'lies, slander and forgeries' that undermined his reputation. One of the Kiszczak papers is a specific agreement, dating from 1970, to spy for the SB. It is signed, in what is clearly the man's handwriting, 'Lech Wałęsa – Bolek'.

Ultimately, though, most Poles don't care about the details. If Lech Wałęsa did make youthful mistakes, they would rather he owned up to them and put the matter to bed. The shining image of the shipyard worker who led his country to independence and democracy has been battered and dented over time, but Wałęsa could never be anything but a national hero in Poland. The truth may not be pretty, but it shows us a flawed fighter whose one-man conspiracy against the Communist regime set half a continent free.

48

ELVIS PRESLEY

WANTED, DESPERATELY, DEAD OR ALIVE

If Elvis Presley is alive and well and living in the sands of Oman, in snowy Norway, in Kalamazoo, Michigan, or, as has been claimed many times, in Tweed, Ontario, in Canada, he must now be into his late eighties.

For a guy who supposedly conspired with those around him to fake his death and vanish at the age of forty-two, that's a long time to stay underground.

Even the fans who used to hope the King of Rock 'n' Roll would reappear and win them the bets that would pay off their mortgages have all but given up. London bookmakers William Hill upped the odds against Elvis making a surprise comeback to 1,000/1 in 2005. You could probably get ten times that now, but it seems nobody much is betting any more.

Other people are still making money out of him, though. There's a new Baz Luhrmann film, starring Austin Butler as the King and Tom Hanks as Colonel Tom Parker, and there's a batch of new Elvis box sets on the way, along with any number of auctions of Elvis memorabilia.

Everybody still wants a little piece of him. And that was

precisely why the rumours were so strong in 1977. Could that feeling of being everybody's property have led him to stage his own death and disappear from public view?

When Elvis was reported dead at his home in Memphis, on 16 August 1977, it looked straightforward enough. The Shelby County medical examiner put down heart failure as the cause of death, without bothering to go into detail about the contribution made by the fistfuls of prescription drugs he took to go to sleep, wake up and get through each day.

As recently as 1994, when the Presley case was reviewed, the coroner, Dr Joseph Davis, sought to rule out the idea that the star's medication had caused his death. 'There is nothing in any of the data that supports a death from drugs,' he said. 'In fact, everything points to a sudden, violent heart attack.'

But it wasn't long before the conspiracy theories started. Elvis was wrecked, bloated, stressed beyond belief. He had big debts, including many incurred in his name by his Svengali, Colonel Parker. He had fans whose obsessive intensity made him fear the deranged loser with a gun or a knife who might seek him out at any time. He'd even managed to get mixed up, through his father, in a complicated deal over the purchase of a jet airliner which had brought him into conflict with the mafia.

Outrageous though it seemed, there did appear to be some logic behind the suggestion that feigning death might free him to live a saner and more private life out of the spotlight.

FAKING YOUR DEATH GETS HARDER ALL THE TIME

The heyday of faking one's own death and disappearing to start afresh somewhere else was the mid-nineteenth century.

Since then, the relentless march of high-speed technologies – telegraph, telephone, radio, TV and, finally, the internet – has made it harder and harder to pull it off.

But faking your own death, or at least talking about other people doing it, was rather fashionable in the mid-seventies. There had been one high-profile British case in 1974, when a former cabinet minister, John Stonehouse, left a pile of clothes on a beach in Miami to give the impression that he'd drowned, only to be arrested in Australia five weeks later. And one of the biggest television hits of the era was a 'faked death' comedy, *The Fall and Rise of Reginald Perrin*.

In America, the most famous case had been a few years earlier. It involved Ken Kesey, bestselling author of *One Flew Over the Cuckoo's Nest*. Kesey had faked a suicide leap, leaving a goodbye note at the top of a cliff and slipping away to Mexico to avoid the drugs charges hanging over him. The ruse failed, though, and Kesey felt the heavy hand of the law on his shoulder the moment he stepped back across the border.

For the usual run of nonentities and bigamists, it might have been possible to make the disappearing trick work. For a celebrity of any kind, let alone a global superstar like Elvis Presley, the chances of successfully faking death and building a new life were not good, even in the 1970s.

The idea must have occurred to many famous people leading highly pressured lives, but none of them actually followed it up. Apart from anything else, all the planning and scheming in the world can't protect a fleeing star from the risk of being spotted. Sooner or later, someone would make the connection and the cat would be out of the bag.

So it is vastly more likely, given his health, his drug habits and his generally stressed and unstable lifestyle, that Elvis simply died – either from a heart attack or an overdose.

The sheer volume of medication he was taking was extraordinary. His private physician, George Nichopoulos, 'Dr Nick', would more or less agree to whatever Elvis wanted. The autopsy found fourteen different drugs in his body, ranging from morphine and barbiturates to sedatives and sleeping pills, antihistamines, laxatives and steroids. Dr Nick had prescribed 10,000 doses of various drugs for Elvis in the first 225 days of 1977, at an average of 44 doses a day.

As always, though, Elvis was full of surprises. The King of Rock 'n' Roll was also the king of contradictions. Despite his health problems and the extra weight he was carrying, he was much more active than people assume.

Elvis had been a serious, and surprisingly disciplined, student of karate for nearly twenty years. He was respected by people he had trained and sparred with in the martial arts community and was known for having quick hands and for his ability to shrug off pain. He had worked hard to improve his skills and reached eighth degree black belt status in 1974. The martial arts kicks, sequences and poses that had become part of his stage act were a good deal more authentic than most people realised and karate obviously had some beneficial effect on his fitness.

But Elvis had clearly been unwell during his last set of concerts, ending on 26 June 1977 in Indianapolis. The girl singer in his band for the previous seven years, Kathy Westmoreland, had been surprised that the next tour, due to start in Portland, Maine, on 17 August (the day after Elvis died), was still going ahead.

'Because of Elvis's worsening health and the way he talked to me the last time we were together, a month earlier, I thought his touring days were over,' she said. 'I told my sister the night before: "Don't be surprised if I'm back home in a day." "Why?" she asked. "Because I don't think it will ever happen, not the way Elvis is feeling," I told her.'

The night before his death, Elvis couldn't sleep, so he woke up his cousin, Billy Smith, and insisted on playing a game of racquetball, starting at 4 a.m. After the game, he sat at the piano in the lounge next to the court and played the old Willie Nelson song 'Blue Eyes Crying in the Rain', before deciding to call it a day just as the rest of the world was waking up.

His girlfriend, Ginger Alden, said goodnight as he headed for the bathroom with the book he'd been reading, *The Scientific Search for the Face of Jesus*, by Frank Adams.

'Don't fall asleep in there,' called Ginger.

'OK, I won't,' said Elvis.

'I SAW HIM AND I KNOW HE'S GONE'

According to the official version of events, Elvis was found dead, on the bathroom floor, several hours later, just after 2 p.m. The county medical officer's report said that he was naked, that rigor mortis had set in by the time the body was examined and that there was 'no indication of foul play'. In the face of the dull facts of a 'found dead' report, it is difficult to imagine that something totally different was going on.

If there was a conspiracy to take Elvis away to a new life, everything must have happened very fast, in those few hours between 8 a.m. and 2 p.m. A suitable substitute corpse would have had to be brought in and loaded with a plausible cocktail of drugs. Elvis himself would have had to be smuggled out, away from Graceland and probably out of the country. A lot of people would have had to be paid off or somehow induced to go along with the story of his death.

There are good reasons why the few people who do try to fake their death often choose drowning. The deception is a lot easier if you don't have to put up a body, with all the complications of getting the appearance and medical and dental details correct.

Afterwards, there were reports that someone looking suspiciously like Elvis had booked a flight to Argentina in the name of Jon Burrows – an alias Presley had actually used in the past to protect his privacy when travelling. There were suggestions, too, that he had been given a new identity by his contacts in the FBI under one of the agency's witness-protection programmes.

Among those who believe Elvis conspired with a few trusted friends to fake his death, leave the old life behind and whisk himself away to start all over again, there is considerable admiration for the way the operation was plotted and executed. But even these diehards admit he didn't get everything right. For one thing, they say, he betrayed his carefully laid plans to do a vanishing act by failing to order any new stage clothing for the tour that was scheduled to start the next day. That's the giveaway, they claim. That's the one slip-up that proves he knew in advance that he wouldn't be around to face the music.

But Linda Thompson was there and she knew he was dead. Linda was Elvis's girl before Ginger. 'He was lying in the coffin,' she said. 'I saw him and I know he's gone.'

She understood what so many people wanted. 'They want to believe that he's off in the Bahamas somewhere – and I wish he was. But he's truly gone.'

Ever since 1977, of course, 'Elvis lives' stories have been a staple of third-rate papers and magazines around the world. He has been seen, apparently, in every state in America, in Germany and Japan, in Guam, in Muscat and the Congo. For a man who never performed anywhere outside the US, he's been getting about quite a bit.

In the end, though, in the absence of totally conclusive evidence, we'd probably do best to trust the bookies. They're usually right about most things. If they're offering 1,000/1 or better against Elvis being alive, it's a pretty safe bet he's dead.